Effective Guest House Management

Third Edition

Ronelle Henning

First published 1998
Second edition 2004
Third edition 2007

Effective Guest House Management

© Juta & Co Ltd, 2007

Mercury Crescent,

Wetton 7780

Cape Town, South Africa

ISBN 9780 7021 7705 7

Disclaimer

Project Manager: Sharon Steyn
Editing: David Merrington
Proofreading: John Linnegar
Cover design: Marius Roux
Indexing: Jennifer Stern
Design and typesetting: Lebone Publishing Services
Printed and bound in the Republic of South Africa by Paarl Print, Oosterland Street, Daljosafat, Paarl

Acknowledgements

Photographs with thanks to Oystercatcher Lodge (top and bottom left) and Aan de Oever Guest House (bottom right). See pages 211–212 for contact details.

Preface

From its humble beginnings over a decade ago, the guest house and bed and breakfast sector of South Africa today offers world-class accommodation in establishments ranging from five-star luxury to welcoming and homely bed and breakfasts and cultural home-stays in the townships. The sector plays a vital role in the development of South Africa as a premier international tourism destination. Its important and essential contribution to the hosting of major international events, conferences and international sporting tournaments like the World Cup is indisputable. It is the fastest-growing sector in the tourism industry.

Starting a guest house offers a relatively easy opportunity to participate in the tourism industry. However it is a highly competitive industry, demanding skills in and knowledge of professional hospitality as well as adherence to of sound business principles. As many guest house owners have little or no formal hospitality training, this book addresses the need for practical hands-on information on effective guest house management to ensure success.

The requirements for making a success of your guest house are presented in this book in an easy-to-follow manner. It is a guide to guest house management for both current and prospective owners of guest houses and bed and breakfasts, from the start-up and business plan, practical suggestions for building and decorating your guest house, the legal requirements, marketing, looking after your guest from enquiry through to check-out, good customer service, your food service and menu planning, cleaning and preparing a guest room, and even dealing with HIV/Aids.

The sections on setting up a website and on online marketing, electronic reservations, business planning and customer service have been extensively updated in this edition to meet present-day demands.

Acknowledgements

It has been my privilege and pleasure to have been involved with the South African guest house industry for more than a decade. Especially gratifying to me is the positive feedback I have received from readers that the previous editions have helped them set up successful businesses. I hope that this new edition of *Effective Guest House Management* will assist new guest house owners not only to realise their dreams of success but also to enjoy being part of the dynamic and exciting tourism industry in South Africa.

I have learnt much from many role players in the industry but would like to mention some in particular: my sister Carolie de Koster for her unfailing enthusiasm for her own guest house, for the business of food as well as for her contribution to the food service section in the book; Carine Willemse for her cooperation and contribution to the first edition and for her immaculate sense of style; André Burger for his work over many years lifting the standards of the industry; Jan Rhoodie for his customer service expertise; my previous business partner, Sarie Mehl, for working with me on many challenging initiatives in the industry, and Karl Seidel, previously vice-chairperson of Guest House Association of Tshwane Pretoria East, for his support and critique of this edition.

Without the patience and encouragement of my husband Lapa and children Constant, Annelize, Caren, Felix and Laetitia it would not have been possible to write this book.

Thank you also to the editorial team at Juta for their professionalism, expertise and support through all three editions.

Ronelle Henning
August 2007

About the author

Ronelle Henning has been involved in the guest house and accommodation industry since 1995, when she started her own marketing and reservations business. *Effective Guest House Management* was researched and written to address a need in the South African guest house and bed and breakfast (B&B) industry for practical information applicable to the South African market.

On the subject of starting and managing a guest house Ronelle has presented seminars and training courses, radio talks and a series on the *Tourism Biz* programme on SATV in 2004. She has been a guest speaker at educational institutions and other organisations and served on the Advisory Committee for Hospitality Studies of the Tshwane University of Technology and the Johannesburg World Summit Company Training Committee. With her business partner, Sarie Mehl, she coordinated the accommodation requirements for guest houses for major events such as the World Summit on Sustainable Development in 2002 as well as for other large international conferences and events. Another initiative was GuestEx, the first specialised exhibition for the needs of the small accommodation industry, in cooperation with Hostex, the hospitality exhibition.

Ronelle was a member of the South African diplomatic service for 14 years and has travelled extensively, staying in B&Bs and guest houses in many countries.

She is married with five children, three of whom are teenagers; additional family members include two miniature dachshunds and two pedigreed oriental cats. Apart from her family and friends, her other interests are travel, cooking and entertaining, gardening, ballet and opera.

Contents

Developing
your dream

Introduction: The guest house business

You dream of owning a beautifully decorated guest house in a picturesque setting, cooking delicious food for interesting guests from all over the world, being your own boss and being able to work flexible hours from your own home whilst earning a good income. Establishing your own guest house seems like the obvious way of making your dream come true.

But what business are you in when you start a guest house?

A guest house provides suitable accommodation and services to temporary visitors for payment. Guest houses are part of the larger hospitality industry, which includes other establishments that provide accommodation such as hotels, motels, lodges and bed and breakfasts, as well as providers of food, such as restaurants, cafés and coffee shops. For the purposes of this book, the term guest house will be used, but the principles and guidelines can be applied to all small, personally managed accommodation establishments, including lodges and bed and breakfasts.

The hospitality industry is a key part of the wider tourism industry and is linked to other tourism product owners, which could be adventure tourism providers such as white water rafting, tour guides, tour operators, travel agents, airlines, rental vehicles, game farms, souvenir and other shops, and any other activity indulged in by people touring or on any kind of visit to another area or country.

Tourism is a huge and growing industry worldwide, and it is a major foreign currency earner for many countries. South Africa's tourism industry has also grown in size and importance over the past few years and its development is officially supported and actively encouraged. South Africa, with its rich natural diversity, beautiful scenery, cultural variety, wildlife, and superb beaches and coast line, as well as other unique experiences, is well positioned to take advantage of this international trend. The country has become a popular international tourism destination. All these tourists need a safe place to stay.

The guest house sector in South Africa really started its rapid growth in 1995, boosted by the Rugby World Cup. Today excellent guest houses or bed and breakfasts are to be found in every corner of the country and the sector makes a vital contribution to South Africa's tourism product and reputation. Guest houses have now become the preferred accommodation choice for many travellers.

Bed and breakfast establishments (or B&Bs) have a long tradition in other countries such as Britain, where there are delightful small B&Bs or elegant country houses in every town. In the United States the inns are ubiquitous, and in Germany the *Gasthaus* is famous. This means that international visitors are well used to the idea of staying in a similar establishment. South Africans have a tradition of warm hospitality and enjoy the reputation of a friendly nation, characteristics that are so essential to the hospitality industry and especially to guest houses.

Major events such as international conferences and major international sporting tournaments like the Soccer World Cup depend on the accommodation provided by guest houses for their success. In terms of the development of quality establishments, the excellent work of professional associations like the National Accommodation Association of South Africa, and marketing organisations such as AA Travel Guides, Portfolio Collection, and Guest House Accommodation of South Africa, means that South Africa's guest houses compete well internationally and have an excellent reputation, often offering a superior product.

This also implies that the guest house industry today is highly competitive, and the highest levels of professionalism are required.

The Star Grading Scheme of the Tourism Grading Council is an internationally recognised benchmark of quality, offering international visitors an easily recognisable symbol of quality assurance.

Checking the realities

Your dream must of course also be financially viable because it is not enough to start a guest house simply because you enjoy meeting people, have the right personal characteristics or have a suitable property. Your personal and economic motives are important, but they must correspond with the business realities of a guest house as a small business enterprise. Although your unique vision will contribute to the success of your guest house, your potential customers will not support it just because you like the idea.

The same rules and risks apply to starting your own guest house as those that apply to starting any small tourism business enterprise. The high capital costs involved in setting up a guest house mean that you cannot afford to experiment, and you certainly do not want to end up in the position where you have spent tens of thousands of rands on the realisation of your dream only to find that you are not getting business and are running at a loss, with an impatient bank manager breathing down your neck.

Your guest house must in the first instance be a small service business undertaking that must provide goods and services to customers to make a profit. You may be selling pleasant accommodation supported by appropriate services, but the principles are the same as for selling shoes or a meal. The four critical elements for success in the tourism and hospitality industry are

* excellent customer service,
* quality facilities and equipment,
* the calibre of you and your staff, and
* sound management of business operations.

These can be achieved with proper preparation and planning, and are dealt with in the following chapters. There are many risks involved in this undertaking, but good planning and careful evaluation of your dream will minimise the risks of your business not succeeding.

Do you have what it takes to start your guest house?

Many guest houses start as the dream of their prospective owners. The attraction of establishing and running a picture-perfect establishment filled with interesting guests is understandable. Remember that to come up with a new idea is not always that easy, and most new guest houses copy an existing idea or some variation of it.

Perhaps you wish to make money or start an alternative career and believe that running a guest house is an easy option, not requiring special training or skills. You may also wish to find something entertaining to do after retirement. Often, once children have left a large and beautiful house, it can be suitable for conversion into a guest house. In the past, managing a guest house was often seen as a hobby or merely something to do to make a little extra money.

Establishing and running a guest house seems at first glance to be a simple thing to do. After all, you may be well known for your excellent cooking skills and friendly nature.

But the guest house industry today is highly competitive, professional and demanding. Managing a guest house is now more often than not the only source of income for the owner and can be done as a side interest only with difficulty. The economic realities demand that your guest house is managed on sound business principles.

The hospitality industry is essentially a service and 'people' industry. While the advantages in terms of being your own boss are obvious, the disadvantages to your personal life should also be considered, such as less personal and family privacy, long irregular working hours, uncertain and fluctuating income, and sometimes unreasonable and demanding guests. You will have to get up very early and often go to bed very late, and your own mood or how you feel must never influence how you treat your guests. Your family's needs will often be placed second.

But running a guest house can also be a very interesting and challenging career as well as a good primary source of income. Consider the pros and cons listed below.

Pro	Con
Interesting and challenging	Repetitive work
Being your own boss	Extra workload
Earning extra money	Fluctuating income
Using existing/retaining home	Loss of family privacy
Working at home	Repetitive work
Meeting new people	Demanding, difficult guests

Personal characteristics

A guest house offers its accommodation and service on a highly personal level. What can be more personal than offering safety, comfort and a good night's sleep? Dealing with people on this level requires that you have particular personal characteristics.

Your personality and credibility as owner are crucial to the success of the enterprise and are in fact some of your biggest assets. Much of what makes a small business successful has to do with the qualities of the owner. You can hire someone with cooking or marketing skills, but your own passion for your business and your commitment to making it work cannot be replaced. Some assessment of personal qualities and entrepreneurial skills is necessary to see whether these businesses are a good match for you and your family.

The personal qualities of a successful guest house owner

Entrepreneurial qualities	You must be willing to take risks and be innovative. You are a self-starter, confident, motivated by success and the desire to create something special and to make enough money. You can take responsibility, make decisions and are enthusiastic about your business. Perseverance is important and you can set long-term goals for success. Although a guest house deals with a specialised and very individual product, it still requires thorough planning, strong motivation, basic business management skills, good decision-making ability and perseverance – all the typical attributes of an entrepreneur.

Communication skills	A confident, pleasant personality with excellent written and oral communication skills coupled with sensitivity about when and how to communicate are absolute essentials. Remember that your guests are not personal friends but paying guests, so be sensitive about when they want to chat or when they would rather be left alone.
Tolerance and patience	People from many different backgrounds, countries, cultures or even moral codes may stay in your guest house. You may be expected to provide special meals or be sensitive to cultural habits, for example how women are treated. It is worth your while to pay attention to these issues; your guest house has to do with people and strangers will be sleeping in your establishment. You will need patience and understanding of their sometimes difficult and unreasonable demands and will have to remain calm in all circumstances.
Flexibility	Although good management will mean that you will have clarity on policies, rates and so on, a guest house is not a school hostel with all the rules written in stone. You must be flexible and willing to make changes in terms of rates, services, times and even facilities, if possible, in order to best meet your guests' needs or to secure a reservation. You should be prepared to offer breakfast at 5 am to a regular customer or give a special rate at other times.
Creativity	One of the outstanding attractions of a guest house is its unique character and the fact that it does not offer another faceless, sterile hotel room but a warm and personable room. This offers you many enjoyable opportunities to express your creative flair. Creating a welcoming and pleasant environment every day is an important task. However, you will also be required to find creative solutions to problems and demands.
Practicality	Everything has to work on a very practical level as well, such as the management, stock-keeping, reservations systems and maintenance.
Good mana-gerial skills and enjoyment of people	This is a people-orientated industry. You will be around people and strangers nearly all the time. You will have to enjoy taking care of them and will have little time left to yourself.
Stamina	The working hours are demanding – from early morning to late at night, up to 17 or 18 hours a day, seven days a week, every week.
Perseverance	Ability to persevere through difficult times and to keep an eye on future success.
Favourable personal situation	Is your personal and family situation such that you can devote the maximum time to your business, or can you only offer limited attention?
Conflict handling	Can you resolve conflict in a calm manner? Can you accept criticism gracefully?
Pressure	There are many pressures in a guest house, ranging from financial to deadlines for breakfast and rooms.
Openness to new ideas and challenges	The tourism and hospitality industry is developing rapidly, and you need to keep up to date with new demands and requirements.
Decisiveness	You should be able to take decisions on your own.
Sense of humour	The ability to laugh can be a lifeline when disaster strikes.

Assess yourself against the requirements below to see whether this business is for you:

	Yes	Should improve
I am a self-starter		
I am well organised		
I work hard		
I like and care equally about people, guests and staff		
I like to be around people		
I can take decisions		
I have financial discipline		
I am creative		
I like finding solutions		
I am tolerant of other cultures and habits		
I like and can prepare food		
I am in good health and have enough stamina for long days		
I am interested in my community and area		
I have travelled and understand the needs of a traveller		
I like to and can communicate well, verbally and in writing		
I am patient and seldom lose my temper		
I have good people management skills		
I do not mind housework		
I am open-minded and flexible, keen to try new solutions and adapt to the times		
I like to please		
I am interested in and know what's happening in tourism and the hospitality industry		
I am a good team player and like to cooperate with others		
I am willing to learn more and to undergo formal training if necessary		
I am comfortable with having strangers in my home		
I am ambitious and want to be successful		
I have the time to spend on building a business		
I am outgoing and courteous		
I will go out of my way to help others and satisfy my guests' needs at any and all times		

My family supports my dream and I will still be able to attend to their needs		
I want my guest house to be the most comfortable and interesting place possible		
People generally like me		
What does your self-assessment tell you about yourself?		

Your personal situation

Your family life

Do you intend to integrate your family life with your guest house activities and, if you do, can your family handle the pressure that necessarily goes with this kind of commitment? Are you prepared to cater for two separate areas in one house?

Do not underestimate the demands and workload of running a guest house and the effect that has on your lifestyle and family. Is your personal and family situation such that you can spend enough time on the business or would you be able to offer only divided attention? The time and labour demands of a guest house are not easy on a young family, and your children should preferably be at a more independent stage. They may otherwise resent the time you spend away from them on running your business.

Is your spouse or partner enthusiastic about the idea? Is he or she willing to wait for attention, meals, and time with you? Is he or she perhaps involved as a business partner? If this is the case, there has to be clear consensus about responsibilities in the guest house.

You may have to get up very early for early departures and wait up late for late arrivals. If your family situation does not allow for this, it will impact on your business. You may have to employ costly additional labour to help with these tasks.

Your family situation will also affect the guest house. Crying children or boisterous behaviour is not compatible with a professional service. Accommodating the physical and emotional needs of your family and your paying guests requires careful consideration. You will have to make sure that there is a clear division between your family's space and that used by the guests, and the two should never be confused. For example, you may never sell a child's room with cupboards stuffed with toys to a guest.

Remember that your pets are also a part of your family. However cute, they are not universally adored by all guests. Some guests may even be allergic to them, but no guests want to be bowled over by an over-eager dog on arrival, have cat hairs cling to their clothes or have the house cat on their laps, or worse, their beds. Scary guard dogs at the front gate will definitely chase your guests away.

Your financial position

Be very honest with yourself about your financial position and what you expect and need from the guest house in financial terms. You may perhaps have to drastically curb some of your more creative impulses and wishes.

Do you have enough money to tide you over until the guest house starts paying its way? What will happen if your new business does not succeed for any reason? Will you have lost all your savings? Can you start all over again?

I have not met a prospective guest house owner who did not have a complete picture in his or her head of the dream guest house. Most happily admit that the development, décor and furnishings are part of the attraction, and the guest house provides the perfect excuse for beautiful linen, fresh flowers or other creative outlets such as impressive breakfasts. These aspects have to bow before the financial realities, as you literally cannot allow your profits to be eaten up or thrown away.

Do not be tempted to spend too much at the early stages, but you have to spend enough to deliver quality facilities and services. Know that it could be some time before you earn an income. Your guests will not pay for your mistakes if you overspend.

Applicable experience

The guest house owner is truly a Jack of all trades, and you should know at least a little about all aspects involved in running the guest house. Large accommodation establishments such as hotels have staff dedicated to reservations and front office management, chefs in the kitchen, accountants, marketing managers and cleaning staff. Your guest house will be providing all these services. Although these are on a smaller scale, you will have far fewer staff, and you and most staff members should be able to perform more than one task in the guest house.

Most guest house owners are either new in business or are entering the hospitality industry for the first time, with little or no formal hospitality training or experience. However, there are many other skills and fields of expertise that will help you to run your establishment successfully. These skills will also ensure that you feel happy and comfortable with what you are doing.

You should also identify the shortcomings in your skills, expertise or knowledge. Ask yourself the following questions: What are the core competencies – those things that must be done well, such as budgeting and food and beverage experience – that are needed for your guest house to succeed? Can you do them or will someone else be doing some of them, which will cost you additional fees? Do you need training in any of these skills?

Relevant experience includes any experience at dealing with the sometimes unreasonable demands of clients, customers or guests. This includes working in a service-orientated business, being a mother or father, teacher, waitress or waiter, having public relations experience, working as an airline flight attendant, or having been involved in the travel and tourism industry.

Good managerial skills, such as managing a household or school, or other committee or professional management experience, will be useful. These skills, as well as financial management skills, can be learnt, however, and there are many courses to assist you.

You will also need food and beverage experience or knowledge of food service and food preparation. Take an appropriate training course or read about the topic. Cooking in a guest house is not the same as cooking at home or for friends, for example. You could run the risk of huge expenditure if wrong decisions literally eat into your profits and you have to throw food away.

Market research

Thorough planning and research in the early stages will save you money. It will help you avoid costly mistakes and assist you in identifying potential pitfalls and problems. It will also help you avoid wrong choices that can have serious consequences for your business. In the planning phase of your guest house, you must make very important choices that will determine the practical working of the guest house and thus, indirectly, its profitability and eventual success.

Why do market research?

Before you lay a brick, buy one extra bed or spend any money on your dream, it is essential to research all aspects of your potential guest house thoroughly. Market research must be undertaken before the guest house is established. However, it should also be done on a regular basis after its establishment to ensure that your services and facilities are keeping up and that your marketing is on the right track, so that you are not wasting money on marketing activities that do not bring in more business. Market research is like taking out insurance against bad planning decisions, and it will increase your chances of success. There are two main areas of focus in market research:

1. The guest house sector of the tourism/hospitality industry.
2. Your target market of potential guests.

Market research will provide you with valuable information about the following:

❀ writing your business plan,
❀ opportunities for your guest house,
❀ the viability and suitability of your ideas,
❀ who your potential guests are,
❀ what their needs and wants are,

- who your competition is and what their strengths and weaknesses are,
- a rough idea of sales potential, and
- developing a sound and effective marketing strategy.

Your guest house should, in the first place, be established as the result of *a need in the market*. It can be very expensive, if not disastrous, to find out that you have completely misjudged the market and that your beautiful guest house is not attracting business. It is not possible for you to force people into buying what you think they want. Your beautifully decorated bedroom and gourmet breakfast will not on their own ensure that you get business if, for example, your rates are not market related or your location is not suitable – factors that your market research will show clearly. Don't be so captivated by your dream that you forget about the hard realities of business. Your research may in fact indicate that you have to make dramatic changes to your original idea or some aspects of it to turn it into a sustainable enterprise. For example, you may discover that although your home may be suitable to convert into a guest house, the location may not be ideal, or it will be very costly to add on all the required bathrooms.

It is vital to have a clear idea of potential business sources before you go ahead with your plans. Many guest houses fail, after a lot of money has been spent, because their market research was inadequate in this regard. Once you start your business, you cannot force people to stay with you and buy your accommodation if you do not offer what they want or meet their needs.

The guest house sector is one of the most competitive sectors in the tourism industry. In order to be successful, you must know as much as possible about the industry, your potential guests and your competitors, as well as business opportunities and possible threats faced by your business. This is why you need to research your target market of prospective guests, as well as the industry and your sector within it.

Finding the answers: How to do market research for your guest house

It is not necessary to employ a team of researchers or to use expensive means to assist you in finding the right information.

Be careful that your market research approach is not influenced by personal preferences. For example, 'This is my dream and it must work.' This approach is wrong. When doing market research, you need to be open-minded and ready to adjust your thinking and ideas.

Start with yourself

Your own travel experiences, knowledge and common sense are very important guidelines in your planning. Ask yourself the following questions: 'What would I require and what do I expect in a guest house?' 'What did I like in guest houses I stayed in and what did I dislike?' Chances are the same things would appeal to your target market too. You may even have been inspired by a particular establishment to start your guest house and may have thought this is something you could do as well. This is why it is invaluable to do site inspections of other guest houses if possible. Remember that your own personality and your excellent service can make or break your business. If you are honest with yourself, you will know that you are not really selling anything intrinsically different from other guest houses, but your own unique manner and your own way can make all the difference.

Don't forget to site-test your own guest house before it opens for guests, by sleeping in every bedroom and using all the facilities as if you were a guest, with luggage. If more guest house owners did this, many complaints of guests would be avoided, such as my own particular irritation when there is nowhere for me to put down my make-up bag in a bathroom.

Reasons for choosing to stay in a guest house

Take note of the reasons people choose to stay in a guest house so that you can ensure that your establishment meets these needs. These have been anecdotally shown to be

* value for money,
* convenient location,
* cleanliness and hygiene,
* appropriate and attractive facilities,
* good personal security and safety,
* personal service (this is one of the major advantages and draw cards of a guest house, compared to an impersonal hotel),
* privacy,
* peace and quiet,
* good home-cooked food,
* attention to detail (the small touches that make the experience special), and
* a 'home from home', but without the normal chaos of family life.

Sources of information

Search the internet on a regular basis for new information about guest houses and tourism developments in your own area, in the country and in other countries, attend trade shows and conferences, and subscribe to magazines or newsletters on tourism trends that may be to your advantage. For example, you may not have known about a new adventure tourism activity that started in your area.

 11

Sources of potential guests

These include major businesses, large institutions, such as educational institutions, travel agents, tour operators, conference venues, shopping centres and tourist attractions in your area. Find out who in the businesses or institutions in your target area is responsible for making arrangements for visitors from out of town. Ask them what type of accommodation they require or what kind of establishment they usually make use of for their guests. Ask what their expectations are, what they are prepared to pay, and whether they are experiencing any problems with their current accommodation providers. Make appointments with personnel managers as they deal with new appointments and transfers. Approach the secretaries of executives, as they generally make accommodation reservations for their bosses and their visitors.

Your local chemist may, for example, know of pharmaceutical representatives who need overnight accommodation, while chain stores will regularly have visiting managers or new staff members from out of town. Many large companies have in-house travel agents to look after their accommodation needs or arrangements with certain travel agents. Contact sports teams, schools and churches in case they have accommodation needs for out-of-town visitors.

Networking in the industry

Contact organisations involved in the guest house industry, such as your local guest house or bed and breakfast association. It is essential to become part of a networking system, as you will be able to learn from the mistakes of others. Most guest house associations are there to assist and advise new guest house owners about required standards, pitfalls, problems and special concessions they may have negotiated for their members. They will also know the local market well.

Local, regional and national tourism organisations

They will be able to assist you in drawing up a profile of the typical visitor to the area and, what is very important, they can supply you with information on peak times and slow times. They will also be able to provide you with information about the other guest houses as well as plans for future developments that could have an impact on the area.

Occupancy rates for your area

There are, for example, statistics available about the average number of nights that visitors spend in an area, the top places of interest, the countries or areas that visitors come from, and the kind of accommodation that they prefer. All of this information will be of value to you in determining your market and, later on, your marketing strategy: if you have a guest house on the KwaZulu-Natal South Coast and are aware that most visitors to the region come from Gauteng while very few come from the Eastern Cape, you will know where to concentrate your marketing efforts.

Existing guest houses in your area

Visit and stay at as many of the existing guest houses in the area as you possibly can, especially your potential main competitors. Ask yourself what you liked or disliked about them. Try to evaluate their strengths and weaknesses to establish what special niche your guest house could fill. For example, how could you improve on your competitors' service or facilities?

New guest houses or hotels in your area

Take note of new guest houses or hotels offering better rates or facilities in your area, as you may need to upgrade your services. It is important to realise that other guest houses are not merely competition. Good co-operation with guest houses in your area will result in better service to your guests. Recognise your impact on your competitors – both good and bad.

The following section provides more detailed information and advice for your research into the guest house sector of the accommodation industry.

Researching the industry/sector

Consider the following questions in your research of the industry:

Need in the market

Is there a need in the market for the accommodation you intend to offer? Is the market oversupplied or are there are some gaps and opportunities in terms of services that you can exploit?

Location

Is your guest house located where it will attract the most business? Location is all-important in this industry. Look at what makes the geographical area good for your guest house, such as a large visitor/tourism base, for example, and also look at the weaknesses of the area, such as high seasonality or lack of roads. Is it close to a business centre, near a hospital, college, university, or a national road? All of these may generate a need for accommodation. Is the guest house easily accessible or visible? It is often better to be visible from the road, albeit a noisy road, than hidden away in a quiet cul-de-sac. Remember that you cannot change your choice of location at a later stage! The wrong location can be a disaster. The location will also influence the services and facilities you need to offer and the rates you can charge. In an urban area, where there are many restaurants, it may not be essential to provide dinner. However, if you are out in the country and far from any facilities, or on a main route, for example on the N1 to Cape Town, you may need to provide some form of evening meal as well. Usually a guest house in a small town cannot charge the same rates for similar facilities as a guest house in a major city. In addition, the country or farm guest house may also get away with fewer amenities and facilities such as *en suite* bathrooms or satellite television.

Type of establishment

What type of establishment are you planning? It is important to establish the type of guest house that will best suit your personality and where in the market you want to be placed, namely at the top luxury end or in the middle or even at the budget end. Not everyone wants to manage a five-star establishment and cater to the high demands of services required. The wide range of types of establishment to choose from is clearly illustrated by the definitions that the *AA Travel Guides* use to classify accommodation.

AA Travel Guides definitions

- *B&B Guest house style:* A B&B is an individually or family-owned establishment which has under 10 rooms, generally not serving dinner, unless in a location where dinner would not be available. It is unlikely to have a liquor licence. This type of B&B is more formal than a Homestay B&B. Guest accommodation may be in a separate house that is used only by B&B guests. The lack of dinner being served and the small number of rooms distinguishes this from a guest house.
- *B&B Guest house with self-catering:* A B&B or guest house that also offers self-catering accommodation.
- *B&B Homestay:* As for B&B Guest house style, but you are likely to stay in the same house as the family and the emphasis is on meeting and mixing with the family. Under 10 rooms, generally not serving dinner.
- *Country-style retreat large:* A country-style retreat is located in a peaceful location offering a tranquil environment for leisure travellers. Emphasis is on getting away from it all. Many country-style retreats restrict access to children. A large country-style retreat has 21 or more rooms.
- *Farm accommodation:* This may be self-catering, B&B or guest house accommodation and is usually located on a working farm where guests are invited to view the farm operations or even participate.

- *Game and/or nature reserve:* A conservation area, either state or privately owned, where an important element of the visit is to experience nature and/or see game. May be a nature reserve where activities such as bird watching and hiking are major attractions or a game reserve where game-viewing can be done but accommodation is less luxurious than at game lodges.
- *Game lodge:* Luxurious accommodation. The game experience is central to the guests' stay. Generally within a reserve offering game drives and all meals etc. as part of the inclusive rate.
- *Guest house dinner by arrangement:* An establishment with anything between two and 20 rooms, where dinner is available by prior arrangement. There are public areas that are solely for the use of guests. The owner/manager may/may not live on site. May also serve meals to non-resident guests.
- *Guest house full service:* Very similar to guest house dinner by arrangement, but dinner is available in a restaurant-style environment.
- *Heritage accommodation:* Accommodation located within a building, which may be a national monument, so that the history of the building is an important element of the experience of staying there.
- *Hotel/guest house garni:* Garni establishments are widespread in Europe. Such an establishment may have the character of a large guest house or even a small hotel. The defining factor is that breakfast is the only meal served on site.
- *Luxury lodge:* This accommodation must be of the highest standard, set in peaceful surroundings either in town or in the country. Furnishings, ambience, food preparation and service should be of exceptional quality. Can be small or large, but whatever the size, personalised service is of the utmost importance.

New business opportunities

Industry and market research will help you to recognise new business opportunities that could supply you with guests, such as a major international conference or a sport event that will take place in your area, other new developments such as a new shopping mall and office complex nearby, and even possible threats to your business like a new hotel opening. You may not have known about the new shopping and business centre that is planned to be built close to your proposed guest house, which may mean that you may attract more business travellers as guests. If so, you will have to ensure that your facilities meet their requirements, such as a desk in every room and a broadband internet connection in the guest house.

Analysing the competition in your market

Who are your competitors? Do similar guest houses operate successfully in the same region or in other parts of the country?

You must know as much as possible about your competitors. You need to analyse their location, guest volumes, hours of operation, the quality of their facilities and their marketing methods, as well as what their guests think of them.

Learn what you can so that you can improve on what they offer. You may discover a particular section of the market that none of your close competitors caters for, such as for the disabled tourist, adventure tourism, the so-called 'green' or ecologically friendly tourism and even agricultural tourism. These could provide you with an excellent and profitable market.

Once you have the information, it is easier to spot opportunities and to decide how to be different, how to price, how to prevent overcapitalising on development, how to market, and how you will convince their guests to switch to you. You may be able to offer a better location, experience, convenience, price, later hours, and additional or better services. You can try to improve on competitors' strengths and exploit their weaknesses.

How much competition is there in your market area?

How many other guest houses are there in your area and where are they situated? Are the guest house sector and/or the accommodation industry growing? Do not consider only the number of guest houses, but also all other accommodation providers. You must make sure that you are not entering an already overfull market. Is there enough business for everyone? Are they prospering or struggling? It is important to determine the size of the market and your potential slice of it. Below is a calculator table for determining market size.

	Example	Your data
Enter the total market size from your research	500	0%
Estimate the percentage of this market who would be interested in your product or service	40%	0%
Percentage taken by competitors	90%	0%
Percentage lost due to external conditions beyond your control	20%	0%
Actual market size	16	0

How to use the calculator:

* Find out the total size of your market by researching directories, statistics etc.
* There will always be a percentage of people in your target market who will not be interested in your guest house.
* Estimate a percentage you would expect to be interested.
* Estimate a percentage you will lose to competitors.
* Estimate a percentage you will lose due to external events/conditions such as: can't afford it, too far away, legal restrictions, etc.

What do your competitors charge in the same region and in other parts of the country? Your rates will be influenced, if not determined, by the rates of your competitors. You cannot hope to recoup overspending on your guest house with higher rates than similar establishments in your area. This will determine the financial decisions you need to take before you start your guest house.

* List the prices of similar services.
* How and why do they differ?
* Do they have incentives?

Knowing what other guest houses charge for the same service will tell you what people will pay. It is important for you to know what local competitors charge, as well as competitors in other areas. Compare the rates with the services and you may even find that as you offer better services you may be able to charge more. The table below should help you in making this comparison.

Competitor name	Location	Product	Price charged

Who are your competitor's guests?

The chances of attracting a totally different target market of potential guests, unless you offer something quite different, are not high. In essence, you will be offering the same product.

What services and facilities are offered by the competition?

Are they all offering optional dinners, satellite television and bathrooms en suite? If you want to charge the same rates, you will at least have to match the facilities they offer.

What is the quality of the experience that they offer?

Do they have star grading, membership of the accommodation association, or an excellent cook, all adding to the experience?

What type of staff do they have?

How many staff members are there, and what is their level of training?

Do they offer value for money?

What do your competitors offer their guests? Can you improve on this and therefore attract guests to your accommodation instead?

Competitor analysis form

The competitor analysis form provided below will help you find the information you need about your competitors. What do they do well? What is done poorly? You will at least have to meet if not improve on what they offer.

Note: Photocopy this sheet to use each time you complete this exercise. Use one sheet per company you visit (or phone). Either you, one of your staff or a friend could complete these surveys. For each item on the list, provide a rating from 1 to 5 (1 is poor, 5 is excellent).

Date assessed		Competitor name						
	Observations	1	2	3	4	5	Comment/action
1	**Outside presentation:** Look for signage, paintwork etc.						
2	**Interior and facilities:** Look for general tidiness of the guest house, internal signage, layout, décor. Does the guest house have a particular atmosphere?						
3	**Services:** Range, presentation, level						
4	**Pricing:** Visibility of pricing, compared to your own prices						
5	**Staff:** Friendliness, dress, name badges, product knowledge, speed. Do they approach you?						
6	**Quality assurance:** Stargrading, membership of local/ national association						
7	**Location:** Potential market in area?						
8	**Market:** Who is making use of this establishment? Unique selling points and competitive advantage						
9	**Hours of operation:** When are they available for their guests, and for which services?						
10	**Marketing and promotion:** Website, brochure, advertising, other						

Researching your target market

As well as researching the accommodation industry and your own sector and area within it, you also need to research and survey your target market of potential guests.

Have you identified potential guests who may have expressed an interest? If so, how many are interested? Market research will help you identify and list all possible sources of business for your guest house and give you a clear indication of who the potential guests to your guest house will be. This is your target market.

For your guest house to be successful, identifying and then satisfying your guests' needs and wants at a profit are critical. You must know and understand your guests so well that your accommodation practically sells itself when you develop your marketing plans. If you do not know who your potential guests are or what they want, you will not be able to reach them through your marketing activities, nor will you be able to satisfy their needs and expectations in terms of the facilities, rates and services you want to offer. As a result, your guest house will not be successful. Remember that as a guest house owner you cannot be everything to everybody. For example, it is not appropriate to cater for families, holidaymakers and serious businesspeople at the same time. You will have to target a specific group of customers and try to meet their requirements as best you can.

Remember that your potential customers have a *free choice* and will not change their needs and preferences to match your establishment; they will simply find what they need elsewhere. If you don't provide what they want, be quite sure that one of your competitors will be pleased to do so.

Your customers' needs therefore determine what they buy. Always keep this in mind. Ignoring their needs and proceeding with your own vision and dream regardless is a recipe for business disaster. The best marketing and the most expensive advertising and promotions will not sell your accommodation in your guest house if it does not meet the needs of a customer. If necessary, change your product to meet these needs. Whatever you do, your rooms, however elegant and comfortable, will not sell if your location, rates, facilities or services are not right for your target market.

Guest profile

Research will enable you to draw up a guest profile describing the requirements of a typical guest that may visit your guest house. It will also show the range and type of services required by him or her such as laundry, meals and snacks, dry cleaning or airport transfers.

The following questions may assist you in drawing up a guest profile indicating the need for services and facilities of different target markets.

How long will the guest be staying?

Business travellers normally stay for one to three days, conference delegates for five days and holidaymakers for a week or more. The longer the stay, the more services you may need to offer, such as a laundry service.

Will your guest stay alone, share a room or bring a partner?

Guests on business generally stay alone, conference delegates may share a room but not a bed, and holidaymakers will bring their families. This information is vital in order for you to decide whether or not you should offer single, double or twin beds, a shower and a bath, or a shower only.

Where does your guest come from?

Foreign visitors may prefer a shower to a bath and need secure facilities for passports and travellers' cheques. Transport from the airport may also be required. South African guests will need lock-up parking facilities.

What is the purpose of your guest's visit?

Why would they want to stay with you? Are they on holiday or business? Are you perhaps offering something different that meets their needs?

What other tourism products will they experience in your region?

This is a valuable source of information for identifying cooperative marketing initiatives with other tourism providers such as tour operators.

At what time of the year will most of your guests stay over?

Coastal guest houses will usually be full over holiday periods, while urban, business-orientated establishments will have little business over these periods. For a few months of the year, guest houses in some areas may be in a position to fill double the number of rooms they have available, while in the remaining months, business can be very slow. Knowing when the busy times and slow times are will assist you in planning your staff requirements, your own and your staff's leave, when to renovate your guest house and how to manage your cash flow.

Have they been to your region before and will they come again?

What potential is there for repeat business from them, for example? How many will visit regularly (i.e. weekly, monthly or annually)?

What level of luxury will your guests require?

High-level dignitaries, diplomatic visitors, top business people and foreign tourists demand the very best in terms of facilities and services. Cash-strapped academics may prefer value for money and clean, comfortable accommodation without extra luxuries.

What special services or facilities do they require?

With some adjustments, your guest house could be made acceptable to specialised niche markets and could benefit from additional business. By ensuring that there is easy access with ramps over stairs and adapting a bathroom appropriately, your guest house could attract disabled guests and thus gain a competitive edge.

Environmentally friendly establishments using so-called 'green' products and policies appeal to a growing target market of ecologically aware people internationally. Adventure travel and cultural and township tourism are new trends, and guest houses could benefit greatly by ensuring that they provide for the requirements of these tourists, who are looking for authentic experiences and would not necessarily require an *en suite* bathroom.

Business people will want to work at a well-lit desk in their rooms. They will require internet access and power points for a laptop computer. A quiet place in which to meet colleagues for a drink at the end of the working day would probably also prove popular with this group. Families will appreciate tea- and coffee-making facilities and a fridge in their room. Business travellers will probably not be keen to share an establishment with families on holiday.

Developing your dream

Backpackers and young tourists, a huge potential market, have also discovered South Africa but they need only basic, budget amenities.

How much will they pay?

What is the financial situation of your target market and what is their ability to pay? How willing will they be to pay what you charge?

What are the emotional needs of your guests?

Remember that your guests are all human, creatures of emotion and not always logical. They often buy with their hearts and rationalise their decisions later with their heads. They form perceptions and often do not tell you what they think or feel. Remember that they buy solutions to problems – they are not buying accommodation for accommodation's sake but are buying a place to stay for a reason. Guests will not make a reservation with you to do something for you, but for what *you can do for them*.

Consequently, the emotional needs of your guests must also be taken into consideration in your planning. Below is a list of the common emotional factors that motivate guests:

✿ convenience,
✿ security,
✿ companionship,
✿ status, the need to feel important,
✿ the need to impress others,
✿ recognition,
✿ fun,
✿ less hassle,
✿ feeling welcome and cared for, and
✿ special, individual treatment.

It is interesting to consider the guest's perception of the value he or she gets from purchasing. Rational value perception includes the following factors: How much does it cost? What is the quality? How convenient is it? Is it reliable? Can you and the business be trusted? Is it safe?

Emotional perception of value will be affected by such factors as how it makes them feel, whether they are given a choice, and whether it is socially acceptable.

You can plan that your services and facilities could meet these needs and add to the so-called feel-good factor – the warm and fuzzy feeling – for your guests. When all else is equal between you and another guest house, the guest will choose the one he or she likes best, often on purely emotional grounds. All people crave appreciation, recognition and acknowledgement of their importance, and the way to create loyal customers is to fulfil such needs.

Compiling your guest profiles

Following your research, you may be able to compile profiles of your potential guests as in the examples below. This will help you to plan your physical facilities to make sure that they are appropriate, and also to set the correct management processes in place.

Profile 1: Typical guests to cities with a high business potential	
Occupation	Businessmen or businesswomen
From where	Other cities in South Africa and/or parent companies overseas
Length of stay	Two to five days
Level of sophistication	High
Preferred location	Near business centres
Size of group	One to three on average (no partners, therefore mainly single occupation)
Level of luxury	From economical to luxury
Essential requirements	*En suite* bathrooms with showers; telephones, desks, internet access, preferably broadband; safe parking, quiet environment (no children); value for money, television, drinks available
Additional services	Dinner and/or snacks on request, meeting facilities, transport and airport transfers
Peak times	March, May–June, September–November
Slow times	School holidays
Profile 2: Typical guests to urban areas	
Occupation	Diplomatic visitor
From where	Countries with which South Africa enjoys diplomatic and/or trade relations
Length of stay	Five to fourteen days
Level of sophistication	High
Preferred location	Near foreign missions (Cape Town and Pretoria) or business centres
Size of group	Virtually always part of a delegation of four or more; often accompanied by partners
Level of luxury	Above-average to luxurious and elegant
Essential requirements	Telephones, television, desks, spacious rooms, internet access, preferably broadband; full *en suite* facilities, separate sitting area in room, good security, all services and dinners, no sharing of rooms, elegant reception area, excellent service
Peak times	Normal business times for both South Africa and the foreign country
Slow times	December–January and June–July

Profile 3: Typical guests to cities and towns with academic institutions	
Occupation	Academic
From where	South African or foreign universities and/or technical universities
Length of stay	As conference delegate: six days
	As academic visitor: up to a month
	On normal business: three days
Level of sophistication	High
Preferred location	Within walking distance of university or technical university campus, research organisations, etc.
Size of group	One to sixteen
Level of luxury	Economical
Essential requirements	Cleanliness, sometimes prepared to share accommodation and even bath facilities, airport transfers, no dinners and/or snacks, internet access, preferably broadband
Peak times	Normal academic year (including July for conferences)
Slow times	October–November and school holidays

Profile 4: Typical guests to a coastal resort	
Occupation	Holidaymaker
From where	Inland South Africa
Length of stay	One to two weeks
Level of sophistication	Middle
Preferred location	Varied
Size of group	Family
Level of luxury	Comfortable
Essential requirements	Often self-catering facilities, television, will share bath, bedrooms, safe parking, children welcome
Non-essential	Telephones, desks, internet access, snacks and/or dinners, transport
Peak times	School holidays
Slow times	Out of season

Using surveys for market information

You can also formally survey your potential target market to get the information you need about your guests. There are websites offering tailor-made surveys, which are an inexpensive and easy option. Another effective method is to get a small group of people together as a focus group, to talk about their needs and requirements. These methods may be a little more expensive but could save you a lot if they help you get your product right.

Developing a questionnaire

A questionnaire will help you collect information from your guests. Here are some simple guidelines:

* Be as brief as possible as you are asking people to give up their free time. Tell them how long the questions will take to answer. You may have to offer them an incentive.
* Be sensitive when asking for personal details, such as name, address, age, and income. Only ask for these if they are going to provide you with useful information. You must assure respondents of their confidentiality.
* Know exactly what you want to find out so the answers people give can be used in a meaningful way. Choose the correct type of question according to the type of information you want (qualitative or quantitative).
    - An example of an open-ended question is 'Please describe your impressions of our reservations service'.
    - An example of a closed question is 'How would you rate our service?' (a) excellent, (b) very good, (c) good, (d) quite bad, (e) very bad.
* Use normal language. Avoid technical jargon and be careful to avoid ambiguity and words that indicate bias, for example 'What don't you like about this bedroom?' This suggests there is something wrong, and may influence the answer. Avoid words such as 'like' and 'dislike'. A better way to ask this question would be 'Please write what you think about your bedroom'.

Choosing the survey sample

Who to survey? Ideally you should survey people in your target market. Try to screen them first.

How many? Generally speaking, a sample of 100 people should be adequate for a small geographical area. Professional market research companies generally use samples of 300 to 1 000. A sample size of 300 will give a maximum error range of about five per cent.

Collecting and tabulating the data

Survey data can be collected in three ways:

* mail questionnaires,
* phone-call interviews, and
* face-to-face interviews.

Person-to-person contact always gets the best response. The phone call method is the least expensive of the two person-to-person methods. Proper tabulation of the data is important so that they can be presented in useable form.

Once you are operating, it is equally important to keep up to date with your guests' needs, profiles and requirements to make sure that you are still on the right track.

Analysing your research results

Once you have conducted thorough market research, you should feel encouraged that your plans are on the right track and know that your guest house will be viable, is correctly located, and will meet the needs of a specific target market with which you feel comfortable. You will be armed with valuable information about your target market and its habits and preferences, and you will be confident that you will be able to answer the key questions in setting up a business strategy for your guest house and be able to add value for your guests.

The following are key questions that should form part of your business strategy:

* Who are my customers?
* What value do I want to deliver to them?
* How will I create it?
* How will I deliver it?
* How will I maintain it?
* How will I measure success and failure?

Your analysis of your market research will indicate where you may need to modify or improve your planned guest house, for example:

* Customers are coming from unexpected areas, and those are opportunities for growth. You could include your product in specific guide books or extend brochure distribution.
* Some aspects of your product may not be working or may even be unnecessary, while others may have the potential for further development.
* You might notice a need for having marketing resources in foreign languages, and/or staff who speak more than one language.
* You might identify an opportunity to target new markets.

With your results at hand, it may be useful to complete the assessment table opposite to evaluate your idea for your guest house, before moving on to the next important stage, the financial planning of your guest house.

List your business ideas below and rate them against the criteria on the right. Rank each of your ideas from 5 (fits the criterion) to 1 (does not fit the criterion).

Ideas (insert a title for each idea)	Different from the competition	Potential revenue is great	Branding possibility	Fits in with key success factors	You are really good at it	You have the capability already to do it	It is inexpensive (or you have the resources) to do it	It fits in with your long-term strategy

It seems that the best option for you is:

Developing your dream

Doing the sums: The business plan

Introduction

Can you afford to start your guest house in the manner that your market research has confirmed? Do you have enough money to establish your guest house, furnish it properly and promote it and also to tide you over until you start to make a profit? It is important to make sure that you are as efficient as possible and that each part of your business pays its way and gives you a return on investment. Find out whether establishing the guest house is financially viable before you do anything else.

The business plan

Your business plan is essential because it forces you to think through your ideas and options. It is a good idea to be pessimistic and to keep your expenses high and income low in your planning. Check your figures with someone in the industry itself, like the local accommodation association. You may be feeling lost with all the figures, but it is vital to get all your figures in order at this stage.

The business plan is the blueprint for your business. Having done your market research thoroughly, you should be in a position to formulate a basic business plan and to do a preliminary costing. A business plan is a statement of what business you want to establish, and what your goals and objectives are. The business plan details how you will generate an income and what the costs of establishing the business will be. It should demonstrate the financial viability of the business, and not only describe the business.

A business plan generally serves two main functions

It provides you with a detailed set of guidelines, setting out how to start your business, what it will cost to set it up, what resources are required to ensure the success of the business, what net income you can expect to flow from the business, and how long it will take for you to reach an operating level where you break even (the break-even point is the point at which income equals expenditure).

The business plan may be used to convince banks and/or investors that your prospective business is viable and can be used to find financial support for the business.

A business plan serves to make sure that you do not forget any small detail and that your guest house will enable you to make a living. Make sure it is clear, well-written and professional in appearance. Be honest with yourself regarding expenses and potential success and rather overestimate expenses and underestimate income.

What should be in your business plan?

Cover page

This contains the name of your guest house, your name and contact details, what the document contains and a one-paragraph summary of the plan.

Introduction

Describe in about 200 words what your guest house is all about and why you believe it will be successful. This section will include the results of your market research and describe who your potential guests will be, what the needs in the market are and how your guest house will meet those needs, the type of guest house that you intend to establish and the services and facilities that will be available, as well as your choice of location. Why would people choose your guest house? What added attractions are there? The introduction has to make a positive impression, as your request for financial assistance may be refused on the basis of this alone.

Business arrangement

You need to decide whether the business will be a sole proprietorship, a close corporation, a company or a trading trust, and the business arrangements need to be clarified (management agreements, lease arrangements and funding options). We recommended that you contact your lawyer and accountant to discuss the options thoroughly in order to decide on the option that will be most suitable to your planned business. Some of the advantages and disadvantages of the most common options are listed in the table opposite:

	Number of people involved	Legal formation	Capital/ financial contribution	Legal liability	Tax status	Distribution of profits	Audit
Sole proprietor	The owner	Nothing needed	Owner's own	Unlimited The guest house is not a separate legal entity	The owner pays tax	Belong to the owner to do with what he or she likes	Not required
Partnership	2–20 partners	Agreement between partners Written agreement recommended	As agreed between partners	Unlimited The guest house is not a separate legal entity	The partners pay tax	Divided between partners according to agreement	Not required
Close corporation	1–10 members	Founding statement to be registered as well as a certificate of incorporation issued Professional help needed	As agreed and limited to members	Limited The guest house is a separate legal entity	The business pays tax	Divided between members according to written resolution	An accounting review required
Company	1–50 shareholders	Memorandum and articles of association registered and certificate of incorporation issued Professional help needed	Limited to the founders of the company	Limited The guest house is a separate legal entity	The business pays tax	Shareholders get a share of the profits in the form of declared dividends	Independent audit by registered auditor

Doing the sums: The business plan

Analysis of the business environment

In this section you provide information about your competitors, business and tourism opportunities in the area and why your guest house will succeed in this environment. These details should be determined by your market research. The performance of the competition will be an indication of the results you can expect. If other accommodation establishments that offer similar products, and are servicing the same market segment, are doing well in the area where you wish to establish your guest house, it may confirm that there is room for more projects of that nature and you can expect your project to perform well.

Marketing strategy

This is where you describe how you intend to reach your target. It is also advisable to consider the trend in the market, in other words whether the market is growing or shrinking, and to take into account the expectations for the future.

Potential utilisation of your services

You need to estimate your room occupancy. This will be influenced by the performance of the competition, by the trend in and future expectations of the market the guest house will be aimed at, and by the fact that the guest house is new and starting from a zero base. The fact that you may be inexperienced and will have to learn how to market the project effectively may also influence your market penetration.

The project

Here you need to determine details of general aspects of the business, the physical infrastructure, the geographical location of the business, the tourism activities (swimming, diving, game drives, walks, trails, or any other activity) and aspects not covered elsewhere.

Organisational structure

Who will do the work? How many staff will you need to hire? What is the potential monetary value of your own involvement in the business? What experience qualifies you to own and manage a guest house? You will need to be a Jack of all trades in the guest house business and will, amongst other things, require marketing, financial and operational skills, which include reception and food and room-preparation skills.

Financial requirements

How much money do you need to finance the guest house? Remember that you will probably not earn any income for the first few months and will need some form of working capital to tide you over.

What is it going to cost?

Set-up costs

A clear understanding of costs is important because if you cannot cover your set-up costs you will have to borrow money or delay your start. Be careful of borrowing too much, as high repayments can stretch your business. Allow for enough money to keep going until your occupancy picks up, which could take a couple of months.

How much money you will need will depend on your decisions regarding the type of establishment you envisage, for example an economical and neat bed and breakfast only establishment or a luxury guest house with all the trimmings and services. This decision should be based on your market.

You have to consider your capital costs as well as your overheads in your planning. Capital costs will include the land, buildings, furniture and equipment. It is better to overestimate how much this is going to be as unforeseen expenses have a way of creeping up on you. Even if you do not have all the correct figures, estimated amounts will give you a feel for the possible costs.

Typical set-up capital costs could include the following:

Description of your needs	Total (R)
Cost of changes to the physical structure of your guest house	
Cost of furniture	
Cost of linen	
Cost of crockery, kitchen equipment, pots, pans	
Office equipment, computers, faxes, desks, internet connections	
Cost of guest amenities	
Cost of interior décor – curtains, flooring, soft furnishings	
Insurance	
Memberships	
Legal fees and permits	
Equipment and assets such as vehicles	
Initial stock	
Lease payments	
Licence fees – TV, radio, satellite	
Stationery	
Advisors' fees	
Training courses	
Initial marketing costs and cost to develop a marketing plan	
Working capital	
Purchase price minus deposit	
Subtotal: Total projected needs	(a)
Contingency fund: Total projected needs	(b)
Total projected needs	(a) + (b)

Consider how you will meet these financial needs. The following are various means of raising capital funds:

Description of your sources of capital	Total (R)
Cash obtained from selling present home	
Cash on hand	
Personal savings	
Other assets	
A loan from the bank to buy a property	
The value of a personal involvement in the guest house	
A loan from a private investor	
A government loan/grant	
Cash flow by means of an overdraft	
Total value of plan (this amount should equal your total projected needs)	

Working capital

An idea of your running costs every month will help you determine the potential viability of your guest house. This is also important so that you know what amount of cash you will need to cover your first months and after that what level of business is required. Even if you don't have guests, as in low-season months, for example, you will still have overheads such as utilities and wages to pay.

It is wise to calculate how much money you have to set aside in order to cover your basic living expenses while the guest house is being established and while you will earn no income.

Regular monthly overheads can include the following:

❀ municipal rates and taxes,
❀ bank fees and interest,
❀ licences and permits,
❀ utilities such as water and electricity,
❀ staff wages, unemployment insurance contributions,
❀ insurance,
❀ lease payments,
❀ postage, printing and stationery,
❀ internet service provider, phones and fax,
❀ bond repayments,
❀ clothing, and
❀ office supplies.

Your salary

You will have to live while your business is being established. Work out what the minimum monthly salary is that you require. Include expenses like travel and car expenses, school fees, clothing, food, medical costs, phones and cellphones, insurance, tax and so forth.

Profit requirements

You are in business to make a profit and that is what your guest house is expected to do. Not only must it pay you a decent salary to live on, it must also give you a return on your investment. Your income must take into account the fact that there is no longer any paid sick or vacation leave. There will no longer be a subsidised mortgage bond or medical aid. The return on your investment should also be higher than if you had simply left your money in the bank. In addition, allow for money for possible growth or improvements to your guest house. Work out the break-even point on the following spreadsheet:

Break-even feasibility test: Example	
What are your monthly business overheads?	R30 000 (annual R360 000)
What is your required annual salary?	R150 000
How much annual profit do you want the business to generate for growth?	R150 000
Enter your investment in the business	R1 000 000
What return on investment would you like to achieve?	12%
How many weeks per year will you be open for business?	50
You need to generate	R15 600 per week

A quick calculation of potential income (more properly termed revenue) will be helpful in this regard:

Revenue example	
Rooms	5
Number of nights open	340
Total potential customers	1 700
Occupancy rate	50
Actual number of nights occupied	850
Average room rate	R300
Average cost per room, cleaning etc	R50
Revenue potential	R425 000

Potential profit calculation

A quick calculation of potential profits will be helpful to give you an idea of business potential. Calculate your potential profit according to the following table. This is the profit forecast table, which shows you your monthly costs and profits:

Profit forecast

Start month (select below)

January

All figures VAT exclusive

Sales revenue	Jan	Feb	Mar	Apr	May	June	July	Aug	Sept	Oct	Nov	Dec	Annual Total
Cash sales	R0	R0	R0	R0	R0	R0	R0	R0	R0	R0	R0	R0	R0
Credit sales	R0	R0	R0	R0	R0	R0	R0	R0	R0	R0	R0	R0	R0
Other income	R0	R0	R0	R0	R0	R0	R0	R0	R0	R0	R0	R0	R0
Total income	R0	R0	R0	R0	R0	R0	R0	R0	R0	R0	R0	R0	R0
Direct cost of sales													
Purchases of stock/raw materials	R0.00	R0.00	R0.00	R0.00	R0.00	R0.00	R0.00	R0.00	R0.00	R0.00	R0.00	R0.00	R0.00
Direct wages	R0.00	R0.00	R0.00	R0.00	R0.00	R0.00	R0.00	R0.00	R0.00	R0.00	R0.00	R0.00	R0.00
Commissions paid	R0.00	R0.00	R0.00	R0.00	R0.00	R0.00	R0.00	R0.00	R0.00	R0.00	R0.00	R0.00	R0.00
Other direct costs	R0.00	R0.00	R0.00	R0.00	R0.00	R0.00	R0.00	R0.00	R0.00	R0.00	R0.00	R0.00	R0.00
Total direct costs	R0.00	R0.00	R0.00	R0.00	R0.00	R0.00	R0.00	R0.00	R0.00	R0.00	R0.00	R0.00	R0.00
Gross profit	R0.00	R0.00	R0.00	R0.00	R0.00	R0.00	R0.00	R0.00	R0.00	R0.00	R0.00	R0.00	R0.00
Overhead expenses													
Accounting	R0	R0	R0	R0	R0	R0	R0	R0	R0	R0	R0	R0	R0
Advertising	R0	R0	R0	R0	R0	R0	R0	R0	R0	R0	R0	R0	R0
Bank charges	R0	R0	R0	R0	R0	R0	R0	R0	R0	R0	R0	R0	R0
General expenses	R0	R0	R0	R0	R0	R0	R0	R0	R0	R0	R0	R0	R0
Insurance	R0	R0	R0	R0	R0	R0	R0	R0	R0	R0	R0	R0	R0
Interest paid	R0	R0	R0	R0	R0	R0	R0	R0	R0	R0	R0	R0	R0

Legal fees	R0	R0	R0	R0	R0	R0	R0	R0	R0	R0	R0	R0
Motor vehicle expenses	R0	R0	R0	R0	R0	R0	R0	R0	R0	R0	R0	R0
Postage	R0	R0	R0	R0	R0	R0	R0	R0	R0	R0	R0	R0
Power	R0	R0	R0	R0	R0	R0	R0	R0	R0	R0	R0	R0
Print and stationery	R0	R0	R0	R0	R0	R0	R0	R0	R0	R0	R0	R0
Rates	R0	R0	R0	R0	R0	R0	R0	R0	R0	R0	R0	R0
Rent	R0	R0	R0	R0	R0	R0	R0	R0	R0	R0	R0	R0
Repairs and maintenance	R0	R0	R0	R0	R0	R0	R0	R0	R0	R0	R0	R0
Staff wages and salaries	R0	R0	R0	R0	R0	R0	R0	R0	R0	R0	R0	R0
Telephone/fax/internet	R0	R0	R0	R0	R0	R0	R0	R0	R0	R0	R0	R0
Travel and accommodation	R0	R0	R0	R0	R0	R0	R0	R0	R0	R0	R0	R0
Other expenses	R0	R0	R0	R0	R0	R0	R0	R0	R0	R0	R0	R0
Other expenses	R0	R0	R0	R0	R0	R0	R0	R0	R0	R0	R0	R0
Other expenses	R0	R0	R0	R0	R0	R0	R0	R0	R0	R0	R0	R0
Total overheads	**R0**	**R0**	**R0**	**R0**	**R0**	**R0**	**R0**	**R0**	**R0**	**R0**	**R0**	**R0**
Operating profit	**R0**	**R0**	**R0**	**R0**	**R0**	**R0**	**R0**	**R0**	**R0**	**R0**	**R0**	**R0**
Bad debts	R0	R0	R0	R0	R0	R0	R0	R0	R0	R0	R0	R0
Depreciation	R0	R0	R0	R0	R0	R0	R0	R0	R0	R0	R0	R0
	R0	R0	R0	R0	R0	R0	R0	R0	R0	R0	R0	R0
Net profit before tax	**R0**	**R0**	**R0**	**R0**	**R0**	**R0**	**R0**	**R0**	**R0**	**R0**	**R0**	**R0**
Tax on net profit	R0	R0	R0	R0	R0	R0	R0	R0	R0	R0	R0	R0
Net profit after tax	**R0**	**R0**	**R0**	**R0**	**R0**	**R0**	**R0**	**R0**	**R0**	**R0**	**R0**	**R0**

Doing the sums: The business plan

Select a month to start	April		May		June		July		Aug		Sept	
	Expected	Actual	Expected	Actual	Expected	Actual	Expected	Actual	Expected	Actual	Expected	Actual
RECEIPTS												
Sales	R0	R0	R0	R0	R0	R0	R0	R0	R0	R0	R0	R0
Other revenue	R0	R0	R0	R0	R0	R0	R0	R0	R0	R0	R0	R0
	R0	R0	R0	R0	R0	R0	R0	R0	R0	R0	R0	R0
	R0	R0	R0	R0	R0	R0	R0	R0	R0	R0	R0	R0
(A) Total receipts	R0	R0	R0	R0	R0	R0	R0	R0	R0	R0	R0	R0
LESS PAYMENTS												
Wages	R0	R0	R0	R0	R0	R0	R0	R0	R0	R0	R0	R0
Drawings	R0	R0	R0	R0	R0	R0	R0	R0	R0	R0	R0	R0
Overheads (rent, power, etc)	R0	R0	R0	R0	R0	R0	R0	R0	R0	R0	R0	R0
Marketing	R0	R0	R0	R0	R0	R0	R0	R0	R0	R0	R0	R0
Repayment of loans	R0	R0	R0	R0	R0	R0	R0	R0	R0	R0	R0	R0
VAT payments	R0	R0	R0	R0	R0	R0	R0	R0	R0	R0	R0	R0
Income tax payments	R0	R0	R0	R0	R0	R0	R0	R0	R0	R0	R0	R0
Materials & stock	R0	R0	R0	R0	R0	R0	R0	R0	R0	R0	R0	R0
Other payments	R0	R0	R0	R0	R0	R0	R0	R0	R0	R0	R0	R0
	R0	R0	R0	R0	R0	R0	R0	R0	R0	R0	R0	R0
	R0	R0	R0	R0	R0	R0	R0	R0	R0	R0	R0	R0
	R0	R0	R0	R0	R0	R0	R0	R0	R0	R0	R0	R0
(B) Total cash payments	R0	R0	R0	R0	R0	R0	R0	R0	R0	R0	R0	R0
(C) Net cash flow (A − B)	R0	R0	R0	R0	R0	R0	R0	R0	R0	R0	R0	R0
(D) Opening bank balance	R0	R0	R0	R0	R0	R0	R0	R0	R0	R0	R0	R0
Closing bank balance (D+C)	R0	R0	R0	R0	R0	R0	R0	R0	R0	R0	R0	R0

Effective Guest House Management

(extend for a full year)											
Oct		Nov		Dec		Jan		Feb		Mar	
Expected	Actual	Expected	Actual	Expected	Actual	Expected	Actual	Expected	Actual	Expected	Actual
R0	R0	R0	R0	R0	R0	R0	R0	R0	R0	R0	R0
R0	R0	R0	R0	R0	R0	R0	R0	R0	R0	R0	R0
R0	R0	R0	R0	R0	R0	R0	R0	R0	R0	R0	R0
R0	R0	R0	R0	R0	R0	R0	R0	R0	R0	R0	R0
R0	**R0**	**R0**	**R0**	**R0**	**R0**	**R0**	**R0**	**R0**	**R0**	**R0**	**R0**
R0	R0	R0	R0	R0	R0	R0	R0	R0	R0	R0	R0
R0	R0	R0	R0	R0	R0	R0	R0	R0	R0	R0	R0
R0	R0	R0	R0	R0	R0	R0	R0	R0	R0	R0	R0
R0	R0	R0	R0	R0	R0	R0	R0	R0	R0	R0	R0
R0	R0	R0	R0	R0	R0	R0	R0	R0	R0	R0	R0
R0	R0	R0	R0	R0	R0	R0	R0	R0	R0	R0	R0
R0	R0	R0	R0	R0	R0	R0	R0	R0	R0	R0	R0
R0	R0	R0	R0	R0	R0	R0	R0	R0	R0	R0	R0
R0	R0	R0	R0	R0	R0	R0	R0	R0	R0	R0	R0
R0	R0	R0	R0	R0	R0	R0	R0	R0	R0	R0	R0
R0	R0	R0	R0	R0	R0	R0	R0	R0	R0	R0	R0
R0	R0	R0	R0	R0	R0	R0	R0	R0	R0	R0	R0
R0	**R0**	**R0**	**R0**	**R0**	**R0**	**R0**	**R0**	**R0**	**R0**	**R0**	**R0**
R0	R0	R0	R0	R0	R0	R0	R0	R0	R0	R0	R0
R0	R0	R0	R0	R0	R0	R0	R0	R0	R0	R0	R0
R0	**R0**	**R0**	**R0**	**R0**	**R0**	**R0**	**R0**	**R0**	**R0**	**R0**	**R0**

Projections

The projections are the forecast of expected income and expenses. Most financial institutions require figures for at least three to five years, with the first year's figures set out on a month-by-month basis. The projections should contain an income statement, a cash flow statement, tax computation and balance sheet. The balance sheet needs to contain a day-one situation and thereafter year by year. It is always advisable to detail all assumptions, as financial institutions will want to analyse the projections and even carry out their own calculations. It may be necessary to seek the assistance of professionals to help you compile the projections.

Cash flow

Your cash flow is the most important indicator of whether your new guest house will succeed or run out of money. It will help you see when money may be tight and help you plan in advance. This is especially important if you are borrowing money from the bank. Most businesses can survive a few months of negative cash flow, but a lengthy period will spell disaster.

Cash flow tips

- A good cash flow is not just a spreadsheet of numbers. It's the document that people who examine your business will spend the most time reading. It must be watertight. If there are gaps, people will wonder what else you haven't thought through. Make a note of the assumptions you're basing the figures on. These will show anyone reading the cash flow how you arrived at these figures.
- Your forecast for the business must reflect a realistic balance between proper sales projections and an accurate costing and pricing of your goods and services.
- The time you spend assessing a realistic sales level is crucial. You should outline exactly how you arrived at the sales figures for each month. Do not forget seasonality, as sales in accommodation rarely stay at the same level throughout the year.
- Once you've outlined the sales for each month, you'll be able to estimate your costs. You need to explain in detail how you calculated these amounts.
- You can be certain about some costs (for example, you can find out your rent), and others will be estimates (power and phone charges).
- Check your capacity. Don't put R50 000 for a month unless you can physically do it. There are only a certain number of hours in the day.
- If you can, find out information such as average net profit and gross profit amounts. If you differ from the average, people will want to know why.
- Make sure your withdrawals from the bank are realistic. Don't take out too much money, or too little.
- Remember once-off items like accounting fees, and your tax obligations. Many businesses struggle to find the cash to pay taxes when they are due. You must get your accountant to help estimate your tax (it is a good idea to register for Provisional Tax, which provides for payment in instalments over the tax year).
- Prepare at least two years of cash flow so you can see what might happen in the second year of business. Don't look too far ahead because longer predictions are unlikely to be accurate.

Sources of income and expenses

Estimating income and expenses

Your income is derived from the number of bookings you receive. This is dependent on your sources of income and the rate you charge. Your income should be enough to cover your basic costs. As a rule of thumb, 33 per cent occupancy should cover your monthly costs. It is advisable that you limit your expenses to about 40 per cent of your income.

Examples of sources of income include the room income from selling the room, beverage income where you may sell drinks, restaurant/food income, renting facilities for functions or conferences, telephone income, gifts and souvenirs, renting equipment such as fishing rods or kayaks, and any other income that your guest house may be able to generate. It is important to collect information about all your anticipated sources of income and expenses. Your income should at least be enough to cover your basic costs.

Remember to treat your guest house like another mouth to feed, as it too will demand that money is spent on it for growth. Work out your own desired income or salary and make sure it is high enough to cover the additional expenses of working for yourself, such as covering for holidays and sick leave.

Collect information about all your anticipated sources of income and expenses. The following worksheets will help you list these estimations. After the first year, it will of course be much easier to project more reliable figures, and they will tell you whether you need to increase your income or expand your business, or whether you have problem areas where too much is being spent. These are guides only and are not exhaustive, and may change according to your own special circumstances.

The direct expenses generally refer to the cost of sales of the various products, while fixed expenses could include items such as audit fees, accounting fees, advertising costs, bank charges, cleaning expenses, water and electricity and staff costs.

Calculate your potential income according to the following table:

Sources of income and expenses		
Types of income	Description	Estimated income (R)
Rooms	Room with breakfast	
Food	Additional meals, dinner, snacks	
Beverages	Drinks, coffee, alcohol, sold separately	
Paid airport transfers	Paid-for transfers to and from airport	
Other: souvenirs, gifts, etc	Special items	

Types of expenses	Description	Estimated expense (R)
Mortgage	Mortgage and interest	
Bank fees	Bank charges and interests	
Wages	Staff and owner's wages	
Rates and taxes	Municipal charges	
Taxes	VAT	
Legal and accounting fees	Lawyers, contracts, accounting	
Marketing costs	Publications, advertisements, website etc.	
Housekeeping stocks and supplies	Cleaning materials etc.	
Utilities	Water and electricity	
Maintenance	Painting, replacements	
Transport	Cars, taxis etc.	
Food and beverage	Food and drinks	
Insurance	Public liability etc.	
Security	Security firms	
Commissions	Referrals from travel agents	
Memberships	Local tourism or guest house associations	
Office supplies	Paper, pens etc.	
Travel	Travel-related expenses	
Linen	Sheets, towels	
Garden and pool	Plants, pool cleaning, mowing	
IT, computers, internet	Technology, internet connections	
Telephones, faxes, cell phones	Rentals and call charges	
Entertainment	Business entertainment	

Pricing structure

The number of bookings you get in your guest house and the price at which you sell the bookings reflect your sales and income in your guest house.

You should know what is meant by *room rate* and *occupancy* and be able to estimate your maximum expenses and income every month. The *break-even* point helps you to clarify the viability of your business and allows you to see how different pricing levels affect the number of sales you must make.

The room rate is the cost of the room and is how much you will charge your guests for the room for one night. It is accepted in the guest house industry that breakfast is included in the rates.

Consider the following aspects when setting an appropriate rate:

❀ What does the competition charge for similar facilities and what value for money are they offering?
❀ Do you offer additional facilities, adding value to your accommodation, such as broadband internet, a king-size bed, unusual and attractive features such as an open fireplace, a spa bath, horse riding or good surfing, or an excellent location in a popular area?
❀ Remember that a double rate is not twice that of a single rate. A single rate is about two-thirds of a double rate. You may wish to sell the room regardless of the number of occupants.
❀ Remember to consider the fact that you may have to pay commission of at least 10 per cent to travel agents and would have a rack rate (see chapter 8), which you use for all guests, and a Standard Tour Operator (STO) rate for the travel trade, which reflects the 10 per cent discount. Do not add commission onto your rates (see chapters 7 and 8 on agents and commissions).
❀ Your rate has to allow for adequate recovery of your costs.
❀ Do not charge so much that your rates are no longer market related and you have priced yourself out of the market, but make sure that your rate covers your service.

Occupancy refers to the percentage of your available rooms sold. You need to estimate your room occupancy in your business plan. Potential occupancy rates according to the number of rooms that you plan to build or refurbish should also be determined by your market research.

Occupancy will be influenced by the performance of the competition, the trend in and future expectations of the target market for the guest house, and the fact that the guest house is new and starting from a zero base. The fact that you may be inexperienced and will have to learn how to market the project effectively may also influence your market penetration.

You can expect to get about 50 per cent of the occupancy rate of your area in the first year and should grow your occupancy by about 10 per cent every year. Because of the effect of seasonality (meaning there are times in the year when occupancy is very high while at other times it can be very low) it is best to take an annual average occupancy rate as you do not want to base your planning on either one of the extremes.

Falling occupancy or occupancy that is not increasing satisfactorily is a sign of trouble and should send up a red flag for you to check all aspects of your planning. Problem areas include wrong location, bad service, too high rates, unacceptable facilities, more competition, ineffective marketing and outside factors.

Your break-even point

Being aware of your break-even point – where your costs are covered and before you start making a profit – will help you in many ways:

❀ You can work out exactly how much business you could afford to lose if prices were increased.
❀ You can work out how much extra business you will need if you increase staff or expand the business.
❀ You can see how much extra work you have to do if you lower your price or offer a discount.

❀ You can use it to predict sales.
❀ It is important to know when you are setting your rates or considering increasing them.

To determine your break-even point you must first break down your expenses into fixed and variable costs. Your fixed costs are the costs that stay the same regardless of your occupancy, such as staff wages, rates and so forth. Variable costs change with increasing occupancy, such as the food you use for preparing breakfast and laundering costs.

What happens if you increase your price or rates? Using the following break-even formula will illustrate the point:

Break-even analysis:

Estimated fixed costs for the year are	R90 000
Estimated variable costs per night are	R25
Current rate/price per night is	R225

Calculation:

Fixed costs	R90 000
Divided by price per room	(R225 − R25 = R200)
This equals	450 bed nights

Or about 8.5 bed nights a week.
If you increase your price to R250, the formula is:
R90 000 ÷ R225 = 400 bed nights.

This means that the number of nights you need to sell to break even is reduced to only 400.

Example: Setting the rates

You may be planning six double rooms and will be able to charge R350 per room for single occupancy. Two rooms occupied at R700 per night represents 33 per cent occupancy. R700 ×30 days = R21 000 per month.

From this you may need to deduct:

Value-added tax (VAT)	R2 625
Electricity and telephone	± 3 000
Food (two breakfasts @ R35 00 each)	R2 100
Salaries and wages	± R2 000
Advertising/marketing	R750
Petrol	R700
Levies, compulsory payments	R500
Total	**R11 675**

This leaves R8 408, and you have still not received any salary or profit. This means that your bond or loan repayment dare not exceed this amount. Remember that it is not wise to over-capitalise at this stage and then to expect your occupancy income to make up any financial shortfall later.

Below is the actual evaluation a guest house owner used to determine his rate. This particular bed and breakfast establishment has eight bedrooms, all *en suite* with full bathrooms (bath and shower), all rooms with television, bar fridge and microwave, and parking in carports behind an electronic security gate. It is centrally situated.

The owner has budgeted his monthly[1] costs – he has no bond repayment – including municipal bills, staff, housekeeper, receptionist and food at R17 400 per month. He included VAT and 10 per cent reservation agent's commission, instead of other marketing expenses.

The guest house owner has 240 rooms available per month; that is, eight rooms on each of 30 nights. To break even at R100 per night (R120 room rate minus R20 for breakfast), R17 400 ÷ 100 = 174 rooms must be let every month. This represents an occupancy of 174 ÷ 240 × 100 = 73 per cent.

In other words, to break even (before making any profit at all), an average occupancy percentage of almost 73 per cent must be maintained throughout the year. In the fluctuating tourism market, it is virtually impossible to maintain such a high occupancy, particularly during the establishment phase of a guest house in the first two or three years of its existence.

If the owner increased the rates to R120 per day (R140 – R20), R17 400 ÷ 120 = 145 rooms must be let every month, representing an occupancy of 145 ÷ 240 × 100 ÷ 1 = 60%. This is more realistic, but still difficult to attain. When his rates are increased to R140 (R160 – R20) per day, only 124 rooms need to be let every month. This represents an occupancy of 52 per cent, which, although still relatively high, is a more realistic and attainable goal.

It is clear that the guest house could not make a profit or even support its running costs at only R120 per night. However, his competitors' rates were between R140 and R175 per night. In order to keep his competitive edge, the owner decided to increase his rates to R150 and thereby to attempt to increase his occupancy rate. This policy has paid off for him.

The reason why this policy has worked for this specific guest house is that both the occupancy percentages and the room rates aimed at per day were realistic figures. The guest house could achieve its goal while still retaining a competitive edge over the other guest houses in the area. The importance of maintaining a competitive edge cannot be emphasised enough. Refer to the calculations when you estimated your possible bond repayment on the basis of what you could reasonably expect to earn in your guest house.

SWOT analysis (strengths, weaknesses, opportunities, threats)

An honest and critical evaluation of the strengths, weaknesses, opportunities and threats will help you capitalise on your strengths, overcome your weaknesses, exploit opportunities and avoid threats (or turn threats into opportunities).

Technical information

The technical information deals with approvals required before your guest house can be established, plans for buildings, and cost estimates for buildings and other immovable assets. It also deals with the technical team to be used and may include architects, builders, renovators, interior decorators, etc.

Conclusion

A concluding statement confirming your faith in the potential of the proposed business will round off the business plan.

---

[1]   One month is taken as 30 days.

Developing a business plan

The KwaZulu-Natal Tourism Authority provides the following useful step-by-step guide to writing a business plan for potential tourism entrepreneurs:

1. Write out what you want to do; i.e. what type of business it is to be.
2. Write out your purpose in starting this business.
3. Write out your short-term (0–3 years), medium-term (3–5 years) and long-term (more than 5 years) vision for the business.
4. Write down a list of what resources you know you need to start your business, e.g. an office, a bank loan, a minibus, etc.
5. Clearly state any uncertainties you may have. For example, you may be uncertain about the type of business structure to create – a company or a close corporation, etc.
6. Identify who your market may be.
7. Identify who your competitors may be and try to find out as much about them as possible, e.g. tariffs, types of service offered, possible gaps or weaknesses in their service, etc.
8. Try to identify those businesses with which you may be able to cooperate. For example, a travel agent would be able to cooperate extensively with tour operators, hotels or taxi services, etc.
9. Attach a cost to each item in (4) and develop your fixed and your start-up costs.
10. Work out how many months your business may have to survive before its income equals the expenditure.
11. Give careful thought to how you will make your business known – how you will market your products or services – and calculate the costs associated with this marketing.
12. Before you spend too much money exploring your business concept, you must draw a conclusion as to whether the concept you have is likely to make a viable business. Then you can try to reach a decision about whether your business idea is worth pursuing immediately, whether the business concept needs to be changed, or whether it should be shelved for a later time.
13. It is very important that you develop as much of the content of the business plan as you can. Then, once you have done all that you can, you should call on the assistance of professionals.

Below is a detailed template for the business plan that should help you in compiling your own one:

1. Business model overview

(Keep this section brief)

Introduction

❀ A brief history of your business (or of the idea that has prompted you to start it).
❀ The purpose of your guest house – why you started it.
❀ Note its location and explain if this is important (or any other competitive advantage).
❀ Describe your accommodation and the services offered.

Current position

❀ What have you achieved so far?
❀ Outline the current position of your business: Where is your business in the business lifecycle (introductory phase, growth phase, mature phase, or declining phase)?

❀ Explain what industry you operate in and where it sits in the business lifecycle (emerging industry, growth industry, mature industry, declining industry).

Competitive advantage

❀ What are the strengths and weaknesses of your competition?
❀ Explain your competitive advantage(s) and the market niche(s) you've identified.
❀ What makes you confident your guest house will continue to grow and endure (longevity)? Why is your business model effective?

Growth plan

❀ Provide a brief overview here of what will be described in more detail in the rest of the plan.
❀ Describe the current reach of your business and explain how this business plan will change that. (An overview of your goals and future plans for your guest house.)

2. Business strategy

❀ Outline your business strategy for:
 – the next year, and
 – the next 3–5 years (choose your own strategic horizon).
❀ Describe your business objectives and goals (make sure they are specific and measurable).

Tactics

❀ Outline the gap between where you are now and where you want to be (as above).
❀ Cover the main practical steps you have to take to get your business from where it is now to where you want it to go. What extra resources will you need?

Strategic impact

❀ Outline the external threats or opportunities that could impact on your business during your strategic horizon in:
 – the next year, and
 – the next 3–5 years (or a horizon of your choice).

Core values

❀ Describe the core values that underpin your business. Explain why these core values are crucial to your long-term business success, how they will affect customers (the benefits) and how they will help to motivate both you and your staff.

3. Marketing

SWOT and critical success factors

❀ Outline briefly your marketing strengths, weaknesses, opportunities and threats.
❀ What are therefore the critical success factors for your business?

Market research

❀ Explain what market research you've done and the methods you used for this.
❀ Outline how on-going market research is built into your daily business operations.
❀ What target market(s) has your market research established?
❀ Explain how intimately you understand these markets (how close you keep to your customers) and how this feeds back into your business (improvements, product/service changes, etc.).

Distribution channels

❀ Describe the current marketing reach of your business (local, national, or international).
❀ In terms of your strategy, what new markets do you plan to access in:
  – the next year?
  – the next 3–5 years?
❀ Describe how you plan to accomplish this.

Strategic alliances

❀ Explain what strategic alliances you have in place or are planning in order to increase your access to markets, leverage resources, etc.

E-commerce and technology

❀ Explain how you're using e-commerce and technology in your business to lower costs, speed up business, access new markets, build online sales, etc.

Marketing plan

❀ Attach the marketing plan of your marketing tactics for one targeted segment. (Complete more promotion plans for other targets for your own marketing purposes.)

Marketing budget

❀ Detail your marketing budget for the year.
❀ Explain how you will monitor it to manage and improve results.

Credibility and risk reduction

❀ Explain your tactics for increasing the credibility of your business and reducing the customer's risk in doing business with you.

4. Team and management structure

Skills, experience, training and retention

❀ Describe the skills, business track record, and experience of yourself and key members of your team.
❀ Outline your team. Explain the key staff, their positions and key responsibilities.
❀ Briefly describe the incentives you've put in place (or are planning) in order to retain them and keep them motivated.
❀ Describe your staff training programme and its budget.
❀ If there are gaps in your team, or you need extra staff to fulfil your short and longer term strategies, outline the gaps here, and who you need to fill those gaps.
❀ Explain how new staff will be trained.

Advisors

❀ Describe your core team of advisors (lawyer, accountant, consultants, business mentor or 'guru') whom you can access for advice, etc.

Management systems

❀ Briefly outline the management structure of your business.
❀ Describe the business systems you have in place to manage efficiently. Do you have written operations manuals in place? House rules for staff (always wear name badges, etc.)?

- ✿ What accounting software or systems do you use? How regularly can you produce financial reports and analyse key business ratios?
- ✿ Cover compliance issues too: e.g. how you prepare for and deal with payroll and employment issues, tax and VAT obligations etc.

5. Financial budgets and forecasts

- ✿ Attach financial budgets and forecasts you are including in the business plan such as
  - – profit and loss forecast,
  - – cash flow forecast,
  - – balance sheet forecast,
  - – capital expenditure budget, and
  - – break-even analysis.
- ✿ Provide brief notes on each of these forecasts. It's a good idea to produce optimistic, pessimistic and realistic versions of the first three.
- ✿ If the cash flow forecasts pinpoint future cash flow difficulties, explain how you plan to deal with these challenges.

6. Summary

- ✿ End with a brief summary of the main points of your plan: where you are now; where you want the plan to take your business.
- ✿ As the market and the world are always changing, outline when this plan will next be reviewed. Write the date into the plan and diarise it. The more frequently it's reviewed the better!

Building and decorating your guest house

Introduction

Your dream of your guest house that will be striking on first impression, with a warm and welcoming atmosphere, provides an important key to the actual planning, designing and building of your guest house. Its exterior and interior are an expression of your individuality, artistic talents and taste, but they must also meet the minimum hospitality requirements and standards of furnishings and facilities. Careful attention should be paid to these aspects at the building planning stage. You will be wise to make sure that your guest house is set up to meet international hospitality standards and requirements.

The building, the interior décor and the furnishing of a guest house will represent a substantial investment of your resources and must be done on sound business principles. The facilities must also meet the minimum industry requirements of providing accommodation for payment.

In converting or building a guest house that will be not only a home but also a working business, bear in mind that all these aspects must be functional and work well, and at the same time must be attractive.

Planning the building

Guest house versus bed and breakfast: What is the difference?

The structure and conversion potential of a specific building will be important to determine whether the establishment will qualify for 'guest house' status, or for 'bed and breakfast' status. A guest house is *not better* than a bed and breakfast, but from both your and your guests' point of view there are definite differences between the two types of accommodation in terms of the facilities and services offered.

The physical criteria for an establishment to qualify as a more upmarket guest house are as follows:

❁ It is a full-time professional and/or commercial undertaking.
❁ The public areas such as the dining room and lounge should be for the exclusive use of the guests and not shared by the family.
❁ The family often does not live on site.
❁ It should have four or more bedrooms (the trend is for more), all with *en suite* bathrooms or at the very least their own private bathrooms.
❁ Meals and snacks are served in addition to breakfast.

A typical bed and breakfast (B&B) establishment, on the other hand, can be described as follows:

❁ It is a family home with less than four guest rooms.
❁ Guests share the lounge or living room and dining room with the family members.
❁ The family lives on the same premises.
❁ Only breakfast is served.

> ### Definitions for accommodation establishments
>
> The difference between guest houses and B&Bs is clearly illustrated by the definitions of the Tourism Grading Council of South Africa:
>
> - *Bed & Breakfast:* accommodation is provided in a family (private) home and the owner/manager lives in the house or on the property. Breakfast must be served. Bathroom facilities may or may not be *en suite* and/or private. In general, the *guest shares the public areas with the host family.*
> - *Country house:* This is a large guest house, usually situated in natural, peaceful surroundings such as near a nature reserve, a forest, a lake etc. It *offers all the services of a hotel, including dinner.*
> - *Guest house:* A guest house can be an existing home, a renovated home or a building that has been specifically designed to provide overnight accommodation. A guest house will have *public areas for the exclusive use of its guests.* A guest house is a commercial operation enterprise and as such the owner or manager may live on the property.
> - *Lodge:* This is an accommodation facility located in natural surroundings. The rates charged are usually *inclusive of all meals* and the experience offered at the lodge, with game drives, battlefield tours, etc.
>
> The KwaZulu-Natal Tourism Authority's definitions also offer some insight:
>
> - A bed and breakfast establishment (B&B) is an informal, periodic accommodation operation undertaken from a private dwelling. The *maximum number of guest bedrooms in a B&B is three.* Any application received by the authorities for a B&B establishment with more than three bedrooms is automatically treated as a guest house.
> - A guest house is a commercial accommodation establishment offering *between four and 16 bedrooms*, which has as its primary source of business the supply of tourist accommodation. Breakfast and dinner are made available to guests, particularly where the latter is not readily available in the vicinity of the establishment.

Structural limitations and potential

For many guest house owners, the dream of opening their own guest house starts with a picture in their minds of a beautiful, elegantly decorated establishment set in a wonderful location or perhaps of a comfortable, welcoming home-from-home guest house. But few owners have the luxury of being able to build and design their establishment from scratch, and many guest houses are initially established in existing family homes.

How much money you have available will play a role in determining the type of accommodation that you can offer, as it is very expensive to add *en suite* bathrooms to all bedrooms and fully equip a kitchen to provide dinner and other meals in addition to breakfast. Be honest about your limitations as far as your existing infrastructure, available capital, family life, natural preferences and available time are concerned, so that you don't find yourself in a position where you haven't really prepared yourself and your family for the consequences of what you have embarked on.

If you are going to use your existing house or any existing building as a guest house, what are the limitations and potential of the building(s) against the framework of the type of guest house or bed and breakfast that you have in mind? Does your house lend itself to a typical guest house form, or does it have structural limitations like smaller rooms or shared bathrooms that will limit it to a bed and breakfast establishment no matter how smartly you furnish it?

Guest houses are established not only in urban areas but also on farms, in small country villages and increasingly in townships and traditional community areas. Limitations of the structure, location or type, as in farm accommodation or in a township, need to be considered. One would not expect a rural or traditional establishment to have *en suite* bathrooms for every room or a separate dining room for guests. This may in fact add to the authenticity of the experience and may even be a competitive advantage.

However, if your structural limitations do not allow for an *en suite* bathroom in an establishment in a city, you may find that it could detrimentally affect the rates you can charge for the room. Do not be disheartened if your present structure does not initially allow you to meet all requirements. Many B&Bs and guest houses start out with only one or two rooms and add more rooms and facilities over time.

Carefully evaluate the existing infrastructure of the home that you would like to convert. For example, you may have an open-plan kitchen, which is not necessarily the best layout for a guest house, as the guests will be able to see exactly what is going on during meal preparation. Also, the existing layout of your home may make it difficult to establish private and public areas for you and your guests. All these should be considered when deciding if your own home is suitable for conversion to a guest house.

Remember that you may be converting your own home so that it is no longer only a home but also an operational business. This means that the building, its furnishings and décor must be highly functional and practical to manage as well as aesthetically pleasing. The safety, security, comfort and convenience of your guests should be well served by the way in which you establish your guest house.

Plan the physical layout of different areas of your guest house very carefully as it cannot be changed without considerable cost or inconvenience to your guests once your guest house has opened. You do not want to close the guest house to make further renovations later on as this will impact on your earnings and you could lose regular guests to other establishments. Furnishings, curtains and carpets can be continually upgraded without interfering with your level of occupancy to any significant degree, but brick and mortar alterations cause huge inconveniences and potential losses of income.

The following are critical features that cannot be changed at a later stage:

❂ *The location of the guest house*: A good location is a vital element of the profitability of a guest house and it is also something that cannot be changed after you have started your alterations. Building a new guest house or renovating an existing house is expensive, but the choice of the right location should secure a good return on investment.
❂ *Size of rooms*: The physical design and size of the different areas in the building and the purpose of different rooms, such as the kitchen and bathrooms, cannot be altered without great disruption and expense.

Aspects that can be changed and upgraded at a later stage include

❂ furniture,
❂ curtains and carpets,
❂ decorating style of each room,
❂ colour of the paint on the walls,

- ✿ tiles and taps,
- ✿ equipment and linen, and
- ✿ finishing touches, such as doorknobs.

Budgetary limitations and profitability

Budget limitations are a fact of life. Choose how and where you spend your money carefully. Few people have enough money at the beginning to do everything they want.

A recommendation with regard to balancing interior decorating and budgetary concerns is to decide what can be upgraded at a later stage with the least inconvenience to guests. It is possible, for example, to upgrade a bedroom with little inconvenience, but changing the service areas is invariably disruptive. Unless you plan carefully, the interior decoration and furnishing of a guest house can drain your budget completely.

Often there are things that you did not think about and that you will have to acquire before your first guest can be accommodated. Prioritise your decorating budget and spend money on your public guest areas first, even if this means that plainer finishes and furnishings have to be chosen for the bedrooms. Some items in your decorating plan are there to create a background, while others form focal points. For each item, you will have to decide what is most important: appearance, durability, practicality, maintenance, cost or comfort. Choose furniture, carpets and curtains that are easy to maintain and keep clean. Focus on the tastes, expectations and comfort needs of your target market rather than on your own needs.

Remember that changing or upgrading guest rooms or public areas may mean that you will have to close the room or area temporarily, which could affect your profitability.

Star grading and quality assurance guidelines

Throughout the world, the perception of people is that when an accommodation establishment is graded, on a scale of one to five, a one-star establishment is normally seen as not luxurious although potentially suitable. No matter what grading you achieve, there is a market and a need for that particular type of establishment. It is not essential for all guest houses to be five-star graded or to be furnished up to that standard.

One of the best ways to make sure you are on the right track is to follow the standards of the Tourism Grading Council of South Africa. It provides internationally accepted guidelines on how to furnish your guest house in order to meet hospitality standards and provide for the comfort of your guests.

A grading is assigned to a property based on the findings noted during an assessment by an appointed assessor accredited by the Tourism Grading Council of South Africa.

Each establishment is thus evaluated individually within its classification category, for example self-catering, guest house, bed and breakfast or lodge.

These are the average gradings that can be obtained by an establishment:

- ✿ *One Star:* Fair to good (acceptable/modest) quality in the overall standard of furnishings, service and guest care. Clean, comfortable and functional accommodation.
- ✿ *Two Star:* Good quality in the overall standard of furnishings, service and guest care.
- ✿ *Three Star:* Very good quality in the overall standard of furnishings, service and guest care.

- *Four Star:* Superior comfort and quality with a high standard of furnishings, service and guest care.
- *Five Star:* Exceptional quality and luxurious accommodation. Highest standard of furnishings, flawless service and meticulous guest care.

The criteria of the grading assessment cover the following areas and are based on guest expectations:

- building exterior,
- bedrooms,
- bathrooms,
- public areas,
- dining facilities,
- food and beverage,
- services and service, and
- housekeeping.

An assessor will evaluate and award each area/item a mark that reflects a balance between its *state of repair, convenience, comfort, quality and adequacy*. The assessor's experience will comprise a balance of these five points and his or her personal taste will not have an influence. The assessor will only look at the workmanship.

The final outcome of this result is to determine whether the establishment is *fit for the purpose*.

Not all areas will be applicable to all establishments. Where an area is not applicable, it will not be graded, and the lack of the facility/service will not count in the overall grading score. In other words, establishments will not be penalised for not having a particular service/facility.

It is important always to be realistic when applying for your star grading. It is not always possible to achieve the highest possible grading because of the financial outlay. It is advisable to start at a lower star grading and upgrade your establishment until you have reached a point where you feel comfortable with your level. The outlay to establish a five-star property is much higher than that of a two-star establishment because a lot more emphasis is placed on quality and detail.

You should note also that the expectation of guests staying in a five-star property is much higher than that for a three-star graded property.

The needs, safety and comfort of guests

The needs and comfort of guests, including their safety, security and privacy, as well as the safety of their belongings, must be taken into account. The general layout of the entrance and reception, parking and access to guests' rooms must accommodate safety and security measures. It is necessary to control the movement of guests, and of outsiders who might gain access to areas where you need to guarantee the safety of guests and their property.

Plan the guest house so that the only guest entrance into the building or complex is through a reception area, past a front desk.

Practicality and ease of maintenance and cleaning

Practicality and ease of maintenance and cleaning are important considerations. Your guest house should have the highest standards of cleanliness and hygiene. This is one area where there can be no compromise, regardless of your level of luxury. Guests will always be impressed by a spotless bathroom and crisp, clean sheets. Choose furniture, flooring, curtains and so forth for maintenance as well as appearance.

How the guests and staff move through the guest house is another vital aspect. Allow for easy traffic flow between the different areas, specifically to accommodate staff members who have to move around as quickly as possible.

The layout of your guest house

The functional or work areas in a guest house

A guest house is a working, functional, business environment. The areas are divided into functional or work areas, and private or family areas. The planning and layout of your guest house must result in clearly distinguishable areas, as outlined below:

- ❀ *Exterior public areas:* The patio, garden and pool, as well as private outside service areas such as the washing lines.
- ❀ *Public guest areas:* The entrance hall, reception area, guest lounge, dining room, guest toilets and any passages, stairways and halls used by guests.
- ❀ *Private guest areas:* The guest bedrooms and bathrooms.
- ❀ *Service areas:* Your private office, the delivery and receiving area, the kitchen, the scullery, the laundry, storerooms and any area the staff use to perform their duties.
- ❀ *Private areas:* The living quarters of live-in staff, their toilets and their tea room, as well as the private area of the building in which the family lives.

Planning considerations

Each of these areas has its own requirements, and careful thought about the activities that will take place in each can make your life much easier once your guest house is fully operational.

This aspect is very important in order to secure the privacy of your guests and your family and/or staff. A separation of 'traffic' with different entrances and a practical layout must be implemented as far as possible.

During busy hours such as breakfast time, it may be necessary to answer the telephone, settle a guest account, open the front door, keep an eye on the preparation of the food and receive an early delivery. If you have to walk from the kitchen at one end of the house to your office at another end, it will be difficult to perform all these functions on your own and you may need extra staff at these times.

It is important to decide whether the family, or perhaps only a manager, will live in the guest house. Should the family share the premises or house, plan the layout in such a way that there is a separate entrance for the family. The family should also have separate recreation areas in the house and in the garden, so that children can watch television and play without disturbing guests. If the private family area too is far away from the front desk and kitchen, you may spend unnecessary time away from your family or be too far from the desk.

These are some important considerations:

- How much privacy is provided for both guests and family?
- How many staff members are needed to manage/serve all the areas where guests may be present?
- How does the layout of different areas influence the 'traffic flow' of staff, guests and family?

If the manager's or owner's office is linked to the reception area on the one side, the kitchen on the second side and the private family lounge on the third side, it should work well, because members of the family are able to reach the office and the kitchen without having to pass through the areas that are set aside exclusively for guests.

Hints on interior, furnishings and general appearance

Although each guest house owner will have his or her own style of decorating, you must keep in mind that guests from all over the world could visit your guest house. It is therefore important to create an atmosphere that will appeal to most cultures and will encourage guests to feel welcome and comfortable.

Although the uniqueness of every guest house is one of the main attractions of this industry, a very individual style of decorating may not appeal to everyone. It is safe to stick to a classic, traditional style that will immediately make most guests feel at home. Be careful of normal family clutter and personal items such as family photographs, which could make your guests feel that they are intruding in your private family area. If you are successful in creating a warm, welcoming atmosphere, your guests will feel special on arrival.

Appearance, durability, texture, practicality and maintenance all play a part in your choice of decorating elements.

Carpets

Carpets are used as a background for other décor items such as curtains, lamps and paintings. It is advisable to choose an easy-to-maintain, hard-wearing and economical carpet, though carpeting in a guest house usually needs to be replaced every five years or so.

Curtains

These add to the visual impression and impact of a room. They should hang to the floor from just below the cornice, or as high as possible. Full-length curtains should drop to about 2 cm above the floor. Curtains that hang from just above the top of the window to the windowsill are used in kitchens, bathrooms and cottage bedrooms, but never in lounges or reception rooms. The length of the curtain can emphasise either the height of the window (in which case it needs to be full length) or the width (in which case shorter curtains should be used). When selecting fabrics for a specific room, you should consider both the practical and the visual aspects.

Use fabrics generously – cheap gingham can look just as good as expensive silk, provided you use enough of the gingham. Skimped curtains without sufficient fullness look inferior even if the fabric is expensive. Always line curtains, with the exception of sheers, and use interlining for thin fabrics. Lining and interlining give thinner curtains the same thick look that expensive, textured curtains have.

Light fittings

Ceiling light fittings can be very expensive and often do little to enhance the atmosphere in a room when they are switched on. Standing lamps and table lamps tend to be softer because the source of light is at a lower level.

However, for practical reasons, it is imperative that the kitchen, the office and other service areas have a strong light source from the ceiling.

Lamps may be switched on during the day when the weather is overcast, or in corners that do not have sufficient natural lighting. Soft lighting will create a sense of warmth.

Paintings and prints

These must match your decorating scheme and style. You do not need to have original paintings. Prints are perfectly acceptable provided they are tastefully framed and hung. A beautifully framed mirror is often less expensive than a painting and adds depth and light to smaller, darker areas.

Ornaments

These should also match your decorating atmosphere. Cluttering will add to maintenance and cleaning. Place ornaments that could be broken out of the reach of children.

It is, however, quite appropriate, and sometimes even expected by guests, to incorporate local, traditional or cultural elements into your décor and interior. A game lodge, for example, can effectively use animal prints, a township B&B can use local arts and crafts, a guest house at the coast can use seashells, and so forth, to add local character to the establishment.

A guest house in a fly-fishing area can use attractively framed prints of trout and fishing paraphernalia with Scottish tartan, as this is also associated with trout fishing in South Africa. Farms and country lodges situated on historic battlefields in KwaZulu-Natal can bring in the 'Boer and Brit' touch, such as posters of Queen Victoria, Paul Kruger and other prints of this era.

General atmospheric touches

In farming and country areas you can opt for Victorian baths in the bathrooms and furnish the verandas with traditional benches ('riempiesbankies'), comfortable deep chairs and lots of plants hanging from the rafters. The garden itself should not be neglected. A hammock, or an outside lapa where a campfire can be made in the evening alongside the barbecue under the starry skies, will add to the experience of being on a farm, at a game lodge or in the countryside.

Colour tips

Base the colour schemes of a guest house on the associations that people normally have with different colours.
- A *deep forest green* has a calming effect on most people, and should make them feel relaxed. It might be too dark for bedrooms, but works particularly well in reception rooms. Lighter shades of green combined with white or near-white have a fresh appeal that can work well in bedrooms and bathrooms.

- *Fun colours* such as light yellow, lime green and lavender could work well in a breakfast room, because guests enjoy cheerful surroundings at the start of a new day.
- A *soft, buttery yellow* has the association of peace, and is a particularly good choice for both reception rooms and bedrooms. Bright yellow, however, should only be used by the very confident!
- *Burgundy red* is a good choice for a formal dining room that will be used mainly at night, because people generally associate this colour with good food, and will be inclined to linger on for the evening. On the other hand, bright red makes people restless and could have the effect that they feel they have to eat and leave the room as soon as possible. Restaurants often use bright red for their interiors to improve their turnover rate per table. Small spots of bright red can be used highly effectively as accents to cheer up a room, but bright red should not be the dominant colour in an interior scheme for any room in a guest house.
- The *classic blue and white combination* often referred to in the interior design world is loved by everyone. This covers anything from aquamarine blue through to purplish blues combined with the numerous shades of near-whites and whites that are available in both paint and fabrics. Turquoise, however, is a variation of blue-green that is often not a popular colour choice when it is used as the main colour in a colour scheme, because it is considered a cold colour. If you want to use turquoise, consider combining it with both green and blue in one colour scheme, which usually makes it look friendlier than when turquoise is used on its own.
- *Pure white* is by far the best choice for bathrooms in general, and can be supplemented by the colour of the bedroom to which the bathroom belongs.
- *Light pink* is generally not suitable for reception rooms or for bedrooms, because most people associate it with a little girl's room. However, a deeper *peach pink* or *watermelon pink* can work very well in almost any area in the house, especially when combined with deep greens, beige and other earthy colours, and even a touch of deep blue.
- It is always an easy option to start decorating a room with the choice of a good quality *floral* (or other multicoloured design) fabric for the curtains or upholstery, and then draw single colours out of the design for wall paint, carpets, cushions, and other extras such as lamp shades and table cloths.
- Paint adds mood and atmosphere to a room but needn't be unnecessarily expensive. It is relatively easy to repaint at a later stage; therefore it is possible to use an economical paint in order to save money. It is important, however, that the room should be painted an appropriate colour, as this will affect the light and ambience.
- In general it can be said that, provided they are chosen carefully, coloured walls, rather than white or cream walls, will be the most cost-effective way to create atmosphere in a guest house. If colour choices are made with the objective of creating a friendly and inviting atmosphere, you can almost always be sure of success.

The guest areas

The recommendations incorporate the requirements of the Tourism Grading Council and would be applicable to a three- to fifteen-bedroom establishment. The layout of these areas must ensure a high level of personal safety and security for your guests and their property, and also enable you to render effective service.

Do not be discouraged if you cannot offer all facilities at the start, but adapt the recommendations below to your own situation. Many successful guest houses build their business over the years and upgrade facilities when funds became available.

Public guest areas

Public areas are for the exclusive use of your guests and their visitors. The following places are regarded as public areas:

* the entrance hall,
* the reception area or office, also called the 'front desk',
* the guest waiting area close to the reception,
* guest toilets,
* the guest lounge,
* the dining room or breakfast room, and
* halls, stairways, landings and passages.

The entrance hall: Making a good first impression

Take time and care to create a smart, impressive entrance and entrance hall with a warm and welcoming atmosphere. You have only one opportunity to make a good *first impression* on your guests, and it lasts for only a second or two.

When guests arrive at your guest house, they subconsciously measure up what they see to what they expected or hoped to find. Your guest house will either match up to their expectations and put them at ease or disappoint them because they expected more. In the latter situation, it will be very difficult to convince them later on that your guest house is up to standard. Your guest's first experience is similar to that of any colleagues who may come to the guest house to visit or pick him or her up for a meeting. If the entrance meets his or her expectations, your guest will feel comfortable about his or her choice of guest house. Use this golden opportunity, not only through the appearance of your guest house but also through the professional and friendly way in which you receive your guests, to capture them as satisfied customers.

A spacious entrance hall that is wide enough to accommodate a number of suitcases and luggage items, without congesting the flow through the area, will make busy mornings, where checking out and breakfast occur simultaneously, much easier.

The availability of capital is always a limiting factor when a guest house is established, so you must establish your priorities if you have to improve your guest house in stages. Always concentrate on the entrance, entrance hall and recreation areas first, because these are what most people will base their opinion on, even though they do not ultimately spend much time in these areas. The part of the kitchen that guests do not see could have concrete work tops initially and later on be fitted with granite, and rooms could be plain at first and then be upgraded gradually, as long as the impression that you want to create at the end of the day is established from the start in the areas guests and their visitors see first.

Hints on creating a good first impression

- The entrance must be kept permanently clean and tidy, even if it means daily attention.
- Use welcoming, colourful flowerpots for the entrance.
- Always have a trained person available to receive guests and attend to their needs.
- Use bold, warm and friendly colours for the entrance hall – an attractive front door and striking entrance hall positively influence anyone's mood the moment he or she walks in.
- Enhance the welcoming message by displaying large bunches of fresh flowers (preferably from the guest house's garden) and playing soft background music.
- Avoid large expanses of bare floors with minimalist interiors, since guests generally adapt more easily to cosy surroundings.
- A clear and attractive name board assures guests that they have arrived at the correct address.
- A welcoming light at night is important.
- Ample parking to offload luggage, preferably under cover for rainy days, will be appreciated.
- The aroma of freshly brewed coffee adds to your welcome.
- A friendly and professional reception procedure creates a positive impression (see chapter 5 for a detailed discussion of this).

The reception area and office

The reception area is the heart of your business. This is where you will meet your guest, where he or she will return for assistance and where you will do most of your administration and control most of the services you offer. If the position of the reception area is such that you can manage almost every aspect of the guest house from there, it is best combined with the office area. Most of your time will be spent there, and the necessary daily filing and updating of administration can be done while you wait for guests to book in or return to the guest house.

Prospective guest house owners often underestimate the space required to accommodate the administrative documents and office equipment necessary to manage a guest house efficiently. A formal reception office always creates an impression of efficiency. It is not appropriate or professional to establish a reception area in a corner of another room, such as the kitchen, dining room or lounge.

The ideal office should have the following:

- desk, office chair and seating space for at least two guests at the desk, where they can sit to settle accounts or discuss their reservations with the manager or owner,
- sufficient space for office equipment such as a telephone, fax machine, computer and printer so that the manager can reach everything from behind the desk, which, to look tidy and professional, should preferably not be in full view of arriving guests,
- sufficient shelving and storage space for files, and
- sufficient display areas for brochures, maps, booklets, etc.

If not provided in guest rooms, a safe should be provided at reception for the secure storage of guests' valuables.

Information on procedures in the event of an emergency should be clearly displayed. This information should be in English and, if possible, multilingual (depending on the establishment's market). Procedures for summoning assistance, in particular after hours, should also be available.

Once registered, guests should have access to the establishment at all times. It is acceptable to provide guests with a key or security code. A key rack should be placed inside or within view of the office.

The reception area should be kept neat and ready to receive guests efficiently. Make sure that you have pens and paper available for guests and all relevant documents relating to the day's activities, such as your reservation sheets, close at hand in an orderly fashion. Keep the area clean and tidy and empty the wastepaper basket regularly.

The lounge

The lounge provides a pleasant place for your guests to relax in. If the lounge area is not close to the office and entrance, seating is required in the reception area for guests who are waiting to check in or out or to be picked up by colleagues for work or meetings. The importance of a spacious lounge must never be underestimated. Often guest house owners don't want to spend too much on these areas, because they cannot be rented out like a bedroom. In fact, the general impression that the guest forms of your guest house will be more favourable if it is clear that you've paid as much attention to detail as you have to cost in the areas that are there purely for the guests' comfort and enjoyment, and not necessarily for the generation of your income.

The lounge will be used by people from different backgrounds, countries and cultural traditions. Create a relaxing, friendly and inviting atmosphere that will appeal to most guests. Furnishings should look soft and welcoming. Use as much upholstered furniture as possible. A traditional, classical sitting-room style is an appealing and safe choice. You will ideally need sufficient seating for at least half your guests, arranged in various seating patterns, if possible, to allow guests to sit alone or in small groups.

A bar fridge or fresh coffee brewing, perhaps with biscuits, attractively set out on a table from which guests can help themselves, will make your guests feel welcome. A communal bar in the lounge where guests can help themselves to cold beverages often works more efficiently than bar fridges in their rooms. The basis of an 'honesty bar' is that guests help themselves to drinks and enter the items they use in a consumption book placed at the honesty bar. Keep the requirements of the Liquor Licensing Act (see chapter 9) in mind when providing alcoholic drinks.

It is more efficient to check the entries in a consumption book rather than the contents of different fridges in the rooms, and it is also easier to keep stocks checked and at an optimal level if all records are kept at one point. (Separate fridges in the rooms can complicate the checking-out procedure, which normally takes place during breakfast time when you least have time to check the contents of individual bar fridges.)

Another possibility is to offer guests all drinks on a complimentary basis. The cost of this extra service could sometimes be less than the cost of the infrastructure needed to control the stocks against a consumption book.

A crackling fireplace in winter and bowls of fresh flowers or flowering plants in summer will contribute to the pleasant atmosphere. Interesting books, new magazines and the daily newspaper on a coffee table, a television and a sound system will always be appreciated and will add to the comfort and enjoyment of your guests.

Be careful of clutter and of displaying too many personal items and family photographs.

The guest cloakroom

Don't forget to make provision for a cloakroom for the use of visitors as well as residential guests. The guest toilet must always be spotlessly clean, so you should check the facility regularly during the day. Make sure there is always enough toilet paper, and that fresh hand soap and clean towels are readily available, as well as space for a handbag for ladies who need to freshen up.

Hallways and staircases

Hallways and staircases often receive little attention when it comes to decorating, but an elegant staircase can be turned into a very attractive feature. Passages and stairs must be well lit at night so that they are easy to negotiate. Stairs must not be too steep or too narrow and safety railings must be provided. A carpet strip down hallways in easy-to-clean, hard-wearing materials would absorb the noise of guests passing other rooms and is preferable to bare wooden floors that could be noisy. Passages should be wide enough for guests to pass each other comfortably even when carrying luggage.

The dining room

A guest house dining room should be spacious enough to offer each guest a separate table and a place setting for each room at full occupation, although not necessarily in one sitting. The dining room should allow for easy, efficient service from yourself and your staff, so plan how staff will move from the kitchen to the tables and also between tables while serving your guests. Allow enough space for the serving area for the breakfast buffet to avoid accidents or spills, which will embarrass or even injure guests. There must be enough space for guests to serve themselves comfortably. Enough space should also be allowed between tables so that guests can move around easily, without bumping into the chairs of other guests.

Guests do not necessarily want to share a table with other guests whom they do not know. Square tables with sides of about 1.5 m can be pushed together to form a large group table or can be carried outside to serve a meal on the patio. Of course, sharing a meal with the family can be part of the accommodation experience for overseas visitors, as in cultural B&Bs on farms or in townships, for example.

Smoking areas

You need to abide by current smoking legislation. It may be difficult to provide a smoking area inside the guest house that meets all legal requirements.

Make ashtrays available on the patio and put a sign up to indicate clearly where guests may smoke. Clean the ashtrays regularly!

Private guest areas

These areas include the bedrooms and bathrooms that are for the exclusive use of the guest who has booked into the room. The privacy, comfort, convenience and security of these areas are paramount. These areas form the heart of the accommodation that you are selling.

Bedrooms

The guest bedroom is one of the most important areas of your guest house, as it forms the core of what you are selling – comfortable overnight accommodation.

If you are planning the layout of your guest house from scratch, you should try to locate the guest rooms in a wing separate from the reception area so that only traffic to the bedrooms passes by.

Non-residents should not be able to look into guests' rooms. It makes management control and security a lot easier when the entrance to the guest rooms can be controlled so that no unauthorised person can reach a guest's room. Rooms should have a private and pleasant view of the garden or swimming pool whenever possible, and definitely not look onto the backyard or washing lines.

Bedroom size: Bedrooms should ideally be large enough to accommodate all the necessary furniture, with sufficient space to allow freedom of movement and access to all the furniture in the room.

If you convert an existing residential home, you will probably have rooms of various sizes. This is quite acceptable and would mean that you will have a variety of bedrooms available – from smaller to larger and from less luxurious to more luxurious. You would also charge different rates for these rooms. Try to accommodate the needs of different guests by providing a choice of bed configurations. If you have twin rooms and rooms with only one single bed, and can change two twin beds with a purpose-made cover into a double bed, you will be able to meet most requirements. It is not advisable to place only double beds in your rooms as you will lose business from people prepared to share a room but not a bed.

If you are able to, build a more spacious structure and improve on the furniture and other details gradually. A spacious room is always appreciated by guests, and guests will usually prefer a plain and larger room to a smart but smaller room. You can economise by using plain interior-decorating finishes that can be upgraded as additional funds become available. Guests will not complain about your plain but spotlessly clean and crisp linen, but will not be comfortable in a cramped space.

However, if you have an existing building, you will have to make the best of the available space. Deliberately choose smaller chairs, a smaller bed (and definitely not two single beds), smaller bedside pedestals and a narrower writing bureau. Be practical with your bedroom furnishings and avoid anything overly dramatic. It is important that everything is functional and comfortable, while being attractive as well. Be careful of overdoing decorations, such as an abundance of scatter cushions which male guests in particular find unattractive.

It should be possible to open all doors and drawers fully.

Bedroom furniture: This should include the following:

* the bed or beds with their headboards and bedside pedestals on each side (which implies a windowless wall of 3.5 to 4 m wide),
* a writing bureau and chair,
* a dressing table and chair close to a power point for hairdryers (this area could be combined with the writing bureau to provide the guest with a clear space to place items and/or serve as a work surface, or to double-up as a bedside table to save space, if necessary),
* a rack or shelf to put suitcases on,
* a shelf for the television set,

❀ a couch or at least one comfortable chair, but preferably two in a double room, and

❀ a wardrobe or hanging space for clothes with sufficient good quality hangers per person and adequate drawer or shelf space.

It becomes clear that, to accommodate all of the furniture above, a room needs to be at least 3.5 m by 3.5 m in size, and preferably even larger than this. Keep one solid wall (without a door, window or cupboards) available for the bed and bedside pedestals. A single bed with a bedside pedestal requires approximately 1.75 m space, a double bed with two bedside pedestals about 3 m, and a queen-size bed with two bedside pedestals about 3.5 m. A king-size bed with two bedside pedestals needs about 4 m, and two single beds placed apart, each with a bedside pedestal, need at least 4.5 m uninterrupted wall space. The ceiling height for the major part of the room should be sufficient for a 1.8 m person to move around without stooping. There should be one window to allow natural light and adequate ventilation. If the window cannot be opened, a ventilation system must be provided.

Beds and bedding: All beds should have a secure headboard. Do not compromise on the quality of the mattresses. They must be comfortable and constructed with a sprung interior and foam or a similar material and should be fitted with mattress protectors or under-blankets. Single beds must comfortably accommodate an average-sized adult and double beds two adults.

Buy the best quality cotton or percale linen you can afford as it will need to withstand much more laundering than normal household linen. It is advisable to have three sets of linen for each bed and it is recommended that all bed linen for all rooms is the same colour. White is perfect, as it always creates the impression of cleanliness and hygiene and would not look faded after many washes.

There should be at least one blanket and one pillow per sleeping space with additional blankets and pillows available on request. Duvets are also acceptable. All sleeping spaces should have an under-sheet and a top-sheet. There should be a pillowcase on each pillow. Non-allergic pillows and duvets are preferable and should be available on request. Use a skirt valance to cover exposed parts of the beds if they are not visually attractive.

Mirrors: Make sure that there is a mirror with sufficient light for guests to apply make-up comfortably, as well as a full-length mirror in the room. The use of mirrors is invaluable to increase the perceived size of a room, and will also almost double the amount of light in a room, especially if positioned opposite a window. A large mirror is less expensive than a small piece of art and can add a vibrant dimension to a room because it is never static. Ideally there should be a mirror adjacent to the dressing/writing table, and lighting intensity in the vicinity of the mirror should be adequate.

Lighting: The bedrooms should be well lit and have a main light. There should be a bedside and/or bedhead light for, and controllable by, each person (the number of people typically occupying a room should be considered when determining the appropriateness of bedside lighting). Twin beds may share a bedside light. A double bed may have one shared bedhead light. All bulbs should have a shade or cover (unless decorative). Emergency lighting should also be provided (candle, candlestick and matches).

Every power socket and light must be safe and in working order. All light switches must be visible. It is advisable for you to sleep in the room yourself before letting it out, to check that everything functions correctly. Make sure that the curtains or blinds open and close easily and that the room is dark enough at night. Curtains, blinds or shutters should be provided on all windows including glass panels and doors to ensure both privacy and/or the exclusion of light.

Beverage facilities, television and telephone: Provide coffee- and tea-making facilities in the bedrooms unless a self-service tea/coffee/beverage buffet is available in the dining room or lounge or appropriate room service is provided. If space and budget permit, a bar fridge with cold drinks and fresh milk will be appreciated by the guests. Make sure the fridge does not run noisily! Place the coffee- and tea-making facilities in an area that is easy to reach and clean.

Unless there is no signal available, a colour television of appropriate size should be provided in each room, or a television room in lieu of a television set in each bedroom.

Although the widespread use of cellphones makes this no longer an essential requirement, bedroom telephones should be provided where appropriate to the market. All in-room telephones should display the guest house telephone number, the reception or switchboard number and the room extension number.

The following are additional bedroom requirements:

✿ a power socket for computer and internet access and sufficient conveniently located power sockets for the safe use of all electrical equipment,
✿ a fan or heater or air conditioning,
✿ ashtrays (if smoking is allowed),
✿ clean drinking glasses for every person,
✿ a clock and a radio or a combination of these,
✿ easy-to-clean flooring and bedside mats,
✿ a waste bin,
✿ a hairdryer,
✿ a basket with fruit/crisps/chocolates/biscuits (complimentary or on an honesty system),
✿ laundry bags and lists if a laundry service is provided,
✿ complimentary stationery and a notebook,
✿ a welcoming letter and a folder with information on local attractions and activities,
✿ a breakfast menu if used,
✿ a 'Do not disturb' sign, and
✿ insect repellent in areas where this may be needed.

The guest bathroom: If you are in the position to plan bathrooms from the beginning and have the space, install full bathrooms with walk-in showers and baths, so that the type of bathroom never needs to be a limiting factor in securing a reservation for a specific room. Some people prefer to shower and others prefer to bath, so a potential booking could be lost because the bathroom does not accommodate guest preferences.

The installation of full bathrooms, if at all possible, will be more costly than bathrooms with only showers or baths, but it is money well spent. If you cannot install a bath in every bathroom, make sure that you have at least one room with a bath, as female guests often prefer a bath to a shower.

All bathrooms should have sufficient space to allow freedom of movement and access to all fittings. If all the bathrooms cannot be *en suite*, every room should at least have a private bathroom for its exclusive use. Different guests can under no circumstances share a bathroom. Note that you will not be able to charge as much for a room with a private bath as for an *en suite* room.

Plan all bathrooms so that there is space for a vanity surface around the basin for a guest's toiletries. Sufficient space should also be provided for items such as soap, shampoo, hand cream and tissues, and for a towel rail, towel shelf or equivalent.

Finishes: A white bathroom is not only easy to clean, but has a fresh, hygienic appearance which is all-important in a guest house. You can also economise by using plain white tiles that can be laid diagonally to add interest, and a triple border of inexpensive shower mosaics will help transform a plain bathroom into something special. Add a dado rail in a different texture or a coloured or granite tile. Use locally manufactured taps that will still be available after five years, rather than imported tiles and taps that might not be available in a few years' time. A cracked or missing tile gives a very bad impression. When renovating an existing bathroom, consider painting the tiles as a quick and inexpensive improvement.

Although expensive, granite tops are attractive and practical as they are extremely hard-wearing and easy to keep spotlessly clean. Marble, on the other hand, is much more porous, lighter in colour and stains easily.

Equipment: Good lighting for applying make-up and a decent-sized adjacent mirror are essentials. A shaver and hairdryer power point will be welcomed by guests.

Bath mats in front of the basin, toilet, shower and bath are recommended and it is necessary to provide sufficient hanging space for towels. Hooks behind the bathroom door are useful for hanging dressing gowns and clothes. Bathroom doors should be lockable from the inside. A dressing gown for use by the guest is optional.

Towels: Do not compromise on the quality of towels. Large towels add to the guest's convenience. White towels are practical and easy to launder and to keep looking new. Worn towels should be replaced immediately. Two sets of towels for every guest per room will be needed if all the towels are the same colour. Buying snag-free hotel-quality towels direct from a reputable hospitality provider will save money and ensure quality.

Provide a generous-sized bath sheet and hand towel for each guest and, if you wish, an extra standard-sized bath towel and a face cloth. Quality swimming towels should also be available at reception if you have a swimming pool. You will need attractive holders for guest amenities such as soap, shampoo and tissues, which should be freshly presented for every guest. Individually wrapped amenities or refillable dispensers can be used according to your own preference. Make sure that the overall impression is one of value for money. Single-ply toilet paper, for example, in a guest house is not acceptable. Extra toilet paper should be available.

Windows: Windows in the bathroom should either be tinted, opaque or made of glass that ensures guest privacy, or, alternatively, covered by an opaque curtain, a blind or a shutter.

The exterior of your guest house

The outside areas, patio, garden and swimming pool make an important contribution to your guest house's overall appearance and add to what the Americans call 'curb appeal'. A stylish name board for your guest house will confirm to your guests that they have arrived at the right place.

A beautiful garden with colourful beds of flowers creates an attractive impression even before a guest enters the guest house. Do not neglect the appearance of your garden; try to match the style to your guest house.

Foreign guests, in particular, appreciate an under-cover patio next to a pool or a lush green garden to enjoy our wonderful climate. Most guests will almost always prefer to enjoy breakfast outside on a patio if weather permits, so it can be worthwhile to invest in a spacious under-cover patio with a pleasant and private view. Provide sufficient seating and patio tables for your guests, and quality deck chairs for the swimming pool.

A shaded seating area under a tree, a tranquil water feature and indigenous plants to attract birds will create additional enjoyment for the guests. Hide unattractive features like backyard walls or the dustbin area with shrubs and climbers.

Keep the pavement and entrance neat and ensure that the name board, driveway, entrance gate, steps and front door are well lit at night.

Service areas

These areas are where the work is done to prepare and provide the essential services to your guests. They should be off-limits to your guests and out of sight and sound, but should be convenient and easy to work in for your staff and yourself.

Delivery entrance

In the layout of your guest house, provision must be made for a separate delivery entrance, so that no goods need to come through the front door. If necessary, the delivery entrance could be combined with the staff or family's private entrance. Staff and members of your family should, if possible, not use the same entrance as guests.

Laundry

Unless linen is handled by an outside laundry service, a private area out of sight of the guests is necessary. The laundry and ironing room must also be planned according to the expected volume of laundry to be done and should have sufficient space for washing machines, tumble dryers, ironing boards, shelves for linen and clothes rails. The ironing room should have shelving for clean linen and hanging space for guests' laundered clothes. A spacious, sunny area for washing lines, well hidden from view, should be able to accommodate all bed linen.

If you offer a laundry service to your guests, provide separate shelving and hanging space, properly marked with the correct room number for each guest, to avoid getting different guests' clothing mixed up.

Staff facilities

Day staff who do not live on the premises will need a dining room or area where they can relax during teatimes and mealtimes. As the pace at a full guest house can become hectic, do not skimp on good facilities that will make your staff feel important and appreciated. Staff members who stay overnight will need accommodation facilities.

Setting up the kitchen

Your kitchen must be designed to enable you to provide meals efficiently and smoothly to your guests. Kitchen and menu planning go hand in hand, and what is installed in the kitchen is closely related to the menu or food prepared in that specific kitchen.

The size of a workable kitchen is influenced by the maximum number of guests to be served simultaneously and by the number of staff employed. An average-sized kitchen of 20 to 25 m² should be sufficient to cater for 12 guests.

Minor additions, such as a few extra shelves installed against the walls or more power points for small appliances, will make a major difference to the flow of the operation, without your having to spend large sums of money initially or engaging in major structural changes like breaking down walls or extending dramatically.

Most guest houses have to cope with a normal domestic kitchen, but you will probably need to add more work surfaces and space to serve food onto plates. A table placed in the middle of the floor will increase your amount of surface space.

Remember that successful guest houses often add more rooms at a later stage, which increases the pressure in the kitchen.

The preparation and scullery areas must not be visible to guests. The kitchen of a guest house therefore differs totally from the open-plan kitchen areas found in many modern family homes.

The kitchen needs to be designed (or redesigned, if necessary, if it is an existing kitchen) to allow for all the actions required to execute the menu – from the time that the food arrives in the kitchen until the time that it is served. In many cases, it is also advisable to plan the menu first and then to decide which appliances, small appliances, kitchen utensils, serving dishes or platters and areas for keeping hot food hot and cold food cold should be included.

The planning, maintenance and management of the kitchen has to be considered as a most important function in any guest house.

Differences between a domestic and guest house kitchen

One of the most important differences between a public and home kitchen is that the kitchen activities should be well screened from the public eye. The initial food preparation and cleaning-up procedures should take place in a scullery area not visible to the guests, and the activities should also not be heard. The serving area for making and serving tea and coffee or drinks may be attached to or be part of the lounge or dining room, so that guests may be served there or serve themselves if they wish. Neat containers with rusks, biscuits, snacks or sometimes covered platters with sandwiches look inviting and will be appreciated by guests who happen to be in the guest house during the day or at odd hours when meals are not served.

A notice board in the kitchen is essential. Any messages, shopping list items and especially all emergency numbers – such as the host or owner's cellphone number and numbers for the fire brigade, ambulance, security assistance and medical aid – can be pinned onto this board for emergencies or to ensure that messages do not get lost.

The kitchen layout

The layout of the kitchen influences the flow of activities. Guests sitting together at a dining table need to be served at the same time.

Increase workspace by placing a kitchen table in the middle of the kitchen floor, or add additional shelves above the work surfaces for equipment or ingredients to ensure that working surfaces are not cluttered.

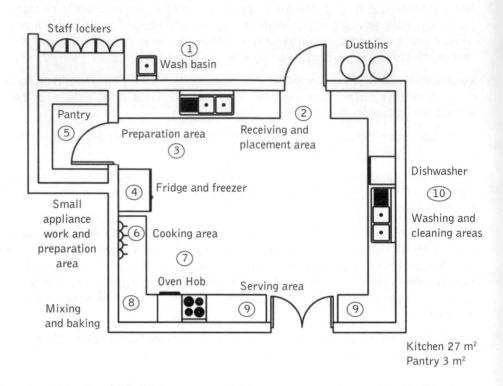

Staff lockers

① Wash basin

Dustbins

Pantry
⑤

Preparation area
③

Receiving and
placement area
②

Dishwasher
⑩

Fridge and freezer
④

Small
appliance
work and
preparation
area

Cooking area
⑥

⑦

Washing and
cleaning areas

Oven Hob

Serving area

Mixing
and baking

⑧

⑨

⑨

Kitchen 27 m²
Pantry 3 m²

Setting up the kitchen according to the flow of activities

1. *Outside wash basin:* An outside wash basin should be placed prominently at the back door for hand washing by anyone who enters the kitchen from outside.
2. *Surface for receiving purchased goods:* To the right or left of the back door you will need a fairly large surface to receive all the shopping brought into the kitchen. Everything that comes into the kitchen is sorted here before storing.
3. *Preparation area and scullery:* A scullery area with a basin, or preferably a double basin and draining area if space allows, is needed for rinsing, draining and drying fruit and vegetables before storing them hygienically. The area next to the fridge is used for further preparation or mixing and processing cleaned vegetables or other ingredients.
4. *Fridge and freezer:* The fridge and the freezer should ideally be placed close to the receiving area and scullery. Bulk buying and advance preparation of dishes are made possible by providing additional fridge and freezer space elsewhere. Wider, larger fridges and freezers, a walk-in fridge or a glass-door caterer's model will be of great help. Bulk packaging does not always fit into normal-sized domestic fridges and freezers and you will consequently have to unpack the contents before storing.
5. *Pantry:* The available storage space will determine how much stock can be carried. A walk-in pantry with neat uncluttered shelves will simplify stock control. If space does not allow for a pantry, shelves or grocery cupboards can be fitted for this purpose.
6. *Small appliance work and preparation area:* The surface next to the fridge is used for further preparation or mixing and processing of cleaned vegetables or other ingredients. Sufficient power points are needed here.
7. *Cooking area:* Following the work surface and small electric appliance area is the cooking and baking area for large electrical appliances. Allowing enough workspace between the various small and large appliances is most important and sometimes not planned for.

8. *Mixing and baking preparation area:* To execute mixing and baking procedures with ease, you will need a surface where all these activities can take place unhindered by other tasks – especially if more than one person works in the kitchen at the same time.
9. *Serving area:* Garnishing and finishing off of all dishes and plating of individual platters is carried out in this area. All finished food and plates are carried from this area to the dining room, so it should be close to the interleading door.
10. *Washing-up area:* All used items from the kitchen and dining room are brought back to this area to be washed, either by hand or in a dishwasher.

Basic kitchen equipment

Although it is not always necessary or wise to purchase the most expensive articles available, evaluate every item and determine whether it is of a high quality and the best value. Kitchen equipment of an inferior quality that will not perform as expected, that will break, become rusty or blunt and useless within a short time is money wasted. Replace a worn-out item with a more modern version. You will need the following items:

❀ apple corer and wedge cutter,
❀ butter ball-maker, butter curl-maker (unless pre-wrapped butter is served),
❀ bread and meat slicers,
❀ chopping boards,
❀ cutters for scones, biscuits, doughnuts and cookies,
❀ dish cloths (washing swabs and drying cloths),
❀ egg lifters,
❀ frying pans, including several non-stick pans (with suitable spoons and lifters), a few heavy-based as well as shallow crêpe or pancake or omelette pans,
❀ garlic press,
❀ heat-resistant glass measuring cups or jugs from small (250 ml) to large (up to 2 litres) – these are ideally suitable for microwave cooking as well,
❀ hygienic chopping boards made of plastic or tempered glass – not wood,
❀ kitchen scissors,
❀ kitchen tongs,
❀ mallet,
❀ meat hammer,
❀ measuring cups and spoons,
❀ microwave-safe heat-resistant glass jugs, bowls and dishes for cooking and heating,
❀ mixing bowls – from small to large,
❀ orange and lemon squeezer,
❀ oven gloves,
❀ pressure cooker,
❀ rolling pin – the kind that revolves around its axle,
❀ scoop to make melon or similar balls,
❀ selection of knives, peelers, cutters, graters and slicers (to prepare julienne strips, for example),
❀ set of good quality heavy-based saucepans,
❀ spatulas in different sizes,
❀ sieves, strainers and colanders in different sizes,
❀ spoons and perforated or draining spoons in different sizes,
❀ steamer, and
❀ whisks, including balloon and flat whisks.

Basic loose-standing small electric appliances:

- ✿ bread and meat slicer,
- ✿ bain-marie (mobile) or heated serving trolleys,
- ✿ chafing dishes,
- ✿ deep fat fryer,
- ✿ electric carving knife,
- ✿ electric frying pan,
- ✿ food processor,
- ✿ grillers and toasters,
- ✿ hot trays,
- ✿ kettle and urn,
- ✿ microwave oven,
- ✿ waffle iron, and
- ✿ wok.

Basic equipment for serving meals:

- ✿ three sets of table linen per table, place mats and serviettes for every guest,
- ✿ enough cutlery for full occupancy,
- ✿ fruit and desert bowls, cereal, side- and dinner plates for full occupancy,
- ✿ fruit juice glasses and jugs for each table,
- ✿ teacups, saucers, teapots, sugar bowls, milk jugs, coffee cups or mugs,
- ✿ egg cups,
- ✿ salt and pepper pots, pepper grinder,
- ✿ toast racks for each table,
- ✿ serving dishes and spoons,
- ✿ holders for cereals, yogurts, fruit,
- ✿ hot tray,
- ✿ bud vases for each table, and
- ✿ trays of various sizes.

Storage space

The need for storage space in a guest house is easily underestimated. In a normal house, the wardrobe in each room can partly be used to store items not in use, but a guest house has to provide an empty wardrobe for each guest. No items that are not used by the guest should be kept in a room. You will need extra storage space for many items in areas separate from the guest rooms.

These are typical examples of items that can take up more space than a normal house offers:

- ✿ heaters, blankets and electric blankets stored during the summer months,
- ✿ fans and outdoor equipment not in use during the winter months,
- ✿ vacuum cleaners and trolleys or baskets with cleaning equipment for rooms,
- ✿ guest amenities such as shampoo, soap, toilet paper, tissues and cleaning products that are always bought in large quantities,
- ✿ stand-over luggage of guests who will return to the guest house after a weekend excursion,
- ✿ items that guests hand in for safekeeping,
- ✿ cash and cheques received from guests,
- ✿ petty cash and the cash float of the guest house,
- ✿ foods that are purchased in bulk and need to be locked away, and
- ✿ liquor.

Managing your guest house

Introduction

Often the primary motive for opening a guest house is not simply to make money. Most guest house owners love serving good food, enjoy the company of interesting people and derive satisfaction from creating beautiful surroundings and gardens. But all these good intentions (and crucial ingredients of a successful guest house) have to be supported by effective and economically sound management.

Effective guest house management should always use the *guest's experience* at the establishment as the starting point.

Always remember that a guest consciously and subconsciously forms an opinion of your establishment when staying there. This should be your strongest marketing tool. However much you advertise your establishment, if the guests who stay there do not experience their stay as pleasant and smoothly run, they will leave your guest house with a negative impression, and will comment on it accordingly. This can do your business much more harm than the good of any successful marketing effort.

For example, it could be a sound financial management principle to limit the variety on the breakfast buffet so that the costs of the breakfasts you serve drop dramatically through reduced wastage of leftovers. However, such measures could result in your regular clients feeling cheated and seeking another guest house where the owners do not limit the breakfasts, and then you will have defeated the whole purpose.

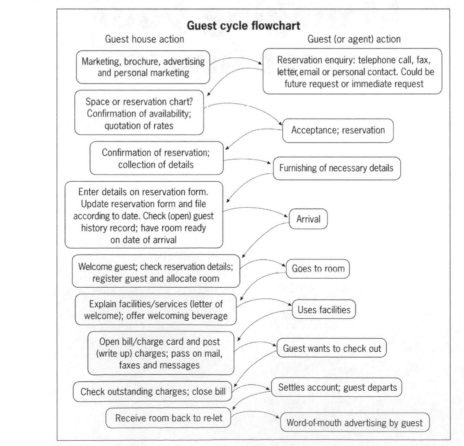

The guest cycle flowchart

Every guest house has to have a clear-cut and well-considered policy about its management of all facets of the business. Every staff member must know exactly what is expected of him or her, and the standards set must be adhered to at all times.

Both your service and your facilities must be maintained at the same high standard on a daily basis to establish a favourable image for your guest house.

Once you are convinced that a guest will have a positive experience throughout his or her contact with your guest house, you can be almost sure that your business is on the right track. The guest cycle flowchart (shown opposite) illustrates this point.

The starting point is to take control of all the contact points between guests and your guest house, so that a guest will have a positive experience throughout his or her contact with your guest house. The best way to ensure that a guest has a pleasant experience is to set up a guest cycle flowchart that covers every possible point of contact between a guest and your establishment, from first enquiry through to the final checkout, with all the steps in between.

Determine a process and policy concerning every aspect of the interaction that normally takes place from the time of a guest's reservation, through his or her stay and up to his or her departure from your guest house. By doing this you can ensure that the necessary tasks on the part of the guest house are executed in the best possible way at each point.

If you analyse all the guest house actions in the flowchart, it becomes clear that the typical course of contact between guest and guest house, from the time of seeing an advertisement to the time of checking out, involves the *effective management* of all the functions of the enterprise. If the impressions of the guest remain positive throughout this contact with your guest house, the chances are good that he or she will return to make another reservation and will initiate word-of-mouth advertising after departing from your establishment.

Running a guest house can appear deceptively simple, but in reality it works like any other business. Sound business principles must be part of the daily activities. Managing a guest house means that the following functions are being exercised:

✿ general management,
✿ the marketing function,
✿ the administrative function,
✿ the financial function,
✿ the human resources (staff) function, and
✿ the production function.

General management

In order to make a management plan work realistically for your guest house, you should keep it simple and easy, so that it can be maintained even during busy times. If this is not possible, you should not even try to have a particular management system in place, because a management system only serves a purpose if it is effective and kept up to date. If the systems you choose are too complicated, they become difficult to complete effectively and create stress.

For example, instead of counting the eggs that you use after every breakfast, it might be more efficient and effective to count the eggs used once a week. Often you can be over-ambitious about checking sugar granules and rice grains, which is pointless if you don't control the general expenditure of your enterprise.

However, it is important to have plans in place in the event of an unexpected or unpredictable catastrophe, in order to protect your business. This will also include having the right insurance in place and protecting the data on your computers against loss.

You must have an up-to-date contact list available of all staff members and clear guidelines as to who is responsible for contacting which staff members. A simple template is provided below. Update the details every three months, and supply a copy to every employee to be kept at home.

Possible disruption	Action	Responsible	Report by	Phone number(s) and email
Loss of premises	Investigate temporary accommodation	Alan	31 July	
Loss of data	Arrange back-up roster Check back-up process does work	Joe		
Loss of computers/server	Secure alternative server Store software off site	Joe		
Fire, earthquake	Check insurances are appropriate and up to date	Jane		
Other: Loss of staff	Make sure skills are transferable	Manager		

The general management of your guest house is designed to realise your short-term, medium-term and long-term planning and objectives for your enterprise.

Your *long-term objective* with your guest house might be to pay off the bond on your property and establish a profitable business. If, by the time you want to retire, you have a paid-up property in a good condition, as well as a steady income, you might be able to employ a full-time manager so that you can relax.

Your *medium-term objective* might be to cover the monthly bond repayments on your property as well as to generate the necessary income to do regular repairs and maintenance, so that your property does not gradually fall into a state of disrepair. In the same manner, your medium-term planning should include covering any replacement costs for items such as linen, crockery and furniture.

Your *short-term planning* in a guest house will always revolve around one objective, namely to keep your occupancy levels and profit as high as possible. Without achieving this goal your medium-term and long-term objectives cannot be realised. In order to keep occupancy levels high, the standard of the accommodation and the service rendered to guests must be reflected in each day's priorities and general objectives for as long as the guest house operates.

It becomes quite clear that whatever you do to manage your guest house, the satisfaction of the guest who crosses the threshold of your guest house is of primary importance. If your guests are not happy, you will not attain any of your goals. Retaining a satisfied guest is much more cost-effective than winning over a new guest.

Effective guest house management will not only give your guest house a competitive advantage but will make your guests feel that they receive good value for money.

The marketing function

We discuss marketing in chapter 7. The most important point to remember about the relationship between marketing and the effective management of your guest house is that you have only a handful of opportunities to convince a guest that you are what you advertise, and that is when he or she makes contact with your establishment, either when making a reservation enquiry or when actually staying at your guest house.

The administrative function

Record keeping is central to good administration and so we focus in this section on systems and categories of record keeping.

Your general administration files

A well-organised filing system is the only way to keep all your important administration records and be able to find and retrieve them when you need to. You should keep the following set of files for this purpose:

* a marketing file,
* a guest reservations file,
* a commissions file,
* a file for your membership of and registration with associations and organisations,
* an insurance file,
* a staff file,
* and a file for records of stock and facilities.

Your marketing file

Keep a comprehensive and well-organised marketing file with all documents reflecting your marketing actions, costs, deals, commission agreements, standard information and rates for agents (which may differ from one to another).

Build up a comprehensive client database of existing and potential clients, and keep detailed records of marketing actions that resulted in more business and those that failed to do so.

Your guest reservations file

The registration forms of all guests who have stayed at your guest house must be kept in this file, which should be archived and kept for at least five years. Make hard copies of your computer records.

Your commissions file

Keep a record of all the commissions you have paid to travel agents, reservation agents, fellow guest house owners and individuals to whom you pay commission for reservations. This file should also be archived and kept for five years.

Your membership and registration files

You will need to keep files for documentation and correspondence regarding your registration with statutory bodies and your membership of organisations.

You will be obliged to register with the following statutory bodies and obligations:

* South African Revenue Service,
* Value-added tax (VAT) registration, if applicable – monthly,
* employee tax – monthly,
* Unemployment Insurance Fund (UIF) – monthly,
* SETA (Services Sector Training Authority) levy,
* Compensation Commissioner – annual levy, and
* monthly municipal levies.

Membership of the following organisations is recommended but not obligatory:

* national, provincial, regional or local tourism bodies,
* regional or national bed and breakfast/guest house associations,
* a central reservations and marketing agency.

Your insurance files

Keep all insurance agreements and policies in a safe place.

Your staff files

Comprehensive details such as the employment contracts, salary payments, deductions, leave taken and UIF contributions of people you employ should be kept on file. Every staff member you employ should have his or own separate file. A copy of the employee's ID document, address and contact details, any disciplinary measures, and pay cheques should be in the file and kept for five years.

Your stock and facilities records

List all the facilities used by the guests. Keep a record of your daily usage of items so that you can control their consumption and replacement. But restock perishables such as food according to your occupancy needs. Keep tight control over the non-perishable items to limit losses and do not forget emergency items and spare batteries for remotes.

Buying stock and facilities control

You must know what stock you have available in your guest house as losses will be financially damaging and your customer service will suffer it you run out of essential basic items. There is no excuse for this, and it is absolutely inadvisable to discover that your coffee cups or teaspoons have disappeared or you have run out of eggs when you have full tables waiting to be served. It is unforgivable not to have toilet paper or any other basic requirement available when needed. Remember items like spare batteries for the remote controls of the entrance gates as well.

Compile a roster according to which you can check all stock and facilities in the guest house, like bed lamps, electrical power points, plumbing items and so forth. A good time to do this is when you inspect the rooms after cleaning.

Control your stock and equipment by physically counting all items such as cutlery, crockery and linen every day, if possible. Check your stocks of the guest amenities and such items as tea bags, small milk canisters and coffee for the rooms.

One way of saving is to compile comprehensive lists of everything used in the guest house, such as cleaning materials, breakfast supplies, products for the general maintenance of the guest house, laundry requirements and garden and pool products. Standardise these products as far as possible and make use of special offers or sales to buy stocks of goods you use a lot of or regularly, such as washing powders, amenities and so on.

Plan your purchases carefully so that you do not have to go shopping every day. Try also to arrange for the delivery of products you use daily in order to save shopping time.

Both perishable and non-perishable food products must be checked on a daily basis. Buy perishables according to your requirements, based on the number of reservations.

You must have sufficient of the necessary items but must also be careful of buying too much as this will lead to wastage and will eat into your profits and affect your cash flow.

It will be well worth your while to join the local bed and breakfast or guest house association, as they have probably negotiated a good discount for their members with suppliers of essential guest house items such as the amenities or even food products.

Have a contingency plan for an emergency such as a power failure by investing in enough gas stoves to be able to prepare breakfast. You must have sufficient torches, candles and gas or paraffin lights so that guests are not left in the dark in their room and can find their way down the hallways to their rooms.

Try to involve your staff members in measures to limit unnecessary expenses, by offering an incentive of some kind or some other form of reward, for example.

General administration hints

- Have a file or form for every possible aspect of administration in your guest house.
- Never try to remember an important piece of information concerning a reservation. Always write it down to ensure that you do not forget and that your service will not suffer as a result.
- Keep notes organised so that similar items are grouped together; otherwise you won't know where to look for a piece of information, and might as well not have bothered to write it down.
- Do the filing regularly, and move a reservation form to the appropriate file as soon as it has reached another stage. A reservation form that gets lost or remains forgotten in the previous stage's file or box can only result in some kind of mistake being made with the reservation.
- The best thing to do with a form in your hand is to handle it immediately and place it in the correct file straight away. Every form should be handled only once at every stage, and the appropriate time to do that is right after the status of a reservation changes – otherwise a mistake could occur.

The financial function

All management functions in a guest house must correspond with the establishment's financial management, and must adhere to the rules laid down in the financial policy of the guest house.

The existence of your guest house relies on *sound financial management* on your part. This is an aspect of guest house management that can seldom be delegated to another staff member. As the owner, you will have to exercise constant control over all areas of your guest house's financial management in order to ensure the financial survival, security and prosperity of your enterprise.

It is important to distinguish clearly between the guest house and your household, at least to the extent that you can be sure of whether you are really making money through your guest house or not. Unless you separate the two, and plan for quieter seasonal times during the year when your occupation levels can drop substantially, you might not be able to survive through the quiet months. The cost of a guest house's infrastructure remains almost unchanged during quiet months, and only economically viable businesses are able to survive these times.

Generally speaking, your guest house should be able to survive financially with the turnover that an *occupancy level of around 33 per cent* will yield, provided that the following aspects are well attended to.

In your financial management plan, you must cater not only for your normal monthly running costs but also for the minimum running costs during quiet months. This means that you must make provision for a healthy cash flow, even while you are waiting for payment from outstanding debtors, or when your occupancy levels drop dramatically.

Try to do as much as possible on cash and as little as possible on credit, because the interest that you pay, as well as escalating monthly commitments, can ruin a business that would have survived bad times if it were not in excessive debt.

Distinguish between items that you need to provide a better service to your guests and those that you need to make life easier for yourself, and concentrate on the former. For example, you do need good quality mattresses and bed linen for your guests, but you don't need to have three sets of bed linen per bed if you cannot yet afford it. Be conservative about buying too much of every item during the first stage of your business when your occupancy levels are still low, and add to your quantities once your occupancy levels justify the expense.

Try to be creative when it comes to regular expenses. For example, your garden needs to be well maintained all year round, so plant shrubs and plants that will yield flowers for your vases throughout the year. Most flowers and greenery that you pay high prices for at florist shops can be grown in your own garden. Apart from the fact that it will save you money, guests will appreciate flowers from your own garden more. There is also little excuse for not growing your own herbs such as parsley and mint, or cocktail tomatoes.

Financial record keeping

Good record-keeping systems provide information for managing finances. The key items in financial record keeping include

✿ *original records*, e.g. keeping your sales slips, receipts, invoices etc.,

- *journals*, which record the details of every transaction in chronological order, e.g. the cash book,
- a *ledger*, where information obtained from journals is made more useable,
- a *trial balance*, which is a list of all ledger account balances taken out to prepare financial statements, and
- *financial statements*, which comprise your income statement and your balance sheet.

The following are the minimum record-keeping requirements for a small business operation:

- a cash book,
- cash control systems,
- an assets register,
- a debtors file,
- a creditors file,
- a bank statements file,
- a tax invoices file,
- a banking book or file, and
- a payments book or file.

Your debtors file

All outstanding accounts of guests, organisations and agents who owe you money should be filed in your debtors file. As you receive these outstanding payments, mark the account as paid and move it to the file where you keep your paid accounts. The file is emptied of all the various accounts on a monthly basis. The record must be kept for five years.

Your creditors file

Invoices of suppliers and organisations with whom you have outstanding accounts should be filed in your creditors file. This will also normally be emptied once a month when you pay these accounts.

Your bank statements file

Keep different accounts separate, for example current and capital accounts (and also archive these statements for five years). Keep all bank correspondence, banked cheques, bank statements and deposit slips in your bank statements file. Make sure that you indicate which payments were made for a particular reservation on the reservation form as well, so that they will correlate with your bank statements. Payments received should immediately be indicated on the reservation form. Keeping a daily record of all payments you receive will make your bookkeeping easier.

Your tax invoices file

Any invoice on which you intend to claim back VAT must correspond with a specific cheque that has gone through the bank. Each proof of a purchase made by the guest house must have a cheque number and cheque date written on it. Such invoices will then be filed in monthly order, according to the sequence in which they went through the bank in that month. They should also be archived for five years. In addition, keep invoices paid for by debit order or direct debit because they will also be reflected on your bank statement. Examples are subscriptions to pay-television services, television licences, electricity bills, cellular or landline phone bills, insurance premiums, credit card commissions, and any other payments on which you want to claim back VAT. Save all your original records such as sales slips, receipts and invoices.

Your banking book or file

Payments into your bank account can be made in different ways, either by yourself or by others.

Payments by yourself are made and recorded as follows:

✿ deposit book: cash, cheques or travellers' cheques (make sure that every deposit slip is dated, stamped and signed by the cashier).

Payments made by others (agents/individuals) are in the form of

✿ bank deposits, which can also be made electronically through internet banking by the customer,
✿ bank transfers, or
✿ secure cash payments directly to your e-enabled website.

If your business has a website that receives online bookings, organise with your bank to get a subscription to its automatic online payments service which will allow you to receive cash payments directly from the account holders. You will get a special payment button on your website, which will create a secure direct payment link. Also find out about secure online payment facilities for direct credit card payments so that customers do not need to provide their credit card details to you.

Always *cross-reference* all the deposits reflected in your bank deposit book and on the reservation forms of your guests. By doing this, you will always know what the source of a deposit was, and which guests' accounts are still outstanding, and which are paid up.

Provide the following information to simplify the process for others to make payments into your account:
• your bank name,
• your bank branch name,
• your bank branch code,
• the name under which your account operates,
• your bank account number, and
• your bank's SWIFT number and street address for overseas deposits.

Your payments book or file

This can be an ordinary A4 hard-covered book in which you keep a day-to-day record of all the different deposits into your bank account. The book should be divided into days, reflecting all cash, cheque, credit card and direct deposit transactions for that day. Remember to check for electronic payments received. Cross-references are made to your bank deposit book, bank statements and reservation forms.

Budgeting

Budgets are based on past experience, the current state of affairs and future expectations. Budgeting will help to provide you with an estimate of the financial requirements involved in carrying out your business plans.

Kinds of budget include

* *the sales budget:* a forecast of your expected monthly income,
* *the materials budget:* your expected purchases,
* *the capital budget:* expected fixed assets expenditure (e.g. machinery and land), and
* *the cash budget:* expected working capital requirements over a specific period.

The human resources (staff) function

The image and success of your guest house will be influenced by each member of your staff through his or her appearance, attitude and actions. All staff members should understand that their job security, besides the success of your guest house, depends on the happiness and satisfaction of each guest. Every staff member plays a very important role so make it a policy to hire people who will not be likely to harm your guest house's reputation through unprofessional or rude behaviour. The saying is to hire people with attitude – the right attitude towards customer service – rather than aptitude, as the skills can be taught. It is vitally important to get and keep the right staff. Employees have to fit in with your management style, be able to do what you want them to and portray a positive, customer-focused image. Incorrect behaviour, such as a surly or unfriendly staff member, could lose you business.

Avoid taking on staff without a satisfactory reference from the most recent employer, as this can pose a security risk.

The first stage in successful recruitment is the formulation of job specifications and descriptions, which clearly define the level of responsibility and skill required. Job descriptions should set out clearly what is expected of staff, listing all tasks and the standard required, the hours of work, daily timetables, and their levels of authority and decision making, if any. Good staff management requires you to make it clear in the job description who supervises whom, and who supervises which tasks, and also to whom each staff member reports. The job description will form part of the employment contract.

Every member of your staff should know exactly what is expected of him or her and how each task should be accomplished. Housekeeping staff should have a clear idea of what a clean and prepared room should look like, how the bed should be made, how the amenities should be set out, and when the room should be ready for the next guest. Front of house reservations staff should know how to deal with enquiries, be computer literate (to use a computerised reservations system if required) and make confirmations and complete final check-out invoices, while the kitchen staff must know how to prepare the breakfasts, plate the food attractively, set out the breakfast buffet and lay the tables in an inviting fashion. Every staff member should know how to treat the guests and how to deal with complaints. You, as the owner and manager, will have to set the standards for all the tasks to be performed to ensure consistency.

Communicate the goals of the guest house – the importance of the guests and good service – to staff so that they can share in your vision. Listen as well to their suggestions for improvements. Studies have shown that it is impossible for employees to provide excellent service if they are not happy in their work. Recognition, rewards, performance evaluation and appreciation are as important as a possible pay rise, if not more so. Small things could motivate staff, such as making sure they each have a business card, giving birthdays off, and asking them what they would change if they could.

The implementation of effective health and safety standards and excellent customer service in your guest house also starts with your staff selection process. The foundation of high standards of hygiene and safety is built by the employment of the right quality staff and the provision of satisfactory training.

Consider the following points when interviewing and appointing cleaning and kitchen staff:

❀ a clean, neat and tidy appearance – persons who cannot take the trouble to present a good appearance at interviews will not respond to hygiene and safety discipline imposed later on,
❀ good dental hygiene,
❀ clean hands with short fingernails and no evidence of nail-biting,
❀ an absence of excessive personal jewellery or make-up,
❀ clean shoes, suitable for the work area,
❀ a belief in the need for hygiene, and
❀ an absence of skin infections.

Staff training

It is essential that you provide your staff with sufficient knowledge and training to avoid mistakes that may result in customer complaints. Cleaning a guest house requires an altogether different approach from that of cleaning a domestic home, where every room will not be made up to professional hospitality standards every day. Make sure your staff members are appropriately trained and resourced with the right equipment to enable them to do a good job. Send them for additional training if required.

In fact, training is an ongoing requirement, both to improve the skills levels of your staff and for their personal development. Subsequently, staff must be motivated and effectively supervised and instructed to ensure that this knowledge is put into practice.

It may be appropriate for you to attend a staff management course as well. You may have converted your home into a guest house, but this does not mean that your domestic staff automatically become guest house staff as the professional requirements are very different.

Although the staff in a guest house will often be involved in general activities, such as reception and kitchen activities, cooking requires specific skills. If there is a team working together in the guest house, different tasks can be assigned to staff members instead of only one person being responsible for all tasks.

Consider training as an investment for these reasons:

❀ it enables staff to fulfil their potential by understanding their responsibilities and improving their skills,
❀ it promotes confidence,
❀ it increases job satisfaction,
❀ it improves performance/morale,
❀ it develops team spirit, and
❀ it reduces the amount of supervision required.

If training is to be successful, you must have a genuine commitment to achieving and maintaining high standards, and this policy must be clearly communicated to staff to engender a positive attitude.

Keeping up standards

Develop standards and procedures to enhance performance standards. Each of these procedures must to be documented to ensure that they are applied consistently. These procedures could include the following:

* customer service guidelines on answering a telephone, dealing with enquiries, reservations and complaints,
* a checklist for serving breakfast, laying the tables and setting out the food,
* a checklist for cleaning and preparing rooms,
* a checklist for stock control of supplies,
* reservations procedures for confirmations etc., and
* regular inspections to ensure that there are no shortcomings in the work done, that procedures are adhered to and that maintenance is up to standard, so that you do not lose business on any of these scores.

The production function

'Production' in a guest house set-up includes all the services that you offer a guest. The services that you offer, such as cleaning, food and reservations, together with your facilities, are what you sell in your enterprise. In this chapter we focus on cleaning. Food is dealt with separately in chapter 6, and the topic of reservations in chapter 5.

Keeping your guest house spotless

Your guests entrust themselves to your care and to your guest house. You have an absolute responsibility to ensure their safety, health and wellbeing while they are staying with you. In addition, the wellbeing and safety of your staff are also vital, as you could not render service of the highest level without them. Compromising on these aspects could not only render you liable to legal actions but would have a very detrimental effect on the reputation of your guest house as well as the success of your business.

A spotlessly clean guest house and guest rooms will most certainly add to the positive impression of your guests, but the best and most expensive curtaining and linen will not hide a dirty room. Your lovely rooms and your overnight accommodation are the most important physical part of what you are selling. As a small business selling accommodation, it is vital that you comply with the professional standards and requirements of the hospitality industry with regard to the health, hygiene and safety of your guest house, particularly concerning the guest rooms and food preparation.

Housekeeping is probably the least interesting part of managing a guest house, but it must be done efficiently. Each guest house has different requirements and facilities. Your housekeeping schedule must suit the layout and infrastructure of your establishment, as well as your personal preferences. The furnishings and decorations in guest rooms are expensive and should be diligently maintained. The signs of a clean guest house are

* well-vacuumed and dust-free surfaces under beds and in corners,
* polished surfaces, tables, baths and vanities,
* smudge-free light fittings and door handles,
* fresh flowers, daily newspapers, recent magazines and clean ashtrays, and
* a tidy garden, clean patio furniture, clean sidewalks and a clean entrance.

Professional room preparation

The requirements for a guest house room and a normal domestic room differ considerably. While most guests like the more homely and informal atmosphere of a guest house, they nevertheless expect a very high standard of room preparation and cleanliness in their guest rooms. You cannot, for example, lock some cupboards in the guest room to store your children's old toys.

Whether you have one room or ten, an *en suite* bathroom or a private bathroom, imported percale sheets or local retail bed covers, a township B&B or a luxury coastal guest house, you can never compromise on the hygiene and cleanliness of the room. A spotlessly clean room is also one of your best marketing features; it is reasonably cheap to achieve and only takes effort and a little time and extra care. However, a dirty room, bed or bath has the potential to close your business down.

A well-prepared room shows that you care and pay attention to detail. It is very reassuring for guests and they will feel safe staying there, content to know that they are staying in a well-managed establishment. Make sure that all the beds are well made and all surfaces gleaming, that there are no blown bulbs or broken equipment, that the television and remote are working, and that the amenities are replaced and there is a spare toilet roll. Put down the personalised welcome letter and check the fresh flowers and fruit in the room. You can extend the service by offering a turn-down service in which the room is tidied, the bed turned down, curtains drawn and lights switched on in the evenings.

The preparation of a room for a professional hospitality establishment needs to follow certain procedures. These procedures will also ensure that the rooms are prepared effectively and without wasting time and effort. Follow a standard routine when cleaning and preparing guest rooms. This helps to maintain a consistently high standard of cleanliness and to save time because you will become familiar with the routine and less likely to forget to perform certain tasks. Working methodically will mean that your rooms are cleaned to a consistently high standard.

Pay attention to detail when preparing a room for guests. Report all problems with a lack of cleanliness or malfunctioning equipment promptly so that they can be attended to.

Consider the guest's comfort and install cooling or heating in the room. On a cold day, switch on the heating and perhaps even warm the bed, or cool the room in the heat of summer. Think of insect control with mosquito nets, window gauze or insecticides. These simple considerations will be much appreciated by your guests.

Remember to check for any belongings that guests may inadvertently have left behind when they leave so that you can send them on to them.

Below are the main reasons for cleaning a guest room:

- ✿ *Hygiene:* Cleaning controls the spread of bacteria that can cause disease or infection.
- ✿ *Safety:* You must meet the requirements of health and safety regulations that make an employer responsible for providing a safe environment for employees and guests.
- ✿ *Maintenance:* Regular cleaning helps to remove dirt and maintain the property and its fixtures in good condition so they will last longer. This is a cost saving.
- ✿ *Aesthetics and marketing value:* Guest rooms and public areas that look good because they are clean and tidy are more inviting for guests. This creates more business because guests are happy to return and spread the 'good word' about the property to other potential clients.

Common cleaning agents

To get the best results when cleaning, you need to be able to choose the correct product for each cleaning job you are required to do. If you select and apply the wrong cleaning agent or mix the wrong cleaning agents, problems can occur, such as surface or colour deterioration.

Preparing to clean the guest room

Daily briefing

Conduct a daily briefing for staff to explain details of the day's events, such as special events taking place in the guest house, priority rooms, special guest requests and extra cleaning jobs to be done. Provide the cleaning staff with a schedule that tells you which rooms they have been allocated for the day.

For security reasons, keys are signed out at the beginning of the shift and signed back at the end of the shift.

Guests' rooms must be tidied and cleaned daily. Do not interfere with or throw away any personal items; that scrap of paper may have an important telephone number written on it. A 'turn-down' service in the evenings will be appreciated, with lights switched on and curtains closed.

Stocking the trolley

This is optional and applicable to larger guest houses. Prepare the trolley with all the things required to do the job efficiently. They include

* cleaning equipment,
* cleaning agents,
* protective clothing, as required (gloves, dust masks),
* fresh linen,
* room stock, e.g. toiletries, toilet paper, tissues, tea and coffee stocks, stationery, etc.,
* garbage bags and bin liners, and
* paperwork, e.g. maintenance reports, lost property reports, linen tally-sheet, room status reports.

To do the job efficiently, a well-organised and well-stocked trolley is very useful and will eliminate the need to run back and forth between supplies and the room. It is a worthwhile time- and labour-saving device, even for a small establishment.

The trolley must be kept tidy so that time is not wasted looking for things. An overstocked trolley increases the likelihood of items on the trolley being damaged, dirtied or stolen, while an understocked trolley wastes time if the cleaner has to constantly return to the storeroom.

Restock the trolley at the end of each shift so that the next shift can begin completely organised and can start cleaning the assigned rooms immediately. Below is a checklist for the housekeeping trolley:

* Are all items on the trolley organised neatly?
* Is the trolley stocked to the level specified by the employer?
* Are sufficient amounts of the required cleaning chemicals available, e.g. all-purpose cleaner, glass cleaner and room deodoriser?

- Are all items of cleaning equipment available, e.g. bucket, mop, lint-free cloth, rags and duster?
- Does the cleaner have all the required paperwork, e.g. lost property, maintenance reports, and so forth?
- Are the guest room keys kept in the designated place to maintain security?

Using the trolley

It is better to push the trolley rather than pull it because one has greater control and there is less risk of injuring one's back.

When cleaning a room, always position the trolley against the wall in the corridor just outside the door of the room to be cleaned. Make sure corridors or fire exits are not blocked. If the vacuum cleaner is beside the trolley, store it neatly with the cord wound up. This allows people to walk freely along the corridor without any obstacles.

Cleaning guest rooms

A set sequence should be followed when cleaning guest rooms. Working in a methodical way helps to produce consistently clean rooms. It also helps to save time because the cleaner becomes familiar with the routine and there is less chance of forgetting to do certain tasks. The easiest is to start at a point near the door and work clockwise around the room.

Each establishment has its own way of cleaning guest rooms. It is important that the extra tasks are performed carefully because they are designed to remove dust and dirt that accumulates from everyday wear and tear.

By rotating these tasks regularly, the guest house can avoid the expense of closing down rooms to perform these tasks all at the same time.

Remember that the guest rooms are off-limits to your pets.

Entering the guest room

Before entering a guest room, always knock and announce yourself by saying 'Good morning/afternoon, housekeeping'. Listen carefully for a reply from the guest. Knock at least three times. If there is no answer, knock again and then open the door, calling out 'housekeeping' before entering the room. It is important to follow these procedures to show respect for the guest's privacy and to prevent an embarrassing situation. Never knock if there is a DO NOT DISTURB sign on the door.

The daily cleaning sequence

All bedrooms should be cleaned and tidied daily, whether occupied or not, so that they are always fresh and ready for an unexpected guest. A daily cleaning sequence is provided below.

1. Make sure that you are wearing gloves.
2. Enter the room. Switch on all the lights and open the curtains. Check whether all the light bulbs are functioning and that the curtains are in order.
3. Bring in the cleaning materials and supplies.
4. Check wardrobes, drawers and under the bed for any belongings left behind if the guest has already checked out.
5. Prepare the room for cleaning – remove all soiled linen and rubbish.

6. Wash used crockery in warm water in the bathroom or replace it with clean crockery from the kitchen.
7. Strip and remake the beds. All linen, including duvet covers, should be changed for new guests. If a guest is staying with you for a length of time, all bed linen – including duvet covers – should be changed every three to four days. This period may be extended for environmental purposes with the guest's consent, usually by leaving a card for him to set out. If he wants his towels changed, he can be asked to leave them in the bath.
8. Soiled linen should be changed as soon as possible. In winter, check that additional blankets are available, that any electric blankets are in working order, and that these are switched off.
9. Dust the room.
10. Clean the bathroom. A variety of surfaces need to be cleaned in a bathroom – it is important to select an appropriate product for each surface. A bathroom is a potential source of infection with germs, mould and bacteria that could be present. The toilet, bathtub, shower and shower curtains or doors, mirrors, pipes at the back of the wash-basin and toilet, and all the corners should be spotlessly clean, fresh smelling and free from bacteria and germs.
11. Wet the surfaces and spray chemicals in the bath, hand basin and toilet, as well as surfaces for vanity cases, any shelves and the mirrors. Kneel beside the bath to clean it, to prevent back strain.
12. Use a separate cloth and sponge for cleaning the toilet. Clean the toilet thoroughly, both inside the bowl and on the outside, as well as the lid, the cistern and the seat. A used toothbrush is handy to clean difficult-to-reach spots.
13. Wipe down the tiles, shower doors or curtains.
14. Replenish and tidy guest amenities like soap and shampoo.
15. Replace towels and bath mats and check whether there is a spare toilet roll.
16. Vacuum all carpet areas.
17. Replenish supplies, such as coffee, tea, sugar and creamer sachets, tissues and stationery.
18. Check that all lamps and electrical appliances are correctly positioned for practical use.
19. Check the magazines, books, information brochures, etc.
20. Check the rooms for cleanliness, faulty equipment and damaged furniture or fittings.
21. Close the blinds, switch off the lights and lock the door after airing and deodorising the room.
22. Finally, record and report the room status. It is important to report any guest house property that is not working or damaged so that problems can be fixed quickly without inconveniencing guests.

Below is a useful checklist for the room cleaner's supervisor to complete:

Checklist for bedroom service		
Tasks	Performed to required standards?	
Checked daily rooms assignment and followed a plan to clean according to an appropriate priority	Yes	No
Followed correct procedure of signing out keys	Yes	No
Trolley neatly stocked with recommended quantities	Yes	No
Trolley stocked with sufficient supplies of cleaning chemicals and equipment	Yes	No

Followed correct procedure for announcing housekeeping services to the guest	Yes	No
Turned on the lights, and checked for lights that are not working	Yes	No
Opened the drapes and sheer curtains correctly	Yes	No
Removed dirty room-service trays or tables and returned to designated area	Yes	No
Washed and dried dirty room crockery and cutlery or replaced with clean items	Yes	No
Removed any rubbish from the room and disposed of it according to the property's procedures	Yes	No
Prepared the bathroom for cleaning using appropriate cleaning chemicals • toilet • shower, bath and tiles	Yes	No
Dusted and polished surfaces: • worked in an appropriate order around room • used appropriate cleaning equipment and chemicals for the surfaces in the room	Yes	No
Cleaned windows and mirrors: • used appropriate cleaning equipment and chemicals • left the cleaned surface free of streaks	Yes	No

Replaced and presented guest supplies according to the property's standards
• Tea and coffee:
   – 2 tea sachets, 2 coffee sachets
   – 2 brown, 2 white sugar
   – 2 coffee creamers, 2 tea whiteners
   – 2 cups, 2 saucers, 2 teaspoons
• Stationery:
   – 2 A4 sheets of writing paper
   – 2 envelopes
   – 2 fax forms
   – 1 guest feedback survey
   – brochures
	Yes	No

Neatly arranged guest's belongings and room items, e.g. ashtrays, directories	Yes	No
Reported lost property to owner/manager/reception	Yes	No
Vacuumed all exposed areas of carpet	Yes	No
Moved appropriate items of furniture and beds for vacuuming when required	Yes	No
Inspected the room using the housekeeping checklist and made any necessary adjustments	Yes	No
Deodorised room with air-freshener	Yes	No
Locked guest room after cleaning	Yes	No
Returned keys to reception at end of shift	Yes	No
Followed procedures to protect guest's security and property while cleaning	Yes	No
Followed correct manual-handling procedures for all lifting, pushing and pulling tasks, e.g. making beds, pushing trolley, moving furniture	Yes	No

Worked in ways to minimise back strain	Yes	No
Followed correct procedures when working with electrical equipment	Yes	No
Kept work area and corridors tidy and free of obstructions that could cause trips and falls	Yes	No
Completed allocated rooms within the given time	Yes	No
Conclusion: The clean room is ready to welcome the next guest to your wonderful guest house		

It may be useful to create a room cleaners' roster, with cleaners working on rooms by rotation. This way, every cleaner has a chance to clean every room, which will ensure consistent standards.

Precautions against HIV

Follow the following procedures:

* Special care is needed when handling or cleaning anything that might have come into contact with another person's bodily fluids such as blood and vomit.
* Make sure that any cuts or grazes you might have are covered with waterproof dressings.
* Make up your disinfectant according to the manufacturer's instructions.
* Put on rubber gloves, and wear a plastic apron if you need to disinfect the contaminated area; use a cloth or mop, but not a scrubbing brush, as this can cause splashes.
* Leave the disinfectant to work – the length of time will depend on the instructions. Then mop up the disinfectant and wash the surrounding areas.
* Without taking them off, rinse the gloves in the disinfectant, rinse and wipe the apron.
* Pour the disinfectant down a sluice or toilet; place the cloth in a plastic bag and put it with the rubbish. Wash out the mop head in disinfectant.
* Leave gloves, apron and mop, if used, to dry before putting away.
* Wash hands thoroughly.

A regular inspection programme

The best way to ensure that the upkeep of your facilities stays under control is to adopt a systematic regular inspection programme according to which you regularly check all the items that may need maintenance. This will prevent an embarrassing situation when everything goes wrong on the same day. Use the times when your occupancy is low to do general maintenance work and to check and clean walls, carpets, furniture and curtains.

Regular inspection of all the areas in your guest house will ensure the following conditions:

* Fixtures, fittings and furnishings are clean and in good working order. Check all lights and lamps daily as part of the daily cleaning routine. Keep stock of all the different types of light bulb that you use in your guest house. Guests have the right to working lights in the room they are paying for, and it is not acceptable to say that you do not have a specific type of bulb in stock. Imported lights and lamps, in particular, may require special bulbs which could be difficult to acquire, so find out who the suppliers of different types of bulb are during the planning phase of your guest house.
* Surfaces are clean and free of marks or clutter.
* Floors and floor coverings are clean and freshly vacuumed, washed or polished.

- Lighting, heating and cooling systems are in good working order.
- Bedrooms and bathrooms have been thoroughly cleaned and tidied, beds made and guest items replenished. Check linen and towels regularly after laundering for stains and wear and tear.
- All areas are hygienic and pest-free.
- The garden, lawn and flower beds are maintained, pathways tidied, outside lights working, the garden furniture clean and the swimming pool clean.
- The condition of the swimming pool's water is checked daily to keep it sparkling blue.
- Plumbing problems and leaking taps can be seen to immediately. Arrange an agreement and tariff structure with a reliable plumber and an electrician for after-hours emergency services. Don't wait for an emergency situation, because emergency service suppliers often take advantage of the fact that you are desperate for their services, and then charge exorbitant rates.
- All electrical appliances are in working order – breakfast without a kettle, toaster or coffee machine will be most inconvenient. Acquire enough gas stoves to get you through a breakfast on full occupancy. Guests will understand power failures, but won't appreciate your failure to make provision for alternative cooking facilities.

Oystercatcher Lodge

TOP: Your guests will enjoy the inviting setting and refreshments in the privacy of their own room. *Oystercatcher Lodge.*

BOTTOM: Guests help themselves to cereal and fruit while their hot choices are being prepared. *Foodlink at Beauvilla Guest House.*

TOP: An inviting buffet of cold breakfast dishes. *Aan de Oever Guest House*

BOTTOM: Make your guests feel special with a beautifully presented table.
Foodlink at Beavilla Guest House.

TOP: The mosquito net over the bed looks very romantic but also has a practical purpose. *Plumbago Guest House.*

BOTTOM: The choice of colours and the seashell design in this stylish bedroom reflect its coastal environment. *Sandals Guest House.*

TOP: Traditional wooden furniture and the small animal designs on the linen give the room a personal touch. *Aan de Oever Guest House.*

BOTTOM: The spotless bathroom has all the modern conveniences in a traditional setting. *Aan de Oever Guest House.*

TOP: A stunning view of the African sunset and a sparkling pool are strong selling points. *Plumbago Guest House.*

BOTTOM: The character and atmosphere of historical homes make them very attractive as guest houses. *Aan de Oever Guest House.*

TOP: Take full advantage of a breathtaking location and view to offer your guests an exceptional experience. *Oystercatcher Lodge.*

BOTTOM: Guests will appreciate an elegant patio to relax and enjoy the South African climate. *Sandals Guest House.*

TOP: The mountains and sunset add to the character of the graceful guest house. *Aan de Oever Guest House.*

BOTTOM: Modern luxury set against the wild beauty of the dunes and coastline. *Oystercatcher Lodge.*

Looking
after your guests
from enquiry to
departure

Introduction

Guests are the lifeline of your business, and reservation requests and enquiries from potential guests are the visible evidence that you have established your guest house in an attractive and appropriate fashion and that your marketing is delivering results. This is what you have been waiting for, and it is crucial that the way in which you deal with the reservation enquiry or request and the manner in which you render the services to the guests are professional and correct in all ways.

In this chapter we discuss how to deal effectively with enquiries from prospective guests and how to make and confirm reservations efficiently. We also guide you in the procedures for receiving and checking-in your guests, preparing guests' accounts, and checking them out at the end of their stay.

Dealing with reservation enquiries

Once you begin marketing your guest house, it is important to be able to handle any reservation enquiries promptly and efficiently. Reservation enquiries can reach you in a variety of ways, for example through your website, telephone calls, faxes, letters or email, as well as the guest who arrives at your front door unannounced, with your brochure or guide in his or her hand.

Reservation enquiries are understood as general enquiries for future reservations. Often a company or agent will not make an enquiry for a specific reservation, but for reservations in general. If you do not have a website, you should have an up-to-date information leaflet available that can easily be faxed or an electronic brochure that can be emailed (see chapter 7 on marketing).

Make sure you have your office organised so that you can immediately supply information concerning reservations. The most important administrative document is your reservation chart. This can either be on a computerised programme, open on your screen, or in hard copy, which should be kept in your office so that you can establish at a glance whether you have a room available or not. If you use a computerised system, it is advisable to print your occupancy graph at least twice a day, perhaps at the start of the day and during the day as well, so that you have a hard copy on which to check availability in the event of a power failure.

You will, of course, also need the necessary reservation forms and other stationery at hand so that you can complete the conversation without having to ask the caller to hold at any stage.

It is important that all contact with guests, whether over the telephone, via fax, or in person, is handled by trained members of staff and not, for example, by young children or untrained staff who cannot supply accurate information and rates. If you cannot find a suitable person to answer the telephone in your absence, arrange for a forwarding facility from your home telephone to your cellphone so that potential customers will reach you automatically when they phone your guest house. Furthermore, never leave your guest house under the management of untrained staff or children when you are expecting a guest to arrive. Hospitality is a 'people industry' and guests expect to be met in person at a guest house by a staff member trained to welcome and check them in, if not preferably by you.

Take note of correct and professional telephone manner and etiquette:

✿ Make sure that your manner and style of talking conveys an impression of warm professionalism and a helpful attitude. People can detect a smile in your voice.
✿ Be enthusiastic and lively in your greeting.
✿ Identify your guest house in a clear manner and give the caller time to absorb the information and to verify that he has reached the place he wants, for example: 'Good evening, Wind in the Willows Guest House, Margie speaking.'
✿ Make careful notes of all important details and repeat contact numbers and details. An incorrect number or email address could lose you business!
✿ If you cannot assist immediately, for example when you need to check a provisional reservation, give the caller a specific time when you will get back to her with confirmation. For example, 'I will call you at 14h00 to confirm availability of the room you wanted'. Do not only say you will call her back later, as she will then look elsewhere and you may lose the reservation.
✿ Remember to thank the caller.

Tips for better phone service

1. Have sufficient telephone lines (especially during sales) so customers do not have to wait for service.
2. Have a speedy and efficient connection. Do customers have to wade through a lengthy electronic menu to get connected?
3. Test how well your employees answer phone calls. Regularly test the friendliness of your business's phone service (for instance, get a friend to phone).
4. Phone staff should be able to handle 95 per cent of all call enquiries without having to refer the call to others. Customers hate being shunted around because the first person who answers can't give an answer.
5. One person (usually the first person who takes the call) should take responsibility for seeing that the customer gets a satisfactory result.
6. Measure how many call enquiries are converted into actual sales.
7. Use standard telephone scripts for your staff (based on best sales practice). They can make a huge difference in delivering a consistently excellent service.

Email enquiries must be responded to within hours. Follow up with a telephone call in order to personalise the enquiry if possible. You must check your email at least twice a day. Most people make enquiries to more than one establishment by email and the one that responds first often gets the business. In addition, quick reaction is equated with professionalism and efficiency, and always impresses people.

If you happen to be out, and a 'walk-in' guest arrives at the door, the staff on duty should know that they should contact you on your cellphone instead of trying to assist the guest if they are not trained to do so. Your staff should know where you are and how long you will be away. Make sure that you are available at all times! This is one of the harsh realities of running a guest house – you have to be totally committed, sometimes for practically 24 hours a day.

Reservation chart

Should a caller enquire about the availability of accommodation for a specific date, you should consult your reservation chart immediately. Below is an example of a typical reservation chart.

Reservation chart for
Wind in the Willows
Guest House

Month: *January 2009*			
Rooms	Blue Room	White Room	Yellow Room
Rates	*R250/R190*	*R300/R225*	*R400/R275*
Beds	*Twin*	*Queen*	*Extra-long king size*
Bathrooms	*Bath only*	*Shower only*	*Full*
Tel Ext.	*x 205*	*x 206*	*x 207*
Thu 01			
Fri 02			
Sat 03			
Sun 04			
Mon 05			
Tue 06			
Wed 07			
Thu 08			
Fri 09			
Sat 10			
Sun 11			
Mon 12			
Tue 13			
Wed 14			
Thu 15			
Fri 16			
Sat 17			
Sun 18			
Mon 19			
Tue 20			
Wed 21			
Thu 22			
Fri 23			
Sat 24			
Sun 25			
Mon 26			
Tue 27			
Wed 28			
Thu 29			
Fri 30			
Sat 31			

In the example above, January 2009 is taken as the month for this reservation chart. January starts on a Thursday, so the corresponding weekdays for every date have been filled in. You should adapt this chart to accommodate the number of rooms in your guest house, and fill in the names or numbers of your rooms where the example has 'Blue Room', etc.

The rooms in the example are arranged from *smallest to largest*, and the prices will reflect this by becoming higher as you move to the right. One advantage of placing rooms in order of size is that you can always upgrade a guest to a bigger or better room towards the right-hand side of the reservation chart. Unless a guest has requested twin beds, for example, and the better room has a king-size bed, it always makes sense to upgrade a guest to a better room if you have one available.

The *rationale behind upgrading* a guest's room is that it costs you approximately the same amount to accommodate a guest in a larger room, and the guest will leave your establishment feeling especially valued and that he or she has received good value for money. It is a good marketing tool as well. Make sure that you always inform a guest that you have upgraded the room without extra cost. This is because the guest might think that the rate paid applies to the larger room, and be dissatisfied when getting a smaller room for the same price on another occasion. In addition, the guest might be concerned about having to pay extra for a better room than the one initially reserved, and your reassurance to the contrary will put his or her mind at rest.

The *rates* are specified in the next line of the example reservation chart. Always specify the single rate (which would be the higher one) first, and then the sharing rate. This will ensure that you do not quote the lower rate instead of the single rate. Depending on the area in which you operate your guest house, and depending on your target market, you will find that you get either single or sharing reservations.

Areas that typically attract tourists and holidaymakers will be visited by more couples than singles, whereas areas that typically attract business visitors will have single reservations most of the time. You could, of course, quote one rate for the room, irrespective of whether the reservation is made for one or two guests, but then you would have to specify, for example, that the room is available for a maximum of two adults plus one child under the age of 12 years. However, this is not a popular option when you have predominantly single occupancy.

In the next line of the reservation chart, you specify the *bathroom facilities*, unless all your bathrooms are identical. If a bathroom has only a bath and no shower, or vice versa, it is always advisable to mention it to the agent or guest who makes the enquiry, so that there is no misunderstanding over the bathroom facilities. It is best to equip all your bathrooms with baths as well as showers, but if you have to make a choice, rather install a shower and no bath than vice versa.

If you have *telephone extensions* in your guests' rooms, you should fill in the relevant extension numbers in the next line of the reservations chart. If you have a telephone system with extensions in all the bedrooms, organise the extension numbers logically so that they will be easily memorised. Make sure that all staff members have memorised the different extension numbers of the rooms. The person who puts a call through to a room must be 100 per cent sure of dialling the correct extension – especially when overseas calls come through at three o'clock in the morning!

The space to the left of the days of the month on the example reservation chart is allocated to the days of the week. These obviously differ from month to month. Complete them appropriately, and mark the weekends and public holidays, so that it is easy to see where the different weeks begin and end.

In any discussion about or confirmation of a reservation, develop the habit of specifically mentioning the day of the week and not only the date. It can happen that people confuse Tuesdays and Thursdays, or that a person looks at the wrong month on the calendar. Such a mistake will normally attract attention the moment that the day and the date don't correspond. The consequences of an error in a reservation because of confusion between days and dates can cause you embarrassment, and can have a financial implication; therefore always double-check. To avoid confusion, remember that reservations are never taken from, for example, the 1st to the 5th, as it is not clear whether the guest will still be sleeping on the 5th or departing on the 5th. To avoid a misunderstanding that could lose you revenue, indicate the date of arrival and the date of departure, and double check the number of nights of the reservation.

It is a good idea to put a loose layer of laminated plastic over your reservation chart to keep it clean, and to use pencil for all reservations until a guest actually arrives. Reservations can then be changed until the last moment, and a neat reservation chart without crossed-out reservations is a prerequisite for correct information and efficient management.

Your reservation chart can be adapted to contain almost all the information used for your housekeeping, administrative and financial management. The more accurate the entries, the less effort you will need to obtain monthly statistics of any kind. Indicate types of occupation (single or sharing), rates charged, commission owed, extra meals enjoyed and any other information useful for your enterprise. Of course, the more information your reservation chart contains, the less it should be kept where guests or staff members could study its particulars. For example, you would not want a guest to know that the secretary of a company receives 10 per cent commission on certain accommodation fees, so don't let a guest see the information on your reservation chart. The best way to keep the information confidential is to have a permanent cover that can be lifted only when you handle an enquiry.

Technology can assist you with the smooth handling of reservations and generally make your life and effective administration easier and more professional. Many computerised reservations systems are currently available that are easy to use and suitable for a small establishment. They will not only help you to render a professional service to your guests but can assist with preparing invoices and generating reports on meals or extra services charged. Most important, such a program is excellent for conveniently keeping details of your guest's previous stays and her preferences to help you provide excellent customer service to her. This way, when your guest calls again, you could really impress her by remembering the preference for a particular room, for example.

If you decide to use an electronic guest reservation and management system, it should be easy to use and to set up the relevant details of your own establishment, such as your guest house name and details of the rooms and rates, as well as any extra services you offer for payment. The system must provide you with the capability to do the following to manage your guest house effectively:

1. *Reservations* should be displayed on a calendar grid for quick visual reference. The grid should provide you with reservations and occupancy reports and projected income based on reservations.
2. The *accounting facility* should consist of invoicing guests for all costs, payment allocations, statements and all the necessary accounting reports such as expenses, outstanding invoices, sales reports, VAT reports, income statements and aged analysis.
3. *Account enquiries* must show the account balance of a guest, contact information and any notes associated with the account. For more information about the invoices making up the account, the detailed invoices may be displayed.

Examples of the various reservation functions that can be performed by a computerised reservations and management system that will save you time and increase your efficiency:

⌂ Account Enquiry   ▭☐✕

Wind in the Willows
Account Enquiry

Account Name | Micro Consulting Services ⌄ | Invoice details

Account Balance | 1881.00

Contact person | Secretary - Emily Williams

Phone No | 021 321 3241

Notes | Order number required
Guests always require airport transfer
Send statement by 25th of the month

F1 = Help

⌂ Reservation Information   ▭☐✕

Wind in the Willows

Reservation for Room 5
Honeymoon suite

Guest name | Melody Mabusa ⌄ | **Reserve**

Arrival date | 08/07/19 ↕ | **Cancel**

Departure date | 08/07/21 ↕   No of nights = 2 | **Guests**

	Select rate	Rate
No of adults	2 ↕ Accommodation - shared occupancy ⌄	450.00
No of children	0 ↕ ⌄	0.00
	Total	1800.00

Notes
Require room from 10am
Special breakfast for 8 at 9:30 on Sunday|

F1 = Help

Screenshots: GuestWise Reservations and Management System

Reservations

Wind in the Willows

Notes - Rooms 1 to 6

Tabs: Rooms 1 - 6 | Rooms 7 - 12 | Rooms 13 - 18 | Rooms 19 - 24

Day	Date	Room 1 Guest	Room 2 Guest	Room 3 Guest	Room 4 Guest	Room 5 Guest	Room 6 Guest
Sun	08/07/06						
Mon	08/07/07	John Smith			Peter Gibbons		PCW Auditors
Tues	08/07/08	John Smith	Mary Jones		Peter Gibbons		PCW Auditors
Wed	08/07/09	John Smith	Mary Jones		Peter Gibbons		PCW Auditors
Thur	08/07/10	John Smith	Mary Jones	David Dube	Peter Gibbons		PCW Auditors
Fri	08/07/11		Mary Jones	David Dube	Pat Mahlanga		PCW Auditors
Sat	08/07/12		Mary Jones	David Dube	Pat Mahlanga	Provisional-Joy	
Sun	08/07/13				Pat Mahlanga	Provisional-Joy	
Mon	08/07/14				Pat Mahlanga	Provisional-Joy	PWC Auditors
Tues	08/07/15				Pat Mahlanga	Provisional-Joy	PWC Auditors
Wed	08/07/16				Pat Mahlanga	Provisional-Joy	PWC Auditors
Thur	08/07/17				Pat Mahlanga	Provisional-Joy	PWC Auditors
Fri	08/07/18				Pat Mahlanga		PWC Auditors
Sat	08/07/19				Pat Mahlanga		
Sun	08/07/20				Pat Mahlanga		
Mon	08/07/21				Pat Mahlanga		
Tues	08/07/22				Pat Mahlanga		

Previous Week | Next Week | Refresh | Print | Save | F1 = Help

Guest Information

Guest Information

Guest Name	Grant Cirus
Phone No	021 184 7750
Cell Phone No	088 986 3265
Fax No	
Email Address	grantc@microcon.com
ID Number	7502025899327
Credit Card No	4444 5555 6666 7777
Card Type	Visa
Next of Kin	Wife
Next of Kin Phone No	088 987 3232
Account Name	Micro Consulting Services
Account Address	P O Box 1095
Account Contact Name	Secretary - Emily Williams
Account Contact Phone	021 321 3241
Account Vat No	442 5687 9564
Special Requests	

Buttons: Add New | Save | Delete | New Account | F1 = Help

Screenshots: GuestWise Reservations and Management System

The programs can be used to easily track your occupancy over a particular period as well. The computer charts work on much the same principle as the manual hard copy charts, and a reputable seller should provide you with some basic training in the programme. In addition, an automatic confirmation letter can be generated to be emailed or faxed and the reservation can be tracked to make sure that you have received the required deposit.

However, it is not advisable to rely only on a computerised reservation system. It is most frustrating for a caller to wait for you to exit a program you may be working on before entering the reservations program to tell him or her whether you have accommodation or not, so keep the chart minimised on the screen. Print a hard copy every day as well, to help you check. Remember to make backups! You could make initial reservations in pencil on your reservations chart and transfer confirmed details to your computer programs. A computer crash or power failure could wreak havoc with your reservations if you rely entirely on the computer.

Do not use your diary to record reservations. Use it only to capture a request when you are not near your reservation chart, but confirm as soon as possible whether you have availability. Sooner or later you will make a mistake with the diary system and could end up with a double booking. Apart from being very embarrassing to you and extremely inconvenient to the guests concerned, this will reflect very negatively on your professionalism.

Confirmation of availability

If you receive a provisional enquiry for accommodation for a certain period and you have a room available, you must confirm as soon as possible by fax or email, as per the examples. Write down everything that is relevant to the reservation in order to ensure that there are no misunderstandings at a later stage. You can use a standardised form or a personalised letter, or attach the form to a personalised email to your guest.

Quotation

You may also be asked for a quotation for the reservation from a business or agent, in competition with other accommodation establishments. If you want the business badly enough, this is a good time to consider offering a special rate or some other enticement to win the booking.

On the next page is an example of a quotation.

Address 62 Willow Lane, Willowmore 1234 PO Box 3300 Willowmore

Tel 0432 44 543 **Fax** 0432 44 542

Email windwillow@guesthouse.co.za
Website www.windwillow.co.za

Wind in the Willows

		Company:	
Fax:		Date:	
From:			

Herewith the quotation as requested:

Accommodation		Arrival:	
		Departure:	
Number of single rooms:	0	@ R365 pp:	R0.00
Number of sharing rooms:	0	@ R285 pp:	R0.00
3rd person sharing:	0	@ R197.50 pp:	R0.00
Number of dinners:		@ R90 pp:	R0.00
Number of braais (Sundays):		@ R120 pp:	R0.00
Total number of rooms:	0	Other:	R0.00
Total number of guests:	0		R0.00
Total number of nights:	0	**Subtotal:**	R0.00
		Total excl VAT:	R0.00
		VAT @ 14%:	R0.00
		Grand total:	R0.00

Booking conditions

Thirty per cent deposit or valid credit card details on confirmation, as per attached authorisation. No refund of deposits if cancelled within seven days of the reservation.

Payment to be made into account:

Wind in the Willows
Account no. 123 567
Happy Bank branch code 7890

We look forward to welcoming you at Wind in the Willows.

Give the guest a limited time within which to confirm. Keep a record in your diary of the date of the enquiry and the date on which confirmation should be received, so that you do not turn away business when the enquirer has no intention of accepting the reservation for the room you were keeping open. People tend to ask for accommodation availability at more than one establishment and neglect to cancel those they do not want.

Cancellation and deposit policy

A cancellation policy is an internationally accepted standard practice in accommodation establishments such as hotels, and it is strongly advised that you protect your business against losses as a result of late cancellations or no-shows, i.e. reservations made by people who have no intention of turning up. If a guest will not commit himself to a reasonable policy, the chances are good that he would not have turned up anyway.

The cancellation policy implies that you have charged a deposit on the accommodation booked. When deciding on the amount for a deposit, it is important to look at how exposed your business is should a booking be cancelled. If a large group makes a reservation taking all your rooms for an extended period of time, your loss will be huge if they cancel at the last minute and you cannot fill your rooms. This would justify charging at least a 50% deposit to confirm the booking well in advance and perhaps even a full payment a month in advance. If one person books for a few nights only, your loss will not be so great so your deposit can reflect that.

✿ Overseas reservations made far in advance by tour groups or agents are often made for long periods of time and for bigger groups of guests. If these reservations are cancelled at short notice or even if the size of the group is drastically reduced and you did not make clear in your cancellation policy that you will retain the deposit, the rooms can often not be filled with new guests and you lose all the revenue for these rooms.
✿ You may lose some reservations because people are normally hesitant to commit themselves too far ahead of time in case their circumstances should force their plans to change at short notice. However, if you have a reasonable policy and timelines for cancellation, this should not happen. Another way around this would be to require credit card authorisation for cancellation charges at a later stage.
✿ You will very rarely be able to recover a reservations enquiry for a room once you have declined it, should a confirmed reservation cancel. You must therefore build in some form of compensation for revenue lost through cancelled reservations if you end up with an empty room.
✿ Cancellation policies normally cover an amount charged as deposit as well as a timeline, which is often staggered. You may, for example, charge one night's accommodation if the reservation is cancelled more than 14 days before the first night and 50 per cent for cancellations less than 14 days before.
✿ It is acceptable to charge individual bookings at least for one night's accommodation in the event of a late cancellation, but cancellation policies that require 50 per cent deposits, which are non-refundable for cancellations later than a week before arrival, are also common in the industry. However, it is not good practice to be so rigid that you charge a hefty cancellation fee if a group, for example, cancels one guest out of five or one night out of a long or large reservation which still remains a good reservation.
✿ You can always be lenient towards regular guests and charge less or nothing at all, but you can never increase or charge a cancellation fee that the guest was not advised of at the time of reservation.
✿ It is a good idea to set your policies in line with those of other guest houses in the area.

Enforcing your cancellation policy calls for fairness and tact as you do not want to antagonise potential guests who may have cancelled for reasons out of their control and may book again in future.

Below are examples of a confirmation letter, a credit card authorisation form and a confirmation form.

Address 62 Willow Lane, Willowmore 1234 PO Box 3300 Willowmore

Tel 0432 44 543   **Fax** 0432 44 542

Email windwillow@guesthouse.co.za
Website www.windwillow.co.za

To: Lookout Travel Agency
Attention: Ms Lee-Anne Jones
Fax: 011 404 4191 (2 pages)
Date: 16 May 2009

Confirmation of your reservation

Dear Ms Jones,

Thank you for your enquiry about accommodation for Mr Peter Brown. I am pleased to confirm the availability of accommodation as requested:

Arrival: Friday 22 May 2009 (14h00)

Departure: Monday 25 May 2009 (10h00)

Room: 1 × luxury suite @ R450 per person per night (single accommodation, bathroom with shower en suite).

Airport transfer: Arranged with Reliable Tours at R150 per trip. Contact James on 082 345 6789. Please pay the driver cash direct.

The rate includes a full breakfast. A three-course set-menu dinner is offered at R150 per person subject to prior arrangement, or we can make a dinner reservation at a nearby restaurant on Mr Brown's behalf.

I attach a credit card authorisation form. On receipt of confirmation, a deposit of 30 per cent of the total accommodation rate (R450 × 3 = RI 350 × 30% = R414) will be debited to Mr Brown's credit card account.

Please complete this and fax it back to us. Alternatively, we will require a payment of 30 per cent deposit into the following bank to secure the reservation:

Bank: Friendly Bank
Account: M Thomas t/a Wind in the Willows Guest House
Account no.:   456789
Branch no.:   1234 Willowmore
SWIFT no.:   ABC 34910

Effective Guest House Management

Please use your name as reference and fax, scan or email proof of payment to us. In terms of our cancellation policy, this deposit is regrettably not refundable for cancellations later than fourteen days before arrival.

We look forward to your reply and to welcoming Mr Brown to the Wind in The Willows Guest House.

Kind regards,
Margie Thomas

Owner and manager: Wind in the Willows Guest House

Credit card authorisation

I, _____, being the legal and rightful card holder of credit card number _____, expiry date _____, CVV number _____, hereby authorise the Wind in the Willows Guest House to debit the said credit card account with a 30 per cent deposit of the total accommodation cost, being R _____.

In the event of this reservation being cancelled within fourteen days of my arrival date, I understand that the 50 per cent deposit will be retained by the Wind in the Willows Guest House, and that a further 50 per cent will be debited against my card account if the reservation is cancelled within three days of my arrival date.

Arrival date: _____

Departure date: _____

Total of _____ nights' accommodation

Total accommodation rate: R _____

Cardholder's signature: _____

Date: _____

Alternatively, you could use a confirmation form such as the example below, forwarded with a friendly covering email or letter.

Wind in the Willows

Address 62 Willow Lane, Willowmore 1234 PO Box 3300 Willowmore

Tel 0432 44 543   **Fax** 0432 44 542

Email windwillow@guesthouse.co.za
Website www.windwillow.co.za

Accommodation reservation confirmation form

Guest: Peter Smith and company

TO: Ms Jenny Miller, Fair Travels

DATE: 21 May 2009

Thank you for your reservation enquiry. The rooms have been booked as requested. I am pleased to forward the confirmation details of your reservation as well as a map to the guest house. Kindly complete the form and fax back to us to ensure the reservation.

Please note: This reservation will be kept for 72 hours only and will be cancelled automatically if not confirmed by returning this form to us.

Booking conditions

A deposit of 30 per cent of the total amount of the reservation must be paid no later than three weeks before the reservation or within 72 hours if the reservation is made less than three weeks beforehand. Full payment must be made if booked less than a week before the start of the reservation. This deposit is regrettably not refundable for cancellations later than 14 days before the reservation.

Details of reservation

Name of person making the reservation: Jenny Miller, Fair Travels

Tel: 018 345 6789
Email: jmiller@fairtravels.co.za
Fax: 018 345 6789

Rates

– R220 pp per night sharing; 10 per cent commission to travel agents

– Bed and Breakfast only

– Dinner R100 pp by arrangement

Rooms

– White room: twin beds with shower en suite

– Blue room (adjacent to white room): twin beds with bath/shower combination en suite

Date of arrival: 29 May 2009
Date of departure: 31 May 2009

No. of nights: 2
No. of people: 4

Expected time of arrival: _____

Late departure (after 11h00 by special arrangement only): _____

Transport required: _____

Airline details, flight number, time of arrival: _____

Total cost of reservation: **R1 760**

Payment required: **Full amount**

Date due: 22 May (Dinner extra)

Names of guests **(to be confirmed, please):**

1.   Mr Peter Smith

2.   Mr Craig Williams

3.   Mr John Maubane

4.   Mr Eric Malopo

Please indicate any special requirements, e.g. dinner, dietary, vegetarian, smoking, physical: _____

Please confirm details as correct or indicate any changes to be made: _____

Name in block letters: _____

Signed: _____   Capacity: _____

Method of payment of deposit/full payment. Please indicate: _____

Travel agent's voucher

Please specify B&B only/all expenses/DB&B/transport personal expenses, e.g. drinks, telephone, laundry excluded: _____

Payment into bank account

Please use your name as reference and fax proof of the payment to (0432) 44 542, or scan or email to windinthewillows@postmail.co.za

Bank: Friendly Bank
Account: M Thomas t/a Wind in the Willows Guest House
Account no.:   456789
Branch no.:   1234 Willowmore
SWIFT no.:   ABC 34910

```
Credit card payment

Name of cardholder: _____

Card no.: _____     Date of expiry: _____

Last three digits on back of card: _____

Signature of cardholder authorising deduction of deposit/full payment

_____

Date: _____          .
```

Acceptance of the reservation by the guest

If a guest or agent wants to take up a reservation, he or she will fax back the credit card authorisation form or send a scanned copy by email, and supply the outstanding details. It is not advisable to forward credit card details on a non-secured email connection and a fax is preferable. You will also need the signature of the cardholder in the event of a dispute. Remember to keep proof of credit card authorisations for at least six months. Alternatively, payment can be made electronically into your account or by direct deposit into the bank, in which case the deposit slips could be faxed to you. Remember to provide the street address and SWIFT number of your bank for overseas electronic transfers. Your account should be linked to internet banking as it would enable you to control deposits received on a daily basis. Remember to keep hard copies of important correspondence or at least make back-ups on separate disks on a daily basis.

It is always a good idea to confirm the reservation as soon as you have received the acceptance from a guest or agent. You can then again mention the amount that will be debited to the client's credit card, if applicable.

From your point of view, a reservation is confirmed and processed only once you have gathered all the necessary information about the guest, agent or company, payment, and any other information that will impact on your planning for the day of the guest's arrival.

❁ Examples of such information are the expected arrival time of the guest, whether or not transport from the airport will be needed, and whether or not any additional meals will be required if you offer them.
❁ In general, obtain as much information as possible regarding the reservation during the first call, and get the rest of the information from the guest on arrival at your guest house. The information you collect at the time of reservation helps to ensure that the room is ready for the guest in time, especially with an early arrival, and ensures smooth procedures for the housekeeping staff.
❁ Directly after a reservation is confirmed, the reservation chart should be updated to prevent a double booking, and the reservation form, together with the confirmation letter, credit card authorisation and guest acceptance, should be filed under the expected arrival date in the reservations box. Each day the preparation of rooms and meals is completed according to the confirmed reservations for that specific day in the reservations box.

- After confirmation of a reservation, the completed reservation form moves to a filing cabinet, either under the day of the current month (e.g. 17 December) or under the month of the reservation. If any additional information has to be recorded on the reservation form at a later stage, any staff member can then find the form by asking the guest what his or her date of arrival is.
- Your filing cabinet should have divisions for each month of the year, and day divisions for the current month.
- The reservation form will stay in the month division until the month of arrival, when it should be moved to the day of that month on which the guest will arrive.
- On the day before the arrival of the guest, the form will be taken out to prepare the rooms list for the next day.
- After the guest has arrived and any outstanding personal information has been completed, the form goes to the expenses box, where all the reservation forms of guests who are currently accommodated at the guest house are kept.

Guest history record

When a guest returns to your guest house for the second time, and it seems as though he or she might become a *regular customer*, you should consider opening a guest history record (see the example below), so that you don't have to ask for the same information each time that person makes a reservation, and any preferences can be noted on the record.

The guest history record should be completed after each stay and then filed alphabetically. When another reservation is received for the same guest, the previous reservation form can be used to complete all the standard details, and only the relevant dates and expected time of arrival need to be confirmed (provided that the other details remain the same).

Guest history record

Name: _____

Company: _____

Address: _____

Account (the way the account is normally settled): _____

Preferences: _____

Arrival: _____   Departure: _____

Room: _____   Rate: _____

Bill total: _____

Rooms list

Once the reservations are filed under the correct date, a rooms list (see the example below) can be set up for the housekeeping staff to ensure that each room is cleaned and prepared correctly and on time.

```
Day:      _____

Date:     _____

Room:     _____

ETA:      _____

Guest:    _____

Arrival:  _____

Stay over: _____

Move:     _____
```

Each establishment should work out its own procedures for the cleaning and preparation of rooms according to a rooms list for each day, to ensure that the room is ready for the arrival of its guests.

Hints for better reservation services

- You have only *one opportunity* to convince a guest that you are what you advertise, and that is the time when he or she makes contact with your establishment when making a reservation enquiry.
- You or a trained member of staff must be available at all reasonable times to take reservations, which will include after-hours times in the evenings and over weekends. Remember that many potential guests may contact you only after their own office hours when they can attend to their personal matters. You will lose business if you cannot be reached. Make sure that you have a clear message on your phone stating reservations hours if you are not available, and follow up on all messages as soon as practicable.
- Your telephone must be dealt with professionally and must never be answered by someone who is untrained or ill-informed. It must be answered promptly (four rings maximum) and professionally. With the availability of cellphones and call-refer facilities on your landline, there is no excuse for not being available to take a reservation at all reasonable hours. Bear in mind that people expect to be helped over weekends and after hours as well.
- Email and a fax machine (that your staff can operate) are essential.
- Take down messages effectively and efficiently, stating the name of the caller, the time of the call and the message, and make sure that it reaches the required person.
- When you receive a message or enquiry, you must react to it immediately. First impressions are lasting.
- When a reservation has been made (for example, a single room for a short period) and a better reservation (for example, a double for a longer period) is received, you must regrettably decline the latter. Stick to the original reservation and resist the temptation to cancel the first reservation. This is part of the risk of the business.
- All reservations must be confirmed in writing, with all the relevant details such as the rates, facilities and available services. Written notification of

your policy on cancellation and deposits is important to protect yourself against late cancellation.

- Double bookings cause embarrassment and reflect badly on your profession-alism. Use your reservation chart in such a way that a double booking can practically never occur.

Welcoming guests on arrival

It is your job to welcome guests and to make them feel at home. If you cannot do it, the other staff member should know about all details of the guest's booking and be able to answer any questions.

Make sure that your reception area is clean and tidy and that there are pens and paper available for the guests.

When guests arrive at your guest house at an arranged time, the room should be ready and they should never have to wait for their room. Their first impression of your establishment will depend largely on how efficiently they are received, the readiness of their room, the welcome they are given, and their general impression of whether your guest house seems to be well managed and organised. However, for guests wanting to arrive earlier than your normal check-in time, you should suggest at the time of reservation that they book the previous night as well to ensure that their room is available and ready for them when they arrive.

People who prefer a guest house to a hotel will normally be looking for a certain kind of atmosphere and homeliness, but they also want to feel that they are booked into an estab-lishment that is held in high esteem and is not just an ordinary house around the corner. Therefore, the person who receives the guests must look presentable and act professionally.

The arrival of guests marks the crucial moment for their first impression – the golden mo-ment of opportunity as it is known – during which they will subconsciously decide whether your establishment meets, exceeds or falls short of their expectations. Use this opportunity to convince guests that they have made the right choice of guest house, and keep this im-pression of your guest house on the same high level with your high standard of service.

After a guest has entered your guest house and has been welcomed, you could ask for any outstanding details or information required for the reservation form. You can ask the guest to sign in, and this is a good time to confirm the guest's method of payment.

You will need the following details of the guest on your check-in form:

- ❀ name,
- ❀ ID or passport number,
- ❀ car registration number, if applicable,
- ❀ contact details, phone numbers and address,
- ❀ arrival and departure dates as well as actual time of arrival, and
- ❀ guest signature.

Make sure that an indemnity clause is printed on the check-in form that the guest signs and that he or she is aware of the clause and its meaning. Once this is signed, it becomes the contract between you and the guest. See the example of an indemnification form on the next page.

 109

Guest Indemnification Form

Date	Initials and surname	I.D./Passport no.	Car reg. no.	Cellphone no.	Signature	Room no.

Indemnity

I acknowledge with my signature that I have read and agree to the following:

❖ That my signature here above is valid as an indemnity for this and any subsequent visits that I will/may make to Wind in the Willows Guest House.

❖ While every reasonable precaution has been taken to ensure the safety of our guests and their possessions, the owner or agents of Wind in the Willows Guest House will not be held responsible for any damage, loss or injury sustained by any cause whatsoever.

You must also display the following in a prominent place in your reception area and point them out to your guest, in particular the emergency procedures:

* guest indemnity notice,
* right of admission reserved,
* cancellation policy,
* methods of payment accepted,
* reception hours, and
* emergency procedures.

Should a guest settle the account by credit card, check the credit card number. Tactfully ask for some other form of identification, such as an identification document (ID) or passport, and make copies of the credit card as well as the ID document. Unfortunately, trusting guest house owners have experienced cases of dishonest people booking into establishments under false names, often paying a portion of their accommodation in cash and then either refusing to pay the rest or disappearing before breakfast with the room's television set and other goods.

Of course, if a guest is tired, offer a refreshing drink first and arrange for the details to be filled in later.

You should then accompany the guest to his or her room. En route, explain the use of facilities such as the swimming pool, the breakfast room and time of the meal, the lounge, how to obtain beverages, where to park, and what the procedure is with room keys. Keep in mind that the guest is not familiar with your establishment, and might not be sure where it is possible to sit and relax, or park a car, and whether it is in order to take a swim, for example. Make sure you point out or explain emergency procedures.

Show him the facilities and features in his room and ask him if you could help with anything else that he may need.

Open bill or charge card for guest

On the reservation form of each guest, or on your computer reservation programme, you should enter the actual time of arrival (ATA) of that person, so that you can be sure of the exact time from which services such as telephone calls must be billed to a specific guest's account. These could all be done on your computerised reservation system as well.

The guest house may open an expenses account for each guest in an expenses book or programme, and enter all expenses incurred by that person in his or her expenses account. When the guest departs, all the expenses are added to the bill and the relevant expenses account in the expenses book is closed.

Alternatively, the guest house may record any expenses incurred by a guest on the back of his or her reservation form, which has been left blank for this purpose. All proofs of expenses will be attached to the form (for example, dry cleaning slips, laundry slips or dinner reservations).

Never leave the administration of charges for the last day of a guest's stay. It is much easier to *post charges to guests' charge cards on a daily basis*. Guests sometimes have to check out at short notice, and the more streamlined your charges administration is, the faster you can provide a guest with the bill.

In addition, the standard time for checking out is during breakfast, and the last thing you need is to struggle with an account that could have been sorted out easily if you had posted the guest's charges on a daily basis. A computerised reservation and management program will be helpful and make it easier and quicker to keep track of costs that must be added to the guest's account.

Hints to ensure the guest's comfort on arrival

- Before you receive your first guests, sleep in every bed, shower in every shower, and test all equipment such as television sets, hairdryers, etc.
- If you do not have a full-time reception service, you must ensure that you or a trained person meets the guest. In fact, people expect to be met by the guest house host personally. Not doing so will create a first negative impression, which you should try to avoid at all costs, as you will find it very hard to change the perception later.
- Do not subject a guest to unpleasant surprises. He or she must get exactly what was asked for and confirmed. After a reservation has been confirmed in writing, under no circumstances may you change any details such as a bathroom *en suite* for a private bathroom across the passage.
- A guest must never be confronted with a change in rates. If you make a mistake in this regard, bear the loss.
- If a guest has travelled far or if your guest house is on a farm, offer to have his or her car washed for a small fee to the car washer. Both your guest and the car washer would welcome this small courtesy.
- Take careful note of a guest's special requirements, such as his or her food preferences (diabetic, vegetarian, *Halaal*, etc.).
- A guest's room must look neat and smell fresh. These criteria also apply to the rest of the guest house, including the garden and swimming pool. Stale smoke and food smells are unacceptable. The only exception could be the smell of fresh baking and freshly brewed coffee.
- Although guests often prefer guest houses to hotels for the personal attention and service, there is a thin line between over-familiarity and personal service. Use only professional terminology to address the guests – no first names or 'darlings', for example.
- Pets and boisterous dogs can create problems, especially if the evidence of the animals' presence is all over the lawns. Most guests do not want to be bowled over by the dog on their arrival nor do they want the house cat to make itself at home on their laps.
- Children must not run loose in the house. In fact, if your family lives on the same premises as your guest house, there must be a clear division between the facilities for the guests and the family home. Under no circumstances should a family room be used for a guest.

Letter of welcome

Write a personalised *letter of welcome* to every guest, and place it next to a bowl of fresh fruit in his or her room. Whether you write personalised letters or not, a general letter of welcome in a folder on the desk in each room will serve the purpose of explaining all your services and facilities to the guest.

Address 62 Willow Lane, Willowmore 1234 PO Box 3300 Willowmore

Tel 0432 44 543 **Fax** 0432 44 542

Email windwillow@guesthouse.co.za
Website www.windwillow.co.za

A warm welcome to the Wind in the Willows Guest House. We hope that you will have a most enjoyable stay with us!

BREAKFAST – Breakfast is served from 07h00 to 09h00 in the breakfast room or on the patio. Please inform reception which time suits you best.

DEPARTURE – Departure time is 11h00. Delayed departures must be arranged with reception beforehand to ensure availability.

DINNER – Dinner is available at R110.00 for a three-course set menu or at R60 for a tray dinner. Please inform reception by not later than 12h00 of the same day whether you will require dinner. Aperitifs may be enjoyed in the upstairs lounge before dinner, and dress is smart-casual. Dinner is served from 19h30.

DRY CLEANING – A dry cleaning service is available. Please contact reception before 09h00 to arrange for same-day service.

HONESTY BAR – The honesty bar is situated in the upstairs lounge. Please make use of the consumption book, specifying items, to avoid any delay on your day of departure.

KEYS – Please do not remove your keys from the premises. Keys may be left at reception.

LAUNDRY – Please place any laundry in the laundry bag provided in your wardrobe, and leave the bag on your bed with the completed laundry list before 09h00 for same-day service. For any last-minute or urgent laundering, please contact reception.

MAGAZINES – Please do not remove any magazines from the premises. They form part of a private collection that we would prefer to keep complete.

MEDICAL ASSISTANCE – Please contact reception on 201 if you require assistance.

PARKING – Secure parking is available on the grounds. Contact reception to arrange for your vehicle to be parked.

RECEPTION – The reception may be contacted by dialling 201. If no reply, please dial 208 – the staff member on duty might be occupied in the kitchen.

RESERVATIONS – Please contact reception to make reservations on your behalf at restaurants or to arrange for tours and excursions, transfers or vehicle hire.

SMOKING AREAS – We regret that smoking areas are limited to the patio and the veranda of the house.

SWIMMING POOL TOWELS – Green pool towels are available from reception.

TELEPHONE – Calls may be made by dialling '0' followed by the required telephone number. Please contact reception for information on national and international dialling codes. External calls are charged at R1.70 per calling unit.

VALUABLES and FIREARMS – All valuables and firearms should be left at reception for safe-keeping.

VISITORS' BOOK – Please make an entry in our visitors' book in the breakfast room. We would be delighted to know how your stay has been.

WAKE-UP CALLS – Please arrange with reception if you require a wake-up call.

At Wind in the Willows Guest House, professional and personalised service ensures that even the most demanding requests are met promptly and efficiently. Please let us know how we can be of assistance to you!

Kind regards,
Margie Thomas

Owner and manager

A guest will normally browse through your letter of welcome to see what services you offer, and whether there is anything that you did not explain en route to his or her room. The guest will make use of the services as explained in your letter of welcome during the course of his or her stay. Ensure that you can provide all of the services you mention. In addition, make sure that you render the services in the best possible way, because these are the criteria by which your guests will measure your establishment.

Every guest house has its own unique set of services, so no two guest houses will have the same letter of welcome.

Departure

If you do not mention a specific required departure time in your letter of welcome, you might have guests who assume that they can vacate their rooms at their own convenience. The adherence to departure times has a direct impact on the degree of readiness of your rooms when new guests arrive, so take a friendly but firm stand concerning departure times, unless a later departure time can be arranged without causing inconvenience to your next guest.

A reasonable checkout time is from 10h00 to 11h00 in order to be prepared for the standard arrival time of 13h00 to 14h00. These are internationally accepted arrival and departure times, and you don't have to apologise to any guest for adhering to them.

You might occasionally receive a request for an early arrival or late departure at the time a reservation is made. Such a request normally has the consequence that you cannot rent the room out either on the previous day or on the following day, respectively. In such cases it is quite acceptable to charge an extra 50 per cent of the normal rate, or you could recommend that they book the extra night, in which case you may offer a discount on the breakfast. It could, however, create a favourable impression for your guest house if you allow a guest to arrive early or depart late without charging an additional rate. In some cases the money that you don't get is worth less than the goodwill you create by extending your hospitality beyond the level that the guest anticipates.

Checking-out procedures

When a guest is checking out on a specific day, his or her account should be brought to a point of readiness on the previous day. Only the remaining few outstanding charges should quickly be added on the morning that the guest checks out. This can be easily done by a computerised in-house management program and would save you time and effort.

Closing a guest's bill

The bill that you present to your guest on his or her departure must be absolutely perfectly correct, as nothing can cause so much unhappiness as overcharging a guest for an item.

You should *check every bill* before it is presented to a guest, because you can never use the excuse that one of your staff members made a mistake with a guest's bill. Check the length of stay and all extra charges. Make sure it is quite clear to the guest what he or she is paying for.

You also don't want your guest's last impression of your guest house to be an unhappy one caused by an incorrect account. Consequently, regard your guests' accounts as one of the most important facets of your enterprise. You can under no circumstances ask for additional payments at a later stage if you have made a mistake.

Guest settles account

The account should clearly state what all the charges are for, such as dinner, or overnight or laundry charges. Compare the charges on the account with the rate you had originally quoted. It will be very embarrassing if you had quoted a special rate or had upgraded the guest to a better room and the cost on the account does not reflect this. Show any deposits or payments received. Make use of tailor-made computer programs to assist you in ensuring that all details are correct.

Payment from guests can be made in any of the following forms, but you are not obliged to accept all of them:

- ❀ *Cash:* Count the cash in front of the guest and issue a receipt, with any change.
- ❀ *Cheques:* You should have a policy regarding personal cheques and whether you want to accept them without prior arrangements having been made. If you accept a cheque, check that all details such as the date and the amount are correct, that it is signed and the payee is correct, and that it has been crossed and no changes have been made to anything.
- ❀ *Credit cards* (Master, Visa, American Express and Diners Club): Remember that you will be liable for commission of on average five per cent per transaction. Check the expiry date and name on the card and, where possible, verify that the card has not been stolen.
- ❀ *Foreign currency* (to be arranged with your bank ahead of time).
- ❀ *Direct deposits into your bank account or internet transfers*: Internet banking is very convenient and will make it quick and easy for you to check whether payments have been received.
- ❀ *Company accounts:* You could open an account for a company (perhaps offering a special rate) that uses your guest house often and bill them monthly travel agency vouchers – check what is being paid for, as personal expenses like meals and telephone calls are often not covered. Remember that the travel agent's 10 per cent commission may be deducted.

- *Government orders:* You need to claim from a government department, which can be a time-consuming task.
- *Electronic transfers:* Provide the street address and bank SWIFT number for overseas payments.
- If a guest does not pay his or her account when leaving (called *direct settlement*), you will send the account to the booking agent, person or company responsible for payment, as indicated and signed for on your confirmation form. However, even when a guest does not settle directly, it is important to have the account ready when he or she departs, and to obtain his or her signature against the final amount. In this way you can prove that you have not added any extra charges to the account. Issue a receipt for payment received, indicating the method and with a 'thank you' note at the bottom.
- In the case of *immediate* (*direct*) *payment* on departure, attach the accommodation account to the reservation form and file it in the reservation forms file, noting the exact payment details and commissions payable in the commissions file.
- In the case of outstanding accounts (*non-direct payment by agents or companies*), attach the account and all other correspondence (for example, an agent's voucher) to the reservation form and file it in the outstanding accounts or debtors' file. Send the account to the relevant agent or company.
- When payment is received from the agent or company, attach the account to the relevant reservation form and file it in the reservation forms file, noting the exact payment details and commissions payable in the commissions file.

Guest departs

When a guest departs from your guest house, he or she should be satisfied with the final account, and, one hopes will enter an appreciative note in your visitors' book before leaving. Say goodbye to the guest in the same friendly and efficient manner in which he or she was welcomed.

You will then have the room back to prepare for your next guest. Your departing guest will leave with a certain impression of your guest house, which will determine the kind of reference he or she will give to other prospective customers about your establishment.

If everything goes according to plan, your *guest should be your best marketing tool*, because he or she speaks from first-hand knowledge and not from hearsay with regard to your guest house. The snowball effect that positive word-of-mouth advertising has on the profitability of your guest house is vital to your success.

Your electronic reservations and management system can prepare your invoices and receipts and show you what your occupancy is over a set period.

Wind in the Willows

112 River Road	PO Box 3276	Phone 015-015015
Willowmore	Willowmore	Cell 093-9876543
White River	6294	Fax 015-015099
Mpumalanga		wwillows@email.com

Micro Consulting Services
PO Box 1095
Parrow

Tax Invoice

No	100
Date	08/07/09

Attention Secretary - Emily Williams

Co VAT No 442 5687 9564

Order No MCS 07/5298

Product / Service		Qty	Rate	Value
Accommodation - single occupancy	Grant Cirus	4	400.00 /person	1 600.00
Dinner / lunch		4	100.00 /dinner	400.00
Beer		8	10.00 each	80.00
Other	Airport transfer	2	90.00	180.00

Sub total	2 260.00
VAT	316.40
Deposit paid	800.00
Amount due	1 776.40

Bank details

Bank	Peoples National Bank	
Account name	Wind in the Willows cc	
Account no	679 002 3294	
Branch	White Streams	Branch code 123498

Payment is due on receipt of invoice

VAT Registration No 44298689

Cpy Registration No C2001/175/044

Looking after your guests from enquiry to departure

Wind in the Willows

Occupancy Report from 08/07/07   to 08/07/20

Room No	Room Description	Days Available	Days Occupied	Percent
1	Blue room	14	4	28.57
2	Yellow room	14	5	35.71
3	Green room	14	3	21.43
4	Maroon room	14	14	100.00
5	Honeymoon suite	14	6	42.86
6	Executive suite	14	10	71.43
	Total - All Rooms	**84**	**42**	**50.00**

⌂ Receipt Allocation   ⬍ ⧠ ✕

Wind in the Willows   *Receipt Allocation*

Account Name | Micro Consulting Services   ▾ | ○ All invoices
                                                              ◉ Outstanding invoices

Guest Name	Trans	No	Date	Trans Value	Payment	Discnt	Pay Date
▶ Deposit	DEP	1	08/07/06	0.00	0.00	0.00	08/07/06
Grant Cirus	INV	100	08/07/06	2567.28	2567.28	0.00	08/07/09
David Dube	INV	101	08/07/06	1881.00	0.00	0.00	08/07/06

Note : Pay date must be entered | Save | | F1 = Help |

Effective Guest House Management

Providing excellent services

Introduction

Your guest house will be required to render professional hospitality services to your guests. This is what your guests pay for and your level of professionalism should be as high as possible.

The services you offer also form part of the product you sell and can be used to give you a marketing and competitive advantage. Which services you provide and how they are offered in your guest house will differentiate your establishment from others. This is critically important to ensure your business success.

The range and type of services may differ between establishments, for example a typical B&B may not offer a laundry service, but services should be structured in such a way that they ensure the comfort and wellbeing of your guests as well as the effective running of your business. Your guest should be the absolute focus and not your own comfort or convenience. Never short-change a guest with bad or indifferent service because it is more convenient for you.

In this chapter we look at those hospitality services that must be available to your guests and those that are optional. We also discuss the importance of professional food service in the guest house.

Front desk (reception/office)

Reception

If your office or front desk is not open 24 hours a day, have a contact number available where guests can reach you out of office hours. A practical solution is to state the extension number of your kitchen telephone or the extension number of your private telephone in your welcoming letter, so that guests can always reach you. It can also shorten your actual office hours significantly if you have the facility to redirect all calls to your private quarters when you feel it is safe to leave your office. It is normally sufficient to have a staff member available for service for half an hour after guests have gone to their rooms – guests will seldom need any assistance after that time.

Distribution of mail, email, telephone messages and faxes

Develop a system that allows your guests to see their messages, post and faxes when they fetch their room keys on returning to the guest house. Keep all messages and faxes confidential, and also guard against supplying information concerning guests to outside callers. You could become instantly unpopular if you answer questions asked by unknown callers about the whereabouts of guests.

Other reservations

It is regarded as standard service to be able to assist your guests with reservations at restaurants or theatres, as well as with arrangements for excursions, tours and car hire. Bear in mind that foreign guests often don't know where to start enquiring about these services, so be prepared to provide assistance and information about any such services that your guests might be interested in. Your guests may even be interested in working out at a local health club, and suitable arrangements would be appreciated.

Telephone

Decide how much you want to charge per external calling unit, and state this amount in your welcoming letter. Invest in a good–quality unit-measuring device so that you can supply each guest with a specified bill for telephone calls. It would always be an embarrassment to your guest house if you were to charge a guest incorrectly, or for calls that person never made.

Make telephone directories of your own area available to guests in their rooms. It is also important to keep telephone directories for other areas in the country available for reference at reception.

Valuables and firearms

If you do not have a safe in each guest room, have a safe-keeping facility available for any valuables ranging from money, traveller's cheques and passports to firearms and stand-over luggage. Exercise strict control over the safe-keeping area, because it will only be as safe as your security measures.

Always issue a *receipt* to a guest when you receive valuables for safe-keeping, and state the contents and amount clearly in order to prevent the possibility of any misunderstanding or claim against you. Guests occasionally forget how much money they handed in for safe-keeping, and they might suspect theft of their money unless you make perfectly sure that you agree on the items or amount handed in. For small valuables or money, it works best if you put the items left with you in a large envelope, with your own and the guest's signatures across the sealing strip of the envelope.

Keys

The biggest advantage of a system that allows guests to take their room keys is that you don't need a staff member to wait for the last guest to return each evening before going off duty. Should you give guests permission to remove keys or the gate remote control, you are entitled to add a key deposit to your room rate.

The following are some of the advantages of not letting keys leave your premises:

❀ You will have far fewer keys to replace (and possibly locks to change), because guests easily lose keys when they take them away from the premises. In addition, guests are inclined to leave with your keys when they finally check out from your guest house, so it pays to enforce a rule to check for keys when guests depart the premises.
❀ You can use your key rack to establish whether a specific guest is in or out when a caller asks for him or her. It saves time for you and the caller if you can immediately take a message for a guest instead of waiting for an unanswered call to return to your switchboard.

If you decide to hand over room keys and remote controls for gates to guests, it could reduce the need for staff during late hours, but this policy has various disadvantages:

❀ Although guests can then enter and leave the premises on their own, you will always need a responsible person on standby for virtually 24 hours a day in case a guest requires something after hours.
❀ If a guest should lose a room key, you will have to replace the key and also change the lock in case an unauthorised person gets hold of the key.

Providing excellent services

✿ A dishonest guest can easily make duplicate keys while he or she is out, and you will never know when to expect the surprise of a burglary without forced entry. An additional disadvantage is that insurance companies will often not cover the losses you suffer in such a case, because entry was gained with a key and not with force.

Whatever your rules are concerning keys, make sure that you always have one set of spare keys for cleaning purposes, and one or two sets of extra spare keys for when guests lose their keys, or for when you have double occupation in a room, and both guests want a key. Keep at least two sets of spare keys for each room – you will make use of them sooner or later.

Wake-up calls

You should be able to offer a wake-up call service. It is obviously extremely important to remember to wake your guests at the arranged time, since they are relying on you to prevent them from oversleeping, and consequently perhaps missing an important interview or meeting.

The best way to make sure that wake-up calls are performed is to note them down on your breakfast schedule. Let the staff member who is responsible for breakfast do the wake-up calls and tick off each guest's wake-up call when it has been done.

Other guest services

Dry-cleaning

Make an arrangement with a reliable dry-cleaner to provide a same-day dry-cleaning service for your guests. It would also ease your schedule if the dry-cleaners could pick up and deliver. Be sure that you can guarantee that your guests' clothes will be handled with the utmost care in order to prevent any damage to clothes or dissatisfaction with regard to the standard of the service.

Guests' laundry

Provide a big plastic or fabric laundry bag in the wardrobe of each room for use by the guests for their personal items to be laundered (not the linen and towels). If you use fabric laundry bags, you could embroider the name of the room on the bag for easy identification of each room's laundry. Create a system to ensure that each guest gets all (and only) his or her own laundry back in the room.

Guests also often need a steam iron and ironing board, or a clothes steamer, a trouser press, a dumb valet, a shoe-polishing kit and a mending kit such as a pin cushion with needles, thread and safety pins.

The best way to make sure that the laundry of different guests doesn't get mixed up is to check the items against a laundry slip when collecting the laundry and then check all items at each stage in handling the laundry until it is delivered back to the room. It is obvious that you should not mix different guests' laundry and wash it together. The only possible way to do different guests' laundry together would be to mark each item with coloured thread or safety pins.

Another possible way to keep the laundry of different guests separate is to have a shelf and hanging space designated for each bedroom in your laundry area. The laundry of each specific guest then goes back on the room's shelf after each stage of the cleaning and ironing process.

The following is an example of a typical laundry request form that can be used to administer each guest's laundry.

Wind in the Willows

Laundry list

Name: _____ Room: _____ Date: _____

Items	Unit price	Quantity	Ironing required or other instructions	Total cost
Dress	R25.00			
Skirt	R10.00			
Blouse	R10.00			
Shirt	R12.00			
Trousers	R10.00			
Shorts	R5.00			
Underwear	R3.00			
Jersey	R20.00			
Pair of socks	R2.00			
Handkerchief	R1.00			
T-shirt	R5.00			
Track pants	R8.00			
Sweatshirt	R8.00			
Sleepwear	R5.00			

Laundry services

Laundry is taken daily, excluding Saturdays, Sundays and public holidays.

Please place all used laundry in the laundry bag supplied in your wardrobe and place it on your bed with this list. A surcharge of 50 per cent of the laundry price will be added per item ironed/pressed. A dry-cleaning service is available by prior arrangement with reception.

Monday to Friday:
Laundry handed in by 09:00 will be returned by 18:00.

Goods are accepted for dry cleaning and washing etc. on the following conditions only:

- While the greatest care is exercised in every process of dry cleaning and washing, in common with all Cleaners and Dryers we do not hold ourselves responsible for:
  - depreciation or shrinkage during cleaning and washing
  - cases where, after the dirt is removed, threadbare marks are visible with other defects of faded and badly worn garments. All goods are accepted at owners' risk only.

- In the event of loss or damage for which the establishment may be liable, the establishment will have the option of either replacing or repairing the article or part damaged or lost, but the liability of the establishment for loss or damage to any article of any kind shall be limited to 50% of the original cost of the article and shall not in any case exceed R10.00 unless the value of such article has been previously declared in writing and special terms made in respect thereof.

- Goods in our care are covered against fire and burglary.

- We do not hold ourselves responsible for damage to buttons, zip fasteners and other fragile goods, but all possible care will be taken in processing articles.

Signature of customer:

Date:

Magazines, books and newspapers

Guests appreciate interesting coffee table books and magazines to browse through while waiting for somebody or relaxing in your lounge. In particular, books and magazines containing photographs of South Africa's beautiful scenery and wildlife appeal to most guests. Make sure that reading material is marked properly so that guests will realise it is your property and should not be removed. It is also essential to have at least one daily newspaper available in your breakfast room.

Medical assistance

Make an arrangement with a general practitioner who is prepared to attend to your guests even after hours, or find a reliable 24-hour clinic or hospital close to your guest house where you could take your guests in case of an emergency. You are advised not to offer any medication whatsoever to your guests as this may leave you open to legal action. Rather refer them to the doctor or chemist.

Keep a well-equipped first-aid kit with everything normally needed in a household (see details in chapter 9, under 'General safety requirements'). You could also keep a small supply of items such as hairdryers, toothpaste, toothbrushes, razors, shaving cream, sanitary items, ear buds, shower caps and other toiletries that guests could have forgotten at home.

Parking

Secure parking behind locked gates on your property is essential. Guests are often careless about leaving their cars on the street overnight, particularly when the car is rented. However, the inconvenience – not only for your guest, but also to yourself – if a car gets stolen is just not worth it. Make a point of encouraging guests to park their cars on your property overnight. It will also be regarded as a special service if you offer to park your guests' cars when they arrive late in the evening. Consider offering also to have the cars washed for a small fee.

Swimming pool

Make pool towels available to guests if you don't want them to use their bath towels. Deck-chairs next to your pool will always be a good investment, especially if your typical guest is a tourist and not an academic or business person.

Visitors' book

Your visitors' book will undoubtedly become a treasured item in years to come. Invest in a good quality hard-covered visitors' book, and encourage guests to write a message in it. If your visitors' book is displayed where guests can read it, they are likely to browse through it and make their own entry without your prompting.

Miscellaneous services and equipment

Your guests may be interested or could need one or more of the following, depending on where your guest house is: an electrical adapter for cellphone chargers, bath robes and slippers, notepaper, envelopes and pens, as well as additional items of stationery, packs of playing cards and other games, insect repellent or suntan lotion, beach umbrellas and towels, binoculars and bird-watching books.

Food service

Your food service is a most important component of what you are selling. Never compromise on the quality and do not underestimate its contribution to guest satisfaction or to the marketing of your guest house.

The popularity of guest houses owes much to the personal and home-from-home character that distinguishes them from hotels. However, the daily management of the kitchen and dining room must be smooth and professional. Planning the menu and keeping shopping lists up to date should be done in advance, preferably on paper, and not left to impulsive decisions.

Catering in a guest house has to comply with criteria that do not apply to a domestic situation. Food should be of the highest quality and attractively presented. Meals should always be adequate and wholesome, but at the same time profitable and contributing to the income of the guest house. Wastage should be combated through good planning or else it will drain the profit made elsewhere.

Purchasing and preparation of food

To run the kitchen professionally, you should have or should acquire the requisite knowledge and skills for this function.

Buy fresh ingredients and do not compromise when selecting and purchasing food. Select the best food available at the best price and then decide on a suitable recipe for the purchase. A comprehensive recipe book and an orderly recipe file will simplify the task and reduce the time searching for a suitable recipe for a good purchase. Rather change the planned menu than use less than perfect ingredients.

Buy only the quantities that will be needed within a few days. Keep an eye on the food, as well as the leftovers, and attend to it before it starts to deteriorate and becomes wasted.

Standardise the items that you need for breakfast, and always make sure that you have sufficient breakfast items in stock to last for at least two days. Purchasing more fresh food than you have fridge or freezer space for can only lead to wastage, but make sure that you do not run out of basic food or cleaning items. You will need to replenish stocks at least twice a week and some items, such as bread, will have to be bought or baked daily. It would not create a good impression if you ran out of basic items such as sugar, eggs or dishwashing liquid!

Develop a system for using the cooked leftovers for your family or for staff meals, but never for guests. By doing this, only the food that guests leave on their plates has to be wasted, and the rest can be used on the same day, so that you start each day with fresh supplies.

Before starting to cook, ensure that ingredients or suitable substitutes as well as the equipment for making the recipe are at hand. Place the ingredients onto the work surface and carry out the preliminary steps, such as cleaning of vegetables or greasing of cake tins in advance to ensure that the main task can be done without interruption.

Breakfast

Breakfast is the most important of the meals served at your guest house and is generally included in your night's rates. A wonderful breakfast is a valuable marketing tool. The standard of the breakfasts you serve will strongly influence your guests' general impression of your establishment. Pay attention to detail, and provide a variety that fits the description of the 'hearty breakfast' you advertise in your brochure. Everyone expects a good breakfast at a guest house.

In a small establishment, it normally works best to ask each guest what he or she would like for a cooked breakfast, and a menu list with choices can be given to the guest the previous evening to fill in. Preparing only what the guest orders will limit wastage and will still provide value for money. The only time it would make sense to prepare a variety of cooked dishes and display these for guests to help themselves would be when you have a large group of guests enjoying breakfast in one sitting, or when the size of your guest house warrants a big supply of hot dishes for breakfast.

Ask the guest at what time he or she would prefer to eat breakfast, and complete the breakfast schedule accordingly. If a guest is not specific about a time for breakfast, fit that person into the schedule in a time bracket during which you don't have many other guests to serve, so that you can give your best attention to each person.

Be flexible about the times you serve breakfast, as this is one of the competitive advantages of a guest house over a large hotel. Remember to serve breakfast fully dressed, with a smile, even at 05h00! It will be quite acceptable not to serve a full English breakfast at such an early time, but your efforts will be gratefully appreciated by a guest who needs to depart that early and you will reap the business benefits from it.

Different guests enjoy breakfasts or meals at different times, and table settings should be cleared quickly after guests have finished their meals, as it is certainly not pleasant for any guest to sit down to a table with a used appearance. Table linen and serviettes should be attractive and immaculate or cleaned before the next sitting, if necessary.

Use a breakfast checklist such as the form below. This not only helps you provide a better service but is also helpful to your planning. You need only make what is ordered and have less wastage of the more expensive items like eggs and sausages.

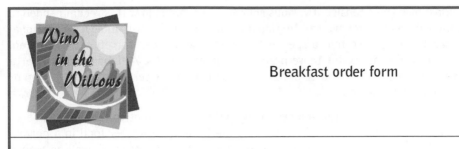

Breakfast order form

Dear guest,

Breakfast is served between 06:30 and 09:30. Should you require breakfast at a different time, please arrange with Reception the day before.

Please complete the form for hot breakfast items and leave it at Reception to indicate your preferences for breakfast.

A selection of cereals, fresh fruit, fruit juices, breads, cheeses and jams and a choice of tea or coffee is served on the breakfast buffet.

Bacon		How many eggs?	
Fried tomato		Boiled: soft, medium or hard	
Pork sausage		Poached: soft, medium or hard	
Boerewors		Fried: sunny side up, over easy, soft, medium, hard.	
Hot oats porridge		Scrambled	
Mushrooms		Omelette	
		Cheese with omelette	
Name:			
At what time would you like your breakfast to be ready?			
Room Number:			

If, for example, you make a late brunch on the patio overlooking the pool a special feature over weekends, you may attract more guests in quiet periods. Your food service offers many wonderful service opportunities with which to distinguish yourself as a special value-for-money establishment and which can be used as effective marketing tools.

The breakfast menu

With the right planning, some pre-preparation the previous day, and many dishes that can be made in advance and successfully frozen until required, breakfast need not be too complicated early in the morning. Many meat, fish and even egg dishes can be partially prepared the previous day. Provide sufficient variation from day to day for guests staying a few nights, as nothing is worse than eating the same dish day after day.

A full breakfast menu will consist of various courses as set out below. It is recommended to compile a file with recipes for typical Continental, American, English and even traditional South African breakfasts, so that a special theme for the day can sometimes be offered. This will also provide variety for those preparing the breakfasts. A light breakfast for a group of women guests will of course be very different from one served to businessmen or a late breakfast for holidaymakers.

Consider health, religious or cultural differences, and make sure that you do not only serve pork sausages, which could offend. It is not possible to prepare *Kosher* food in a normal guest house kitchen, but a good vegetarian range will cater for *Kosher* as well as *Halaal* guests.

Full breakfast menu

1. **Fruit juices**
   With a wide choice of quality juice available, a choice of at least two different colours is recommended. Orange juice is always popular. If only one or a few guests are served, use smaller jugs and refill as necessary to prevent fresh juices from standing out at room temperature. Juices may ferment if exposed to warm temperatures. Never mix old and new stock.

2. **Fresh fruit selection and occasional stewed dried or canned fruit**
   Fresh fruit in season should always be a part of the menu, whether washed and displayed in an attractive bowl or peeled and arranged decoratively on a platter or mixed into a fruit salad. Fresh fruit and stewed, dried or canned fruit may be combined.

3. **Breakfast cereals/home-made or purchased muesli and yoghurt selection**
   Have a wide selection of cereals available for the guests to help themselves from. Refill sealed glass containers regularly. Serve warm and cold milk, sugar, cream and plain and flavoured yoghurts. One brand of cooked cereal, especially in winter, may be a good idea.

4. **Egg dish or choice of eggs**
   Eggs are synonymous with breakfast. Eggs should always be fresh and perfectly prepared, whether boiled, poached, fried or scrambled or turned into dishes such as omelettes, oven-baked soufflé omelette, frittata, or boiled eggs in sauces, such as a piquant curry sauce.

5. **Fish and meat dishes**
   Fish is popular, whether it is steamed, poached or grilled with a parsley, caper, lemon butter or cheese sauce, or smoked fish like steamed kippers or poached haddock or even fish cakes. Serve at the most two meat dishes per day, such as boerewors, sausages, savoury mince, bacon or mushrooms and chicken livers.

6. **Vegetarian dishes**
   Fried or grilled mushrooms and tomatoes, spicy cheese or vegetable sauces and bean and legume dishes, spinach and feta cheese sauce, bean and chickpea casseroles, or fried eggplant (aubergine) slices with grilled tomato and mozzarella cheese can be served.

7. **Side dishes**
   Grilled bacon strips, fried or grilled tomatoes and mushrooms, fried bananas or banana fritters can be offered.

8. **Bread and bread roll selection, scones/muffins/croissants/crumpets/waffles/pancakes**
   Serve regular, white, brown, whole wheat and rye bread toasted or plain and scones, muffins, etc., occasionally.
9. **Butter/cheese/jams and preserves/marmalade**
   Serve with the baked products.
10. **Tea selection/coffee/hot chocolate/milk and sugar**
    A variety of teas, including Ceylon, rooibos and Earl Grey and the best filter coffees are essential in a guest house. Hot drinks must always be steaming. Serve warm and cold milk, white and brown sugar, honey and slices of lemon with the drinks. Decaffeinated coffee, cocoa, malted milk and other popular drinks should be available on request.

English breakfast

This menu includes the elements of an English breakfast consisting of bacon, eggs, sausage, tomato, mushrooms and toast.

Continental breakfast

A selection of cereals, fruit, breads and pastries, served with jams, preserves, cheeses, cold meats and tea, coffee and fruit juice is provided for guests to help themselves from.

Traditional breakfast

Hot porridge is served, such as mealie-meal or oats, with eggs, boerewors, bacon and toast with tea and coffee.

Dinner

It is the choice of the host in the B&B or guest house to serve dinner or not. The provision of dinner will generally be more of a service to your guests than a source of profit for your guest house. Particularly if your establishment is small, work out a roster of three main courses for dinner for each day of the week, with different proteins but similar vegetables and starches, and let the guest choose an option in the morning when he or she reserves dinner for the evening. If a guest house has a liquor licence and beer and wine are also sold, it will certainly make a vast difference to the profitability of being on duty till evening and then clearing and preparing for breakfast the next morning.

Make arrangements with guests to book dinners early in the day – specify a time, for instance, of no later than 14h00 to allow sufficient time for planning the evening meal. Food prepared in excess that cannot be frozen or re-used will lead to substantial financial losses.

Do not offer an *à la carte* choice to guests if it means that you could be left with food that you haven't used. Even if your staff members use all the food that hasn't been used for your dinners, it does not make sound economic sense because you would be unlikely to buy fillet steaks and fresh kingklip for your staff, as you would probably need to do for your guests.

Offering dinners in a guest house can be either a pleasure or a problem, depending on how it is handled. The right choice of recipes and efficient planning will ensure that you do not have any last-minute hitches. Without good planning, hours may be spent in the kitchen evening after evening. If your chef or cook is well trained, the menu can be more complicated and extensive; if not, make use of less complicated recipes that can be prepared earlier in the day and served at dinner time. It is advisable to choose dishes that can be prepared in large quantities and then frozen in single portions, or to prepare food that is quick, yet impressive and palatable.

It has become popular to offer a so-called tray dinner only, which means that you would present a tray with a light starter, main meal and desert to the guest to enjoy in the dining room or on the patio, but you will not be expected to serve the guest. Guests can be very demanding and could expect the same standard of continuous service from you as they would get in a restaurant, quite forgetting that you will have to get up early the next morning to prepare their delicious breakfast and may also need the time to rest or catch up with administrative tasks.

On the other hand, planning the food service efficiently may add considerable extra income. Although it is difficult to lay down rules for costing of meals, a general guideline could be that a meal should not cost more than one-third of the selling price to prepare, and preferably even less. List the prices of all your ingredients for the meal, for example one litre of milk at R6.90 will serve ten guests. Calculate the cost of the meal per guest per item. The cost of milk per guest is R6.90 divided by ten = 69c, and so forth. Add the cost of labour and electricity, which is usually regarded as three times the cost of the food.

Health and hygiene in the kitchen

To protect yourself and those who will be served by your kitchen, it is important to have a clear concept of what hygiene is and how and why it should be practised. It is important to understand the dangers that may lurk and the preventative measures that can be taken to prevent any adverse effects caused by unfit food.

The kitchen staff

Kitchen staff should already be trained or they will have to be trained for the specific tasks they will be responsible for, whether making salad, frying eggs or garnishing and serving the food in an attractive fashion. Table setting and serving must all be taught. It is the responsibility of the host or owner to describe all the tasks correctly, so that every person working in the kitchen knows exactly what is required of him or her. All members of the staff should know how all the appliances work, the level of hygiene required and other safety measures.

Correct food handling

This includes all measures necessary to ensure the safety and wholesomeness of food supplies. Correct food-handling measures apply to every stage in food production and supply, such as packaging, storage, distribution and retail handling when offered for sale or supplied to the consumer.

Sound hygiene can only be practised if standards for food handling are clearly outlined. Food service operations at all levels should take place in such a way that they present no risk of illness from the food served or from the persons preparing and serving the food. Protective measures should be intact in every area of the food line. Food should be protected from the risk of contamination of any kind.

To protect fresh food that arrives in the kitchen, it is essential to ensure that no contamination will take place due to infected equipment (correct method of cleaning each piece of equipment is vital!), work surfaces, containers or contact with spoilt food in fridges or freezers. Germs can be transferred by staff members who are infected (with even just a common cold) or who do not adhere to the rules of personal hygiene and cleanliness, including clean overalls and well-scrubbed hands.

Avoiding food risks

Organisms that occur naturally in food can cause decomposition or deterioration if care is not taken to prevent them from multiplying to such an extent that they become toxic and pose a risk to consumers. An example would be fresh chickens that are not kept thoroughly chilled (at specified temperatures) at all times to prevent increase of the natural bacteria to concentrations that can cause food poisoning. Potentially harmful bacteria in food can be destroyed by cooking, processing or irradiation to ensure safe food with a much longer shelf life. But, after you have treated the food in one of the ways listed above, you should once again protect it from contamination and treat it as perishable.

Procedures to control safety and wholesomeness of all food products must legally be part of the running of any public kitchen. Every food handler should be aware of high-risk foods that support the multiplication of pathogenic bacteria. These include cooked meat, poultry or fish or products including gravy and stock, such as pies. Any products containing milk, cream, eggs or cheese rank high in this category – examples are confectionary containing custard, or savoury pies with cheese and bacon or ham. Mayonnaise made with eggs should be treated as highly perishable.

Keep food clean and covered and really cold at all times.

Safe storing of frozen food

Spores and significant numbers of pathogenic bacteria are usually able to withstand freezing and prolonged frozen storage. After a suitable lag phase, survivors will commence multiplication on thawing. Strict precautions must therefore be taken in the manufacture of frozen foods to ensure the absence of pathogens and the correct freezing temperature. If food is frozen too slowly or at a temperature not low enough, or if there is a breakdown in the cold chain at any stage, the quality and safety will be affected.

Most domestic freezers operate at −18 °C and at this temperature a gradual loss of flavour and a toughening of texture occur. Above −10 °C, spoilage organisms – especially certain yeasts, moulds and bacteria – commence growth and, together with biochemical reactions, they cause serious problems, including souring, putrefaction and rancidity.

Cleaning and disinfection

Cleaning schedules are a communication link between management and staff and are necessary to ensure that equipment and premises are effectively cleaned and, if necessary, disinfected as frequently and as efficiently as possible.

Store chemicals, hazardous materials and cleaning agents safely away from food to avoid contamination.

It is advisable to compile a cleaning schedule for each working area. The cleaning schedule itself must be clearly and concisely written, without ambiguity, to ensure that instructions to staff are easy to follow and result in the objective of the schedule being achieved. Written schedules should specify the following:

- ✿ what is to be cleaned,
- ✿ who is to clean it,
- ✿ when it is to be cleaned,
- ✿ how it is to be cleaned,
- ✿ the time necessary to clean it,
- ✿ the chemicals, materials and equipment to be used,
- ✿ the cleaning standard required,
- ✿ the precautions to be taken,
- ✿ the protective clothing to be worn, and
- ✿ who is responsible for checking and recording that it has been cleaned.

Food poisoning

Food poisoning can be considered an emergency, as it can be life-threatening. Every kitchen should have a notice board with emergency phone numbers for medical assistance, poison centres, the environmental health department and the fire brigade, so that staff are able to act instantly and correctly in case of any food- or kitchen-related emergency. Any person preparing and offering food to the public has legal obligations to ensure good standards of food hygiene. The human cost of food poisoning or infectious disease due to poor hygiene is very high – these can even result in death.

Loss of working days and decreased productivity due to persons becoming ill after eating contaminated food can be serious in some cases. Minor or severe gastric disturbances or occurrences of food poisoning can seriously harm the reputation of the guest house, from bad publicity or outspoken guests who have had a bad experience. Costs such as medical and medicinal expenses can be high, especially in cases where hospitalisation may be necessary. Legal or civil action may also be faced due to serving or selling unfit or unsatisfactory food.

The applicable laws and regulations require the following:

- ✿ A person whose fingernails, hands or overalls are not clean should not be allowed to handle unpacked food.
- ✿ A food handler shall wear overalls that are in a clean and sound condition and should be used for one shift only, and be washed after every such work shift. The overalls must be kept in a changing room, central storeroom or locker when not in use.
- ✿ Unpacked food shall not be handled by any person who has not washed his hands thoroughly with soap and water or cleaned them in another effective manner:
  - – immediately prior to the commencement of each work shift;
  - – at the beginning of the day's work or after a rest period;
  - – after every visit to the latrine or urinal;
  - – every time after he has blown his nose;
  - – after his hands have been in contact with perspiration or with his hair, nose or mouth;
  - – after handling his handkerchief or belt or a refuse container or refuse;
  - – after handling raw vegetables, fruit, eggs, meat or fish;
  - – before handling ready-to-use food.
- ✿ An area or facility where food is handled shall have one washbasin for every 15 persons or part of such number in service.

- A person in control of an area or a facility where food is handled shall ensure that sufficient supplies of soap or cleaning materials, nail brushes and clean, disposable towels are supplied to all hand basins.
- No person shall smoke or use tobacco in any other manner while he is handling unpacked food or while he is in an area where unpacked food is handled.
- No person suffering from an infectious disease, or suppurating abscess, or a sore on his body, or who is a carrier of a disease that can be transmitted by food, shall be allowed to handle food or touch any utensil, implement, equipment or anything used in the preparation of food or be present in any area or facility where food is handled.
- 'Clean' means free of any dirt, or impurity, or undesirability, or pollution that is unhygienic; no remains of cleaning materials or disinfectants, and no more than 100 viable micro-organisms per cm^2 upon analysis.
- No crockery, cutlery, utensils, basins or any other such facilities shall be used for the handling of food if they are not clean or if they are chipped, split or cracked.
- Any utensil or item that is suitable for single use only shall be stored in a dust-free container until used; and shall not be used more than once.
- No person shall:
  - handle unpacked food in such a manner which brings it into contact with any exposed part of his body, excluding his hands;
  - lick his fingers when he is handling unpackaged food or material for the wrapping of food;
  - cough or sneeze over unpacked food or food containers or facilities;
  - walk, stand, sit or lie on unpacked food.
- Surfaces must be cleaned and washed before food comes into direct contact with them, and shall be washed as and when necessary during the handling of food so that cross-contamination of food that comes into contact with surfaces is prevented.
- A food container shall be clean and free from any toxic substance, ingredient, or any other substance liable to pollute or contaminate or spoil the food in the container.
- Food that is displayed or stored:
  - shall not be in direct contact with the floor or any soiled surface;
  - shall be free from dust or any other impurity.
- Any shelf or display case used for the storing of food shall be kept clean and free from dust or any other impurity.
- Perishable food is stored at a temperature below 10 °C, provided that this requirement shall not apply to:
  - food kept heated to a temperature not lower than 65 °C;
  - any food which, in order to avoid spoilage or other deterioration, is kept at room temperature for a suitable period to allow it to cook;
  - fresh fruit and vegetables;
  - any other food which is so resistant to spoilage that it need not be kept at a temperature below 10 °C at all times.
- Every chilling and freezer facility used for the storage, display or transportation of perishable food shall be equipped with a thermometer, which at all times reflects the degree of chilling of the refrigeration area of such a facility, and which is in such condition and placed in such visible position that an accurate reading may be taken unhampered.
- The following shall be available in respect of food premises:
  - liquid-proof, easy-to-clean containers with close-fitting lids for the effective removal of refuse arising on the food premises.

✿ A person in charge of food premises shall ensure that:
  − refuse is removed from the food premises as often as is necessary and whenever an inspector requires it to be done;
  − refuse is stored or disposed of in such a manner that it does not create a nuisance;
  − refuse bins are cleaned regularly and disinfected whenever necessary.
✿ All food premises:
  − shall be rodent-proof in accordance with the best available method;
  − shall have effective measures to prevent the access of flies or other insects to a room or area where food is handled.
✿ Surfaces and facilities shall be:
  − cleaned and washed before food comes into direct contact with them for the first time, during each work shift;
  − washed, as and when necessary, during the handling of food, so that cross-contamination of the food that comes into contact with the said surface or facility is prevented, and the surface may contain:
    − no more than 100 viable micro-organisms per cm^2 upon analysis;
    − no remains of cleaning materials or disinfectants that may pollute the food.
✿ No person shall keep or allow any animal in an area or facility where food is handled, unless such an animal is a guide dog accompanying a blind person.

How to prevent food poisoning

It is in the hands of the cook to protect those who eat out of his or her kitchen and to ensure that only completely safe food is served. Food poisoning should be considered in a very serious light and should be prevented at all costs. Never serve or even taste any food that appears to be dubious. Be wary of any of the following signs:

✿ a strange colour,
✿ a strange wet or slimy exterior coating caused by bacteria on the surface,
✿ a bad odour, or
✿ any signs of fermentation.

Do not try to disguise bad food in any way. It is certainly recommended not to swallow food that tastes wrong, bad or strange in any way − remove it from the mouth and rinse the mouth with water or a mild salt and/or vinegar solution. Induce vomiting, if necessary, if bad food, especially fish, which can be lethal, has been ingested.

Food poisoning can range from a mild to an acute attack. The onset is usually sudden and brought about by unknowingly eating contaminated or poisonous food. Symptoms generally include

✿ abdominal pain,
✿ diarrhoea,
✿ nausea and vomiting, and
✿ a feeling of weakness or running a temperature.

The causes of bacterial food poisoning

Bacterial food poisoning consists of contamination of high-risk food with food-poisoning bacteria, multiplication of these bacteria and then consumption of the infected food.

To control and keep contamination of food to an absolute minimum:

❀ Raw and cooked food should be kept separate at all stages of preparation, storage and distribution.
❀ Equipment, work surfaces, cutlery and crockery should be hygienically cleaned every time after and, if necessary, again before use.
❀ Purchase the right kind of cleaning materials and soap products and use as recommended by the suppliers.
❀ When using poisons and disinfectants (e.g. to kill rodents or insects or disinfect floors), take care to carry out instructions correctly and never allow them to come into contact with food.
❀ Make sure that kitchen cloths and pot-holders are always clean (wash daily!)
❀ Handle food, especially cooked food, with the utmost care and with implements, not hands.
❀ Personal hygiene should be a high priority.
❀ Stick to rules of constant hand washing and not touching hair, faces, noses, clothing or shoes while working with food.
❀ Consider floors as being highly infected, even directly after they have been washed or scrubbed.
❀ Keep raw and cooked foods covered at all times to protect them from contamination by rodents, cockroaches, flies, insects, animals and birds.
❀ Discard any dubious or unfit food immediately.
❀ Do not mix fresh and old supplies when making a new dish to serve to guests, for the concentration of harmful bacteria in old food will immediately infect the fresh food and render it unfit for use.
❀ Do not feed contaminated food to any animals.
❀ Dustbins offer a breeding ground to germs of all kinds and should be kept covered and placed far away from any critical preparation areas, as well as disinfected thoroughly on a regular basis.
❀ Whenever waste materials or dustbin lids have been handled, hands should be washed thoroughly before returning to the food preparation or serving stations.
❀ To prevent natural bacteria in food from multiplying, store food out of the dangerous temperature zones, which lie somewhere between 5 °C and 65 °C.
❀ Refrigerators must be maintained at the correct temperature and once food is removed for preparation, carry it out promptly.
❀ Cool cooked food quickly, avoiding exposure to the lukewarm temperatures that are favoured by bacteria for multiplication.
❀ Dried foods should be stored in such a way that they will not absorb moisture and become damp, as toxins can form under damp conditions.
❀ Natural bacteria in food are destroyed by thorough cooking, using suitable preservatives such as vinegar or salt (to create an unfavourable environment for bacterial growth), or processes such as pasteurisation, sterilisation or canning, which are mostly also based on heating to the desired temperature.
❀ Water supplies should also be safe and immaculately maintained, for they can lead to infections of many kinds.

Nonbacterial food contamination

Apart from the bacterial poisoning, food can also be contaminated with moulds or viruses that are found hidden in many places in unhygienic kitchens.

❀ Physical contamination by foreign bodies, including hair, soil, insects, bits of paper, plastic, metal or string, is not acceptable but not as dangerous as the less noticeable contamination.

❀ Chemical contamination can take place if any dangerous chemicals or even their fumes come into contact with raw or cooked food.

A well-run, organised kitchen will be protected from such contamination in most cases, as most food-poisoning outbreaks are caused by the negligence or ignorance of food handlers.

In severe cases of food poisoning, it is advised to call in the services of the local health department to investigate the possible causes of the outbreak and advise on the steps needed to prevent any further spreading. Try to retain samples of possibly infected foods in sealed containers to aid investigation.

Safety measures in the guest house kitchen

To prevent accidents, teach the correct procedures for cooking, frying with oil, carrying bowls with hot food (not overfilled!), for table service, and particularly for the serving of hot food and clearing used areas afterwards. As part of the general safety training programme, consider safety in handling candles, matches and gas stoves and, in opening sparkling wine bottles. Ensure that leftover liquor is put out of temptations way from fellow staff members.

Marketing your guest house

Introduction

There are many questions that you will be asking yourself when you want to market your guest house. These could include the following:

✿ Why do marketing?
✿ What are you marketing?
✿ What is your market position?
✿ Who are your competitors?
✿ Can you create more value than your competitors?
✿ What is your brand?
✿ Who is involved in marketing/promotion at your guest house and how are they involved?
✿ How do you market?
✿ What methods are you using or should you be using to promote/market?
✿ What should be the elements of your marketing strategy?
✿ How do they rank in importance?

This chapter, with chapter 8, will assist you to answer these questions in relation to your own guest house to enable you to develop your own marketing strategy.

What is marketing in a guest house? Many current and prospective guest house owners often find marketing their business quite daunting and shy away from it. They see marketing as a separate function from their main activities, such as providing quality accommodation, good meals and an efficient reservation service. If you follow the basic rules of marketing, have done your market research and understand that marketing is an integral part of what you do and what the guest house offers, it should be fairly straightforward.

Marketing is basic to your business because it is your guest house as seen from the final result, the guest's point of view. Remember that the success of your guest house is not determined by you, but by your customer, your guest. Your guests are the whole purpose of your business and clearly you cannot survive without them. Effective marketing means that everything you do has to focus on the customer's interests, welfare, convenience and happiness.

Marketing, especially in a service business like a guest house, is therefore the processes you put in place to create, communicate and deliver value to your guests. It is a way of always thinking of the guest first in everything you plan and do – of a totally customer-centric business philosophy – so that you implement processes to suit the customer, not to suit yourself.

Marketing is also the way in which you showcase your guest house's facilities and services to current and potential customer guests, in order for them to buy your accommodation. It is not a separate function from all your other activities and your guest house's facilities. It has to do with every single aspect of your guest house, from your lovely bedrooms to the way you cook the breakfasts, and every aspect has a direct effect on your marketing.

There are many such examples in a guest house which, if not properly considered, can totally undermine or destroy your marketing efforts. The following aspects, for instance, can cause customer dissatisfaction and be a marketing disaster:

✿ nearly everything in the bedroom and bathroom, such as waiting too long for a blown light bulb to be replaced, or having cushions too hard or too soft, inconvenient electrical connections, too small a desk, and so forth,
✿ the general cleanliness of the guest house,
✿ a late wake-up call,

- eggs overcooked, or
- mistakes on a final invoice.

The list is endless and can include both the facilities and the services. Of course, marketing is not only the responsibility of the owner or marketing staff – every single person involved with your guest house has a marketing role.

Marketing your guest house entails making sure that your potential guests (your target market) find out about your guest house in order to make use of what you offer. Effective marketing forms a bridge between you and your target market, your potential guests. Your marketing plan or strategy will give you the framework for identifying opportunities for bringing value to your customers and for delivering that value at a profit.

Your marketing plan will make it possible for you to identify your competitive advantage and to differentiate your guest house from others, and will help you decide on how best to serve the market in a sustainable manner. The following sections will give you the framework of marketing in the context of a guest house and will look at the basic elements of marketing, the objectives, the strategy and tactics and also how to check that it is working.

Take note of new developments that may influence your business and adapt your marketing decisions accordingly. Do not become disheartened when your marketing actions are not immediately successful, but don't hesitate to make changes to unsuccessful actions when necessary. Since you have done your market research before establishing your guest house, the actual marketing should now be relatively easy and enjoyable.

Practical marketing concepts

The foundation of marketing a guest house is the same as the four elements of all marketing: *product, price, position* and *promotion*. These elements are commonly known as the four Ps of marketing.

Product

The *product* of any business is what is made and/or sold to customers. The product sold in a guest house consists of both tangible and intangible elements. It includes your physical accommodation facilities, the services you render such as food and laundry services and the front of house services like reservations, as well as how efficiently your guest is served.

The following are the three essential elements of the product:

- physical (tangible),
- service (intangible), and
- processes (both tangible and intangible) – the customer's journey through the guest cycle, from enquiry to arrival, stay, departure and all contact points on the cycle.

The physical, tangible features of your guest house, such as a welcoming lounge, a hearty breakfast, a comfortable bed and a clean bath – can be seen, touched and enjoyed by your customer. These tangible aspects have been discussed in chapters 5 and 6. However, you are selling not only these aspects; an important part is the expectation the potential guest has of the experience and how he or she will be treated, which are all intangible aspects linked to customer service. Both of these aspects are two of four critical factors for the success of your guest house. If you do everything to the best of your ability, these factors will improve your chances of success:

* excellent customer service,
* quality and appropriate facilities,
* sound business management of all processes, and
* the calibre of you and your staff.

Your own individual mix of service and accommodation – incorporating your key selling points – could involve the following:

Example 1:

* conveniently located for your target market,
* comfortable and clean twin accommodation at reasonable rates,
* basic facilities such as an *en suite* bathroom, television and telephone,
* breakfast only, and
* safe parking.

Example 2:

* situated in exclusive, quiet suburb,
* luxury and spacious accommodation,
* conference facilities,
* accommodation for a fairly large group (ten or more),
* sixteen-hour reception, room and bar service,
* all meals, snacks, etc.,
* television (including satellite), fax and email,
* indigenous African décor and atmosphere, and
* pool and patio.

Customer service in a guest house

Excellent customer service is the absolute determinant of success in the guest house business. Outstanding service is the one element that will distinguish you from your competitors. It provides you with many powerful opportunities to gain a competitive advantage. It need not even be expensive and only requires a way of thinking, enthusiasm and willingness from you and your staff.

> *We are what we repeatedly do.*
> *Excellence then is not an act, but a habit.* – Aristotle

Customer service is more than a friendly smile: it is a set of skills that can be learnt. It is not only a business philosophy but a way of looking at all your business ingredients, from your bedrooms to your reservations, and how they best serve the interests of your customer.

Excellent customer service is far more important than the quality or expense of your interior décor. It will provide you with many advantages and will save you thousands in marketing expenses by ensuring that you get word-of-mouth referrals and return-business, the two best sources of business for successful guest houses.

The service objective today is very simple: it is to get your guests to say 'Wow'!

Guests expect that, at the very least, their basic needs will be taken care of. Service can fortunately almost always be improved upon.

Service outcomes and reactions	
Service falls below expectations	Negative reaction
Service meets expectations	Neutral reaction
Service exceeds expectations	Positive reaction and guest delight

It is interesting to note that there is a strong personal involvement of customers in the service they receive, much more so than, for example, when buying a new pair of shoes. Studies have shown that people believe that they are partly responsible or to blame for the kind of service they receive, good or bad. They think that their own actions somehow contribute to the service they receive. This makes them less likely to complain about bad service and more likely to take good service for granted.

People also perceive choosing a service product (and the guest house and accommodation industry are essentially service businesses) as more risky than purchasing a physical item. Think of how carefully you choose your dentist, for example. Once customers have chosen a service – and have had their needs satisfied – they remain far more brand-loyal to service providers than with goods such as groceries or clothes. This makes it more difficult to lure customers from the competition but easier to keep them when they are happy with your establishment.

This is also why it is so essential for you to get some form of quality assurance, whether through star grading, being a winner in a national competition or at the very least through belonging to an accommodation association or body. Achieving all three will of course be preferable, as they will offer reassurance to guests that they will be staying at a reputable establishment that will look after their needs well. Such credentials are also valuable to you as a very important marketing tool to support your marketing claims.

 141

Everyone in your guest house has to take responsibility for providing good service. People will forgive a bad cup of coffee that is presented with a friendly and helpful smile. They will not forgive or forget an unpleasant service encounter. This unpleasant encounter can be with anyone dealing with your establishment, from a staff member to management. And, unfortunately, people not only remember, they also spread the word.

A challenge that guest houses face in their marketing is that potential guests are hesitant about booking accommodation in a guest house unknown to them. This is simply because of the bad experiences people have had at other guest houses.

Have no illusions about the potentially catastrophic effects that bad service can have on your guest house. It could close you down. Do not underestimate the power of the internet to get the message out.

Examples of bad service

- Guests were not welcomed in a friendly way on arrival and made to feel at home, the facilities were not explained to them, they did not know when breakfast was served or, worse, there was a problem with the reservation confirmation.

- The facilities were unacceptable, not of good quality, noisy, small, etc.
- The guests did not receive what was promised to them, for example a double bed was booked and they were given a twin room, or there was no desk to work at or a bad reading light next to the bed.
- They feel they did not receive value for money and that they were over-charged, compared to other guest houses, or there was a problem with the final invoice and they were incorrectly billed.
- The guest house owner took personal attention and hospitality too far, or conversely was not friendly enough.
- They did not enjoy the atmosphere of the guest house, disliked the décor, the look and feel of the establishment, or even something like the music playing, the cat on the chair (cat hairs on suits) or the dated magazines in the lounge.
- Their requests or complaints were not promptly attended to, or not attended to at all, and they were kept waiting for an essential item or service.
- The guest house manager was inflexible in meeting their needs, such as an early breakfast for an early departure.
- The guest house, bathroom or linen etc. was not spotlessly clean.
- The guest house manager or a staff member did not treat them courteously or with respect, whether in person or on the telephone.

How to provide excellent service: The competitive edge

As the service provider, you should always remind yourself that your guest might be seeing a completely different 'picture' from the one that you are seeing, without either of you being wrong. Based on the same set of facts, any two people will provide two different versions of them. As we all have our own uniquely formed filters in our brain that process incoming information, we will each form our own unique set of perceptions through this process.

What can you learn from this principle and how can you safeguard against a one-sided view of your own service?

- Ask other people whom you trust for their opinion of your service.
- Challenge yourself to look at the various aspects of your service from different 'angles' at regular intervals.
- Test your own service – become your own client. This is a very effective method of evaluating your service and amenities. Spend a night in your own rooms as if a guest, and use all the facilities.
- Listen to criticism/complaints with an open mind, knowing that these provide the opportunity to test your own views and to improve your service.

The following factors influence people's perceptions of service:

- *Responsiveness:* How do you respond to your customer's needs?
- *Reliability:* Will you deliver the same level of service every time?
- *Assurance:* Does your service instil confidence in your guest?
- *Empathy:* The way you deal with your customer's need.
- *Tangibles:* The physical environment that you create for your customer.

People are persuaded more by the depth of your conviction than by the height of your logic, more by your enthusiasm than any proof you can offer. Your conviction, your enthusiasm, your belief in what you are doing are what sells. Your feeling, your emotions, your sincere interest in your product and prospects are persuasive. Your optimism, your assurances, your hope, when combined with knowledge of what you are doing, enjoyment of what you are doing and the faith that you and yours are the very best, create an unseen force that cannot be resisted.

Create your own service model

You need a plan to help you to construct or deliver any product or process successfully. Wherever possible, systematise the customer service process so that it operates consistently.

The service model should enable you to deliver a service that incorporates the factors mentioned above and should reflect the core values of your business, such as integrity and loyalty. This model should therefore allow your vision to be converted into action. The model is also a map for your staff to follow at all times and should also provide a framework according to which they can be evaluated.

Although there is no single model available that will guarantee successful service delivery, there are basic concepts that should be included in your model.

> **Your service model**
>
> *Purpose:* You must know the reason for the business's existence and what you want to achieve with it. What is your vision?
> *Plan:* Your business plan for achieving your vision.
> *People:* Your human resources – what are their strengths and weaknesses and what skills need to be acquired?
> *Processes:* The administrative systems, the booking facilities, food and beverage controls and marketing strategies.
> *Performance:* Does delivery of your service take place and does it reflect your vision?

One crucial concept should at all times be enforced in your service model, and that is the proven fact that service is a process or chain of events and never a single event. Although the process is made up of numerous 'single events', you will never succeed in delivering competitive service when you focus on the event and not the process. Once again, the old saying that the chain is only as strong as its weakest link comes to mind.

One unpleasant incident can ruin a number of pleasant ones and might just last longer than other memories that the customers take with them on leaving your business. An incorrect account, an overdone egg, an unfriendly waitress, a broken bed light, will undo all the other pleasant experiences. You cannot afford to be right only 90 per cent of the time in terms of service rendering in the guest house business! Only 100 per cent is good enough. It usually takes only more effort, time and care to get right and does not cost much.

Remember that good service is rendered not only to your guests, but to all the people involved in making reservations with you. Do not forget the following people, and treat them courteously and professionally. Always make it easy, convenient and, above all, pleasant for them to do business with you:

* the secretary or personal assistant who makes a reservation on behalf of a guest of the company she works for, or on behalf of her director,
* travel and reservation agents and tour operators, and
* colleagues in the guest house and tourism industry.

Your team

No business can invest too much in its human resources. Minimum standards should be set for staffing levels to ensure customers are treated quickly and fairly. Having happy staff is critical if you are relying on their contact with your guests. You cannot afford to have the wrong people on your staff – hire people with the right attitude and train them well.

Your first priority is to share your vision and the purpose of the business with your staff or team and explain it to them. Ensure that they understand the terminology and phrases you use and be very sensitive to cultural difference and/or interpretations. Give them the resources to deal with your guests.

All staff working on the premises should be involved, as you never know who might be called by a guest to assist with a problem. Therefore the gardener (as an example) should understand why the guest is there and know how to deal with the guest should he come into contact with him.

A very useful tool is to create your own Quick Reference Guide for delivering the expected service. This guide will ensure that processes are maintained and levels of service are achieved. The guide can even be printed on small cards to be carried by all staff and should be known by heart. The guide can include, for example, a standard greeting and instructions on how to deal with a problem. Ensure that customer information is easy to access and understand for all guests and staff. Consider displaying these in other languages if necessary.

The 'WIIFM' (what's in it for me) principle is commonly used to emphasise the importance of explaining to your staff what your business has to offer to them, such as job security, the ability to support their families, and skills and opportunities. They must be made to realise the importance of competitive service and the benefits for them that are associated with it.

Coaching your staff on basic life and social skills will help them to realise the importance of aspects such as personal hygiene, a proper dress code, personal appearance and manner of speech. As we have emphasised above, make sure that you and your staff see the same 'picture' at all times, and remember to practise what you preach.

Serving customers is the lifeblood of a guest house and the ultimate expression of its purpose.

The guest

Providing exceptional customer service is about putting your customer first in order to ensure his or her satisfaction, which will eventually lead to your success and financial reward. If you put service first, the income will surely follow. You may sometimes have to forfeit short-term gain or profit in order to build a relationship with a new guest or to ensure his or her satisfaction.

The more I know about my guest, the better service I can deliver to him or her. Once you know who they are, what they want and what they will do, you will be able to serve them like no other. Invest in a process that will enable you to know as much as possible about your guest, even before the guest arrives. Many current computerised reservations programs make it easy to store information about guests' preferences for future use and to help you remember that Guest B likes a double bed with a bathroom and hard boiled eggs for breakfast. Remembering and paying attention to small details like these goes a long way to ensuring happy and satisfied customers who feel that you really care about them and make them feel special!

Information is a powerful tool, but it needs to be processed to become what is referred to as 'business intelligence'. In other words, obtaining the information on your guest's culinary preferences provides the edge only once that information has been passed on to the kitchen and the plate of food in front of the guest reflects that information back to the guest in the form of the great meal containing the food that he or she wanted. It is therefore vital that information is kept up to date and made available to all staff through a structured process.

Various tools are available to obtain such information, and most guests would willingly provide most of what you need, so don't be afraid to ask questions. Prepare a list of possible questions that can be used at any given time to obtain the specific information that will enable you to deliver competitive service.

Regular surveys or other methods to get feedback are important tools to use. An example, which also includes some market research questions, is set out below.

This visitor summary template is for you to complete yourself by asking the questions as your guest books out. Alternatively, you can use it to gather the data from guests' written responses. Edit the questions you would like information on.

Customer survey
Please help us to provide an even better service by filling out this brief questionnaire. All information is confidential, and your name is not required. Please be as honest as you can.
What brings you to the area?

Business	Leisure/holiday
Visiting local companies	Main holiday
Passing through on business	Short break
Attending a conference	En route elsewhere
Working locally – temporarily	Family/social event locally
Other	Sports event/entertainment
	Other

How did you find out about us?	
Recommended by friend or colleague	Internet
Booked by visitor information centre	Just passing and saw sign
Picked from guide book (which one?)	Other

How did you enjoy our service and facilities?				
	Excellent	As expected	Could be better	Disappointing
Welcome on arrival				
Overall efficiency				
Overall cleanliness				
Services				
Quality				
Cleanliness				
Comfort				
Experience				
Service				
Food quality				
Menu				

Are there any areas where you think we do things exceptionally well?

Are there any areas where you think we need to make some improvement?

	Yes	No
Do you feel we provide good value for money?		
Would you use us again and/or recommend us to friends and colleagues?		
Thank you for taking the time to help us to improve our service to you.		

By spending a few minutes with the guest on arrival, by keeping a record of your guest's preferences and comments and getting your staff to report any useful piece of information, you will quickly be in a position to spoil your guest. The lady doing the room will note what pillow the guest preferred or how many blankets he or she used, the barman will note the drinks and the chef the way the guest liked the eggs. The guest will be impressed and will notice the fact that you are interested in him or her. Most guests are more than willing to pay a premium for that kind of attention and service, and this will create strong customer loyalty. It does not cost much, only attention to detail, to gain the competitive edge through this route.

Does the guest have confidence in you to deliver the expected (in his or her mind) service? Remember that the guest's experience is in your hands and therefore you control and determine his or her experience! This entails your changing the angle from which you deliver service from 'what can I give the guest?' to 'what does my guest want?' Service should always be user-friendly and not provider-friendly.

Through effective communication, by being sensitive, by understanding that there are other 'pictures' out there, by bearing in mind that it is a process, by involving all staff and by keeping notes, you can deliver competitive service at any time.

Dealing with a difficult guest or complaint

Create a recipe for dealing with difficult guests and refrain from
- blaming other people,
- attacking the guest,
- defending your actions/business, and
- making excuses for everything.

Problem solving

It has been proven that unaddressed complaints are by far the biggest reason why people no longer support a particular service. Responding quickly to guest problems is a key factor in providing quality customer service. You can no longer respond to a complaint with a general response like, 'We'll get back to you soon.' You must respond quickly, specifically *and* effectively to remain competitive today. You must do everything possible to serve the customers until they say, 'It works for me.'

In fact, problems provide you with an excellent opportunity to improve the quality of your service, as you may be able to eliminate procedures or systems that prevent you from taking care of your guests and building up guest loyalty. Effectively dealing with complaints and the way this is done is one way of reassuring guests that they will be looked after, and is a very powerful marketing tool. Ignoring complaints is, on the other hand, a recipe for disaster. You should display a 'whatever it takes' attitude about complaints.

The guest needs a solution to his or her grievance or problem and is normally not interested in your explanation. Therefore you should rather use the process outlined in the box below.

Positive problem solving

The positive problem-solving formula is summed up in four Fs:

Feelings:
- Greet appropriately, make eye contact, smile, use positive body language.
- Compose yourself, look interested, let the guest speak, listen.
- Paraphrase and express sympathy.
- Thank them and apologise for the problem.

Facts:
- Clarify the problem.
- Get the facts.

Fix it:
- Promise to do something immediately.
- Find ways to offer help.
- Offer solution options – guide the guest from the problem to the solution, apologise again as appropriate.

- Invite the guest back.
- Thank, greet and re-offer services.

Follow-up:
- Keep in contact with the guest.
- Learn from the complaint.
- Share the information.
- Report the problems to someone who can change or improve the situation.

How to provide better service

Good customer service is more than the friendly smile; it is a mindset and a set of very specific skills and actions that can be learnt. It is beyond the scope of this book to deal with this topic exhaustively, but much has been written by various experts about this. We recommend that you read as much about this topic as possible as improving your customer service will continue to benefit your business.

Establishing effective customer service procedures is helpful to assist in providing better service.

The following is a list of tips for better service:

❀ Ensure that all customers leave your guest house feeling they are special and individual persons.
❀ Place the interests of your guests above your own. Don't park in the best spot! Whether applied literally or metaphorically, this is a classic error and should be avoided. How often do we see the best parking spots reserved for the owner or staff? What signal does this send a prospective customer? Take a look around your business and see if you're occupying the best and most convenient spot for your vehicle, your chair or anything else.
❀ Build customer expectations. Do more than expected. The phrase 'under-promise and over-deliver' is the perfect standard for customer service.
❀ Greet guests with enthusiasm and friendliness.
❀ Be alert to guests' needs and respond with help and enthusiasm.
❀ Accept responsibility for each guest's concerns and follow through to a satisfactory conclusion.
❀ Ensure that every member of staff accepts responsibility for the environment and for keeping the facilities up to standard.
❀ Provide every guest with a unique experience to ensure he or she returns again and again and also tells others.
❀ Give your guests better value than they expected.
❀ Good service is consistent – always the same, every day.
❀ Remember your guests and their details – show them you care.
❀ Give the best quality you can, all the time, and in the same way every time.
❀ Quick reaction to requests, enquiries, acknowledgement of emails, etc. is seen as excellent service; slow response, although possibly appropriate, is seen as bad service.
❀ Be concerned about your guest's comfort.
❀ Don't cut costs or the value of what you offer.
❀ Highlight intangibles such as truth, honesty, integrity, investing time in your guest.
❀ Communicate with your guests and potential guests.
❀ Effective communication starts with *effective listening*.

- Manage your image. Anyone representing your business either adds to or detracts from your image. Control your image by establishing policies and procedures. Ensure that your image is constantly under review and that under no circumstances do you allow your image to be compromised.
- Give business to others. There are occasions when what you have to offer is not what a customer needs, or you can only provide part of the service that is required. You can really add value if you are knowledgeable and help customers to obtain what they require, even if it means introducing them to your opposition. Businesses that are committed to serving their customers don't rest until each customer is satisfied. Be creative with each referral; it will pay dividends in the long term.
- Follow-up and feedback: Service doesn't stop when the sale is concluded; this is the opportunity to reinforce and expand a relationship. Follow up customers to ensure their needs have been met, ask for feedback on the key areas of your business relationship and show your sincerity by making changes whenever relevant. Listen to feedback, make changes, experiment and acknowledge input.
- Say *thank you*. Say it everywhere. Say it on your invoices; say it out loud; say it to your staff. Never conclude a sale without a thank you and continue to let your customers know that you appreciate them.
- Remember that good service can be a small impromptu act, such as offering a map or carrying a bag into the guest house. Train staff to look out for such opportunities to be helpful.
- The key encounters that occur between a customer and your guest house are the so-called 'moments of truth' and what your guest thinks about you is the result of these encounters, from first enquiry to check-out. Think of all the places that make up your guest's experience and especially those that are critical to the guest's perception of quality. How he feels at each moment of truth is what he will go on to grade the quality of your service.
- Saying 'No' to a guest can be done only with the manager's permission.
- Ask yourself the following questions and train your staff to do as well: 'If I were the guest, how would I feel about this? Would this explanation satisfy me? Does this rule/procedure make sense to me?' Consider the slogan TLC - Think Like a Customer.

The ten most important phrases

- The 10 most important words: *I apologise for our mistake. Let me put it right.*
- The 9 most important words: *Thank you for your business. Please call us again.*
- The 8 most important words: *I'm not sure, but I will find out.*
- The 7 most important words: *What else can I do for you?*
- The 6 most important words: *What is most convenient for you?*
- The 5 most important words: *How may I serve you?*
- The 4 most important words: *How did we do?*
- The 3 most important words: *Glad you called.*
- The 2 most important words: *Thank you.*
- The 1 most important word: *YES.*

Price

Value for money

The next important 'P' is price. The golden rule here is 'value for money'. A person's decision to make a first reservation in a guest house is often based on the convenience of the location and the right price or rate. Guests will return if your service and facilities are good enough.

In guest house terms, price refers to your *rates*. This is an area where many guest houses and bed and breakfast establishments experience problems. The price of your product is calculated in terms of your costs, the competition or what other guest houses are charging for the same facilities and services, and what a customer is prepared to pay. Refer to your original market research regarding the calculation of your rates, costs and budget (see chapters 1 and 2 for pricing structures).

You may discover too late that you have charged unrealistically high rates or that you cannot cover your costs and the debts you have incurred, having spent too much on the building or interior decorations.

Do not expect your guests to pay for your mistake of over-capitalisation. Your rates must provide for a full recovery of costs as well as an adequate profit. If you do your market research properly, you will know what the market can bear in terms of rates.

What should your rates include?

Rates normally include bed and breakfast, while dinner, other meals, drinks, telephone calls, laundry and so forth are quoted and invoiced separately.

The rate for two people in the same room is not simply double the single rate. The accepted ratio is that the double rate should be about one-third more than the single rate. It does not really cost you much more than an additional breakfast and the washing of extra towels to accommodate two people in one room. The practice of some guest houses of selling a room at a set rate regardless of how many people it accommodates is not popular with guests, as it makes single occupancy very expensive.

Commissions

Your normal rate is what is known as the 'rack rate' in the travel trade. Travel agents expect to be quoted the same rack rate as your other guests, and commission is then paid on the normal rack rate for bed and breakfast only. Alternatively, you can offer a special STO or Standard Tour Operator rate, which will normally be 10 per cent less than your rack rate to account for the commission the agent will add to the cost when selling the room to his client. The principle behind this is that the customer should not pay more for the room by booking through a travel agent than by booking directly with you. You can expect to pay between 10 and 20 per cent commission to travel agents on the basic rate.

Do not add the commission onto your rates but pay it out of your normal rates. Adding the commission on will make both your guest and agent unhappy and you will appear greedy, which is not a good image to have for the sake of a few rands.

Additional services like laundry and dinner are usually excluded from commission. Pay the commission promptly to travel and reservation agents as they can save you considerable advertising and marketing costs. Remember you are paying for actual business received, not for hoped-for business as with advertising. You are reaping the benefit of their marketing and advertising at very little cost to you, and looking after your relationships with agents can be very beneficial financially as they are able to make a lot of reservations with you. They deal with many accommodation establishments, from large hotels to small B&Bs. Be professional in your business dealings with them.

Be prepared sometimes to wait a little longer for your payment, for example when travel agents make use of your establishment. Do not pester or nag large organisations for payment. Hotels operate on a 30-day period for payment and if you wish to compete for the same business you should do the same.

Using rates as a marketing tool

Rates are a very powerful and important marketing tool in the guest house industry:

- Use pricing as an effective promotional tool with features such as weekend rates, winter rates and corporate rates.
- Distribute information on special weekend rates or on new services you may have introduced, such as offering dinner or airport transfers, and communicate them to previous guests and clients.
- Offer special rates as an incentive to a valuable source of guests, for example, a major local institution that requires accommodation for visitors on a regular basis, or lower your prices outside of peak periods.
- Give discounted rates for group reservations. It is always worth your while to give special group rates and to let tour operators stay free of charge when they bring a group with them.
- Offer lower rates to guests staying longer than a week.
- Offer weekend specials, low-season specials, midweek specials or bridal specials.
- Be flexible with your rates. An empty room is unacceptable and last night's empty room cannot be sold again. It is always worthwhile to offer a special rate for a long-term or group booking.

Keeping the competitive edge

Never compromise on the value of the product; that is, the quality of your facilities and the service you offer. No matter what the price is, whether it has been raised or lowered, if the current price is seen to be good value, then the price is right and your rooms will sell. You will need to gain a thorough knowledge of your own costs, your competitors' rates and the services they offer, to determine your price while simultaneously keeping a competitive edge.

If you set your rates too low, you may sell more rooms, but your profitability will suffer and you will make less profit per room. If you set the rates too high, you may make more profit per unit, but are likely to sell fewer rooms. One way of avoiding this, if the layout of your guest house allows it, is to offer a variety of rates. Usually, a guest house owner will decide whether he or she is in the luxury or higher end of the business, selling fewer rooms at higher rates, or the lower economy end, selling more rooms at lower rates.

It is *not essential* that your rates should be lower than those of your competitors. You could also gain the competitive edge by offering more value for money and better service. This is a safer way to attract business to your establishment than through low rates, because your rates could become too low to provide for a full recovery of your costs and for an adequate profit.

Offering the lowest rates is an easy tactic but really is the last option, as it could be very difficult to make sustainable profits. A better alternative would be to cut only a few prices on some products, such as weekend accommodation. As long as your service is superior and your other competitive advantages are in place, such as outstanding facilities and location, you can be the most expensive guest house and that would be quite in order.

Be flexible and sensitive to the market. If you know what your costs per room are, you could offer a special low rate, which would at least cover your costs during slow times. Lower rates than you would ideally like to charge could also help to win over new customers or lure them from the competition. This could help you to get yourself established in the market. The policy of lowering your rates in order to attract clients is known as *yield management*.

Do not fall into the trap of being greedy when things start going well, or panic when things are not going well and the bank needs to be paid. Erratic fluctuation of rates will drive your customers away and make them feel exploited. Sudden extreme increases as well as reductions in rates will make valuable customers feel exploited. Take a long-term view and be prepared to build your guest house's business up slowly. In this way, you will ensure that loyal customers return regularly and it will eventually save you money in expensive marketing activities.

Position

Position is concerned with where you wish to place yourself in the market, at the higher luxury end, the lower budget end, or somewhere in the middle. For example, are you planning a standard homely bed and breakfast offering limited services, or perhaps a more formal luxury guest house with 16-hour reception?

Remember, you cannot be everything to everybody and cater for all tastes, needs or budgets. Know what you are and where you should place yourself in the market. It should suit your own personality and style and, as you must be comfortable with the type of establishment, the kind of guests it will appeal to and eventually serve. You should be happy to work long hours in it.

The attraction of the guest house industry to potential guests is precisely to be found in the wide variety and individuality to choose from and because there is an establishment to suit every taste and pocket.

Promotion

How will you best be able to reach your target market? You want your guest house to stand out from the crowd.

By now you should thoroughly know your customers and their needs, and direct your promotional efforts towards satisfying those needs so that you obtain maximum customer satisfaction and maximum profit. Emphasise the benefits that guests will experience at your guest house and your points of difference from your competitors. You can focus on what makes you unique and on your own combination of key selling points.

> **Examples of key selling points**
>
> - Excellent location, near a particular facility, attraction, beach, business, hospital etc.
> - High quality assurance and Star Grading, B&B Association membership
> - Additional services and facilities: conference or meeting room, business facilities
> - Broadband internet and email facilities
> - Special attractions, view of mountains, sea, even star gazing
> - Ecotourism experience
> - Cultural tourism or accommodation
> - Traditional cooking
> - Hearty breakfasts using local produce
> - Country breakaway, peace and quiet, safety, security, nature
> - Honeymoon suite
> - Historical house or area
> - Walking trails, horse riding, wine tasting, gourmet dinners, game watching
> - Babysitting

The various methods of promoting your guest house will ensure that you bring your guest house to the attention of your potential guests, wherever they are.

You know from your market research where your guests come from, what they would read, what they have in common and what would appeal to them. Put yourself in their shoes. What would appeal to you? Be creative, but bear in mind the cost and expected effectiveness of your marketing activities.

The image of your guest house

Your guest house image is simply your marketing brand. First, consider what kind of image you wish to project. This is what will make it stand out from your competitors and what will differentiate it. This will create the best possible first impression. You have only one chance to make a first impression and make sure that however guests come into contact with your brand, through a brochure, website, or letter, or on the pavement, that the impression is positive as well as consistent.

Your brand is a name, a term, a sign, symbol or design, or a combination of these intended to identify your products or services to differentiate them from those of competitors. It is a promise to deliver consistently a specific set of features, benefits and services. Brands have the following values, which are all applicable to a guest house:

- *Functional value:* Perception of functional capability, what can I do with it, is it good for my purpose?
- *Social value:* Perception of brand being associated with a particular social group – does it meet my social aspirations?
- *Emotional value:* The brand's ability to arouse particular feelings – do I like it?
- *Epistemic value:* Trying a new brand to satisfy curiosity – but if it does not meet my needs, I will not try it again.
- *Conditional value:* Perceived utility from a brand in a specific situation – it has limited use for the time and purpose.

It is crucial to have a clearly identified image for your guest house, as you are basically selling the same as other accommodation providers. What makes you different and special? Why would people choose to spend a night with you and pay for it? What can they expect? And will you live up to their expectations?

Think of any major international hotel group. You know exactly what to expect and what you like and dislike about it. In the highly competitive guest house market, it is essential that you define your image so clearly that you stand out in the minds of your guests and potential guests.

You will need to make important decisions regarding the image and identity of your guest house, as this will influence your marketing decisions and will form an integral part of your marketing and promotion strategy.

The name of the guest house

The importance of an appropriate and effective name must not be underestimated. The name should clearly portray the identity that you wish to give your guest house.

Is there an interesting historical connection to your premises or the surrounding area? Is the location of your establishment outstanding? Location, history, politics and aspects of the area can all be sources of inspiration – the wind, mountains, battlefields, ostriches, anything really. Think of names with positive mental images. Whatever you choose, it should be easy to pronounce, spell and understand over the telephone. Do not leave the formation of your image to chance. Once established, it can be difficult and confusing to change, not to mention the wasted advertising and marketing costs.

Choose a name that is easy to remember, which is appropriate and descriptive, and which captures the mood of your guest house. A shorter name is preferable to a long name. It is easier to remember and can be enlarged in an advertisement.

Do not call your guest house 'Manor' or 'Lodge' if it consists of only two or three rooms or 'Cottage' if it is a luxury mansion. Avoid names that may confuse your establishment with another business, institution or monument in the area. Ensure that your name cannot be confused with another rival establishment, for example 'Constantia Lodge', 'Constantia Guest House', 'Constantia Bed & Breakfast', or similar-sounding slogans such as 'Be our Guest' and 'Be my Guest'.

It is advisable to register your guest house's name to ensure that it cannot be used by another establishment, thereby creating confusion on the internet or, worse still, losing you business, as has happened to some guest houses. Browse through a B&B or guest house guide to confirm whether your chosen name has not already been taken or is overused.

Be careful of names that cannot be pronounced or that may have a slightly strange or inappropriate meaning in another language and may mean something different to diverse people.

The name that you have chosen for your guest house must comply with the Business Names Act 27 of 1960. This Act protects businesses and avoids the duplication of names. The Registrar may order a person to cease using a specific name for a business if he is of the opinion that the name might deceive or mislead, cause annoyance or offence, or is suggestive of blasphemy or indecency.

It is a legal requirement that the following particulars have to appear on all your business correspondence, orders for goods or statements of accounts of your guest house:

- the name, title or description under which business is conducted,
- the physical address of the business,
- the name under which the guest house was registered or established if the business is carried on by a corporate body with a different name,
- the name of every partner if the business is structured as a partnership,
- the current or, where applicable, previous given names, initials and surnames of every person carrying on the business, and
- the nationality of the persons carrying on the business, should they not be South African citizens.

Contravention of the above renders a person, on conviction, liable to a fine.

Other elements reflecting the image of your guest house

Physical and aesthetic appearance

The physical and aesthetic elements of the interior and the exterior of your guest house play an important role. What does your guest house look like?

Quality assurance

How many stars have been awarded to you, are you a member of a B&B or guest house association, or have you been a finalist/winner in an accommodation awards competition? Such credentials will reassure potential guests that they are making the right choice in coming to you.

Personal treatment of guests and customer service

This entails the manner in which guests are treated from first contact to checkout and involves all aspects of your customer service. How do you answer the telephone? How efficiently and promptly are reservations dealt with? How are guests greeted on arrival?

Your writing style

All correspondence with guests should carry the clear message that you wish to help them and provide for their needs. Liberally use words and phrases such as 'Thank you for your booking/enquiry', 'I trust that this will be of assistance', 'Is there anything more I can for you?', and 'Do you need any further assistance/information?' If you cannot provide for a particular request, suggest an alternative and ask whether it will be in order.

Your stationery

The image of your guest house must also be conveyed by your business cards, brochures, leaflets, stationery, letterheads and invoices. The same image and character must be conveyed throughout. An attractive logo can assist in portraying your image.

Use appropriate designs that complement the general character of the guest house. A game lodge should not use a nautical or flowery theme, for example. When in doubt, opt for something that is plain rather than too elaborate. This will also be much more economical, will serve the purpose just as well and could easily be done on a desktop computer. No matter what the character, all of your guest house stationery (letterheads, complimentary slips, invoices, etc.) must be professional, with no spelling mistakes or grammatical errors. Remember that since you are operating a full-scale business enterprise, these items are essential, not optional, to the successful running of your business.

Small personal touches

These details are important, such as a room smelling of fresh flowers from the garden, or the smell of home-baked cookies and fresh coffee brewing. These things will all help to make an indelible impression on your guests and can give you the competitive edge.

Behaviour and appearance

Remember that the image of your guest house is also reflected in the behaviour and appearance of everyone associated with the guest house and every member of staff. Are you a credible business owner, honest in your dealings with people, a member of the local association, contributing to the community in some way?

Other guest houses

People will also judge you by their experiences, good and bad, of other similar establishments. It is important that you also assist in raising the standards of your competitors so that you do not become labelled by default through their errors or bad images.

Your marketing strategy

You will now be in a position to formulate your own unique marketing plan or strategy, which will include some of the elements discussed above.

The actual marketing mix, or range of marketing options that you will be using, is important. The marketing plan will help you to plan your future objectives realistically and in an ordered fashion. What do you expect your marketing to deliver? For example, are you aiming for a 30 per cent increase in occupancy or spend from the target group? It is important to keep track of the success of each method.

Where do you wish your business to be in one or five years' time? A marketing plan will give direction and consistency to your actions. It should address ways in which to get new customers as well as to encourage return visits from previous customers. Your plan will cover:

* *Who you are targeting:* Identify the exact types of customer you want to reach.
* *Your objectives:* Clear objectives of increased occupancy or spend.
* *Your plan for implementation:* What methods will you use? (Discussed in chapter 8.)
* *A timeline:* When will it happen?
* *Your budget:* What can you do with available funds, how much can you spend?
* *Evaluation of success:* Did it work?

Your target market

This is where you decide precisely who you want your marketing to reach. This could be:

* existing customers or – more narrowly defined – customers spending R1 000 a night,
* new customers sharing the same characteristics as your current customers, such as business people, hikers, or
* people from a different area sharing the same profile as your existing customers.

The point is to decide who you are going to spend most of your marketing efforts on as it is impossible and far too expensive to try to reach everyone. Remember that even if you have the most loyal of guests, you still need to acquire new customers because existing customers can move away, and in any event you want to grow your business.

Timeline

Setting deadlines is equally important and you should also think about the best time to carry out each tactic. Map out when and how you will spend your marketing funds for the year to avoid spasmodic and ineffective marketing or budget blow-outs. You may be influenced by seasonal issues but need to get maximum exposure from your available funds and even out troughs and peaks in your income.

Your marketing budget

Precise targeting of who you want to reach with limited funds is vital. You could, for example, target existing guests who spend more than R1 000 per visit, or a new target group identified by your research. Set a definite target, for example: 'to assess the customer satisfaction of all guests who spend R1 000 and encourage them to increase spending by 30 per cent.'

In drawing up your budget, you should also consider your yield from marketing. How much profit do you need to recover from your promotion to make the exercise worthwhile?

For example:

You want a yield of 5 times for advertising. The advert costs R3 000, so five times gives you a return on investment of R15 000. If your profit per guest is R150, you need 100 guests to get your return.

To work out your budget, you can consider the following options:

* Pay whatever you can afford when you can afford it. This is the worst option.
* Do the same as your competitors; you assume they know what they are doing and follow suit. The second worst choice.
* Percentage of sales – you budget a small percentage of your sales, less than six per cent.
* Set objectives and targets and budget accordingly. This method has the best chance of success.

Using the last method, list your ideas and the costs in priority order and calculate the annual cost. Set an upper limit of, say, five per cent (more at start-up, at least 10 per cent) of sales. Discard options that are too expensive or not targeted well. You can spend twice as much for the same results if you are not careful.

Split the budget among your different promotional choices, such as those below:

Advertising	10%
Tourism magazine	5%
Annual travel guide	15%
Networking	5%
Trade show exhibit	20%
Website	20%
Direct selling – phones, etc	5%
Brochures	15%
Contingency	5%
Total	100%

Consider aspects such as time versus money — some cost-effective strategies take more time than others. For example, building a word-of-mouth reputation involves hard work, good service and effort over a long time, while advertising is quick and expensive. You may have lots of time and no money or vice versa. You must commit both time and money to some measure to market your business.

Do a SWOT analysis

It is useful to do a *SWOT analysis* to assist you in your marketing planning. This is an analysis of your current position under the headings Strengths (S), Weaknesses (W), Opportunities (O) and Threats (T). Strengths and weaknesses must be measured against your competition. You need to maximise your strengths and minimise your weaknesses. Here is an example of a SWOT analysis in marketing terms.

Strengths

Confirm the following:

✿ Is your service excellent and/or do you provide a wonderful breakfast?
✿ Are your rates better than the competition's while offering the same level of facilities?
✿ Are you visible and easily accessible?
✿ Are your staff friendly and well trained?
✿ Do you have a unique selling point?
✿ Are you seeing any results from your marketing plan?
✿ Are you offering a unique experience/service/facility that may give you a competitive edge?

Opportunities

You must capitalise on the opportunities that could benefit your business by, for example, making use of new marketing media such as the internet.

✿ Are there any new trends in the market? South Africa's emergence as a conference destination could, for example, provide guest houses with additional business.
✿ Is the profile of visitors to the country changing? If there are more visitors from Germany, perhaps you should consider marketing in Germany, in German on your website or, better still, appoint someone who can speak German.
✿ Are there any opportunities your competitors may be missing that you could exploit?

Threats and weaknesses

These can impact on your business, and serious weaknesses could even close you down.

✿ Are your rates far too high for the market?
✿ Perhaps you are difficult to find or your facilities and service have failed to keep up with your competition?
✿ A new guest house with better facilities could have opened around the corner from you.
✿ What are your other competitors up to?
✿ External factors outside of your control could have a serious impact on your business, such as the state of the economy, crime and safety, new legislation, changes in interest rates and international incidents like 9/11 or a pandemic, industry trends and environmental changes.
✿ Threats and weaknesses must be minimised as far as possible in order for your marketing plan to work.

Know your product

Keep fully up to date with what is happening among your competitors and in the marketplace, so that you can adjust your day-to-day marketing tactics accordingly. Read the newspapers, business news, tourism and industry publications and scan websites for new trends, competitor developments and innovations as well as potential threats. What new advertising techniques are being used? Are your competitors changing their rates? Why are they changing their rates? Have they added a new service? Has their share of the market improved? It is equally valuable to find out why your competitors may not be succeeding and how this could affect your business and profits.

Your long-term marketing objectives and the aims that you wish to achieve through marketing – increased occupancy would clearly be one – will determine your strategy and plans. Marketing is about making the future of your business happen. It is a long-term investment and you must keep a long-term view in mind. It is not a quick fix for short-term problems.

Set your goals

Set clear goals, for example a 20 per cent increase in occupancy within six months, 15 per cent increase in business customers, or existing customers to increase their spend. You must be able to monitor your marketing to know whether it has been successful.

Decide what to do, when to do it, where to do it and whether your budget can afford it. You should always spend at least 20 to 25 per cent of your management time on marketing-related activities, and about 75 per cent of your time on these at the start of your business.

Marketing must never stop. It involves each and every member of your establishment and should become a way of life for everyone involved in your enterprise.

When you know your product, its strengths and weaknesses, and your customers' needs, go out there, fulfil those needs, and tell others about your success. Sell your product in the ways that will best reach your customers, whether by advertisements, personal visits and the effective use of price, or by means of other promotions. Your own knowledge forms the basis of your marketing mix – the ways in which you bring your product to potential customers. Make sure that you deliver what you promise.

Find out what marketing is working

With the form overleaf, you can ask each customer who enters your premises about why they came in. We have entered some marketing methods for you already and left some fields blank for your own unique ones. When you have asked a hundred or so customers, you should be able to build up a bit of a picture of the success of your various marketing methods.

Example marketing method	
Yellow pages	
Newspaper adverts	
Networking	
Website	
Tourism magazine	
Radio adverts	
Television adverts	
Fliers	
Word of mouth	
Article in media	
Referral from other guest house	

To conclude this chapter, here is an example of a six-month marketing action plan for a guest house at the coast, including costs:

Marketing action plan

Action	Jan	Feb	March	April	May	June	July
Annual membership Guest House Association R300 per annum	R300	0	0	Hosting meeting R150	0	0	0
Travel magazine ad 6-month special R3 000	R500	R500	R500	R500	R500	R500	0
Website hosting R260 per month New design/upgrade of website R1 200	R260	R260	R260	R260	R260	R260+ R1 200	R260
Personal marketing R1 775 per annum	No	Breakfast for local travel agents R500	Visits to secretaries of local businesses R300	Personal visits to conference venues R300	Telephone survey of potential business in area R500	Tourism Association function to network R125	Visit to university foreign guest dept R50
Annual star grading of Tourism Grading Council R1 300 per annum	0	R1 300	0	0	0	0	0

Prize sponsorship	No	No	No	School golf tournament R500 + R200 for leaflets	No	No	No
Low weekend/ week rates 15 per cent discount	Yes	No	No	Yes	No	No	Yes
Annual advertisement in *Portfolio of Places* R1 600	0	0	0	1 600	0	0	0
Accommodation Awards entries AA Travel Guides: R800	0	R50	0	0	0	R800	0
Local chamber of business: R50							

WELCOME

8

Getting your guest house noticed: How to promote your guest house

Introduction

Your guest house, its services and lovely facilities must be noticed in order to attract the attention of buyers. Your brochures, advertising, other printed material, website, public relations and networking are all the methods that you will be using to promote your guest house to your potential guests. You will reach your potential guests through different media and different methods, and it is therefore important that you diversify your promotional efforts.

Your resources should all emphasise your competitive advantage and unique selling points. Your guest house should stand out from the crowd. The various methods and tools you use to promote your guest house will ensure that you bring it to the attention of your potential guests.

Marketing collateral and technology: Websites, brochures, advertising and publicity

Website marketing

A well-designed website is now the top method of choice of promoting your guest house and it is becoming essential to have one. The internet is today the preferred source of information for many; it is now a more popular source than printed materials and its reach is far wider than any brochure or advertisement. There are many advantages in setting up a good website, not the least being that it is accessible all over the world at a time and place that suit your potential guest.

If you don't have a website, you will be missing out on many potential guests who use the internet to search for accommodation. The question therefore is not whether you can afford to have a website but whether you can afford not to have one, as it is an essential promotional and communication method in the world today.

Many email service providers offer free hosting space that you could use for your website. However, a website is not simply an online brochure, and a few other rules apply to setting up a website. Potential guests today want to see before they buy, and they have been spoilt by the quality and variety of material on the internet. You will lose reservations if you cannot refer enquiries to view a website as well. The time saved is also quite obvious.

However, note that the internet is a very quick and hugely competitive medium. You must check any possible reactions or enquiries from your website at least once a day, if not more often, and react to them immediately, even if you only confirm receipt and advise that full details will be provided at a set time. Do not delay, as you will lose the sale. People have come to expect virtually 24/7 service, all day and at any time, from the internet.

A website offers the following advantages to a guest house:

- ✿ an opportunity to sell a room at the last minute,
- ✿ the latest and most up-to-date information about rates, specials, etc.,
- ✿ fast and easy changes and updates of information, virtually instantaneous,
- ✿ a choice for users to select aspects they are interested in, and the possibility of providing more comprehensive information than the printed media,
- ✿ all-hour accessibility from the comfort of your own home, eliminating the need to visit a travel agent,
- ✿ faster and much cheaper communication than traditional media such as publications, with changes or corrections, e.g. about rates, being easier to make,

- the ability to track enquiries and to measure the effectiveness of the promotional method,
- online links to other providers such as tour operators or tourism information, providing a one-stop information centre, and
- an equal opportunity for all suppliers, big and small, to reach the market.

Developing your website and costs

You could build your website in stages, starting with a very simple brochure-like site which you can then expand as you grow more confident. There are excellent template programs available which make setting up a website very easy to do technically.

Development costs fall into the following areas:

- *Buying a domain name:* This is the main part of your website address or 'URL'. How you choose your domain name is critically important to ensure that potential guests can find you when they search the web. Choose a name that preferably contains your guest house name as well as the description, so be sure to include 'guest house' in the domain name.
- *Site hosting costs:* The costs depend on the size and sophistication of your website, and also on the volume of visitors (or 'traffic') that your site receives. You generally pay the fees monthly to the internet service provider. If you have an email account, you may be entitled to a certain number of pages or a certain size site free. Hosting packages vary from very basic to very advanced, but hosting services generally allow for upgrades when you need them.
- *Web design and development:* This is usually offered by the hosting service, but you are free to choose any design and development provider.
- *Maintenance of the site:* It will be far cheaper (and quicker) if you can do this yourself. It is not difficult at all and your site should be planned so that you can do this. Hosting services usually provide online guidance.
- *Appropriate software to manage the site:* Arrange security and a secure server certificate if you plan to take online reservations and payments by credit card. This is usually part of the package that you negotiate with the hosting service.

The design and structure of your website

It is a good idea to look at a variety of websites and see what you like and dislike about them. Look at the site navigation – this is how you select links to move from one section to the other. Is it easy to find the information you want? Does it download quite quickly? Does it look inviting? Did you find it easily when searching? Is the structure for finding information intuitive? Make a note of what you like to make sure you include it in your own site. Look out for good ideas. It could be something as simple as giving the local time if you often have guests from overseas.

Remember that your site should reflect the same brand image, colours, styles and fonts as the rest of your marketing and brand collateral, including stationery, brochures, reservations letters and signage.

Don't forget to ask your guests what information they would like to see on your pages and what they like on other pages.

We recommend that you use a skilled website designer to help you set up the website and the design of your site's architecture. There are also templates that could be used as well. It will be worthwhile for you to attend a short web-design course offered by one of the many programmes available, so that you can manage and update the site yourself on a regular basis.

Most simple websites contain the following:

- Homepage: An attractive first page briefly stating your key marketing messages, who you are and what you are about, with a very descriptive image or photograph and your logo. It must make the visitor want to read more about your guest house.
- Details and gallery: More precise details of the rooms on offer, services available etc., and a link to a gallery of photos of the rooms, garden, dining room and so forth. A photo of the guest house team can also be good to include.
- A page with prices, booking conditions and cancellation policies, if not included above – the information on the rates list as described under the section on brochures will be suitable.
- Reservations page: You may wish to link this to an online payment facility that could be provided by your bank;
- Your contact details and address, etc.
- An easy-to-read map.

Writing for the web and other points to remember:

Research shows that users 'skim and scan' rather than 'read' to find what they want. Users read 20 to 25 per cent more slowly online.

- Write briefly and succinctly, making ample use of headings, bulleted points and new paragraphs. Write in small content chunks in a friendly, approachable manner. Paragraphs should contain a single idea in at most three to four sentences or 50 to 70 words. Sentences are focused and short, with a maximum of 15 to 20 words.
- Don't crowd pages with irrelevant information or promotion.
- Design each page so that it could be an effective entry point into your website and stand on its own to promote your guest house.
- Links should be in context and created by a keyword – for example, 'Room rates' instead of 'for room rates click here'. The 'click here' usage is now seriously outdated.

The content should of course be useful. Is it what users need to help in their decisions or actions? Is it up to date and still relevant?

- Your website should provide the essential information in as few words as possible. Reading a website can be compared to reading banners along a highway.
- Photographs should all be optimised for the website for quick downloading and should be resized accordingly. It is not necessary to have a 5 MB photo on the website, and large photographs that take too long to download will make people click off. Photographs should be resized to no larger than 72 dpi. Use thumbnail links of small photos on the main pages to larger images that can be viewed.
- The images could show guests enjoying themselves and the experience of being in your guest house, but make sure they give permission to use their images in terms of privacy laws! Have the photographs taken by a professional photographer.
- Select the right search words to list your site. Remember that the internet is not a neatly ordered library, but the right search words will guide visitors to you. Search words are the most likely words that people will use, such as accommodation, guest house, B&B, inn, country house. Add words like the area you are located in and special services, such as fishing.

Best practice for readability includes the following:

* dark font on a white background, or a high-contrast dark text on a light background,
* fonts that are no smaller than 10 point; a font like Verdana is very popular for clarity (avoid italics), and
* avoidance of things that move and background images.

How to make your website work for you

So, by now you have a website, it looks good and your webmaster keeps on telling you that this is the best thing on earth! So why are you still not happy with your website? Is it because the site is not up to standard or is it because your site does not get enough visitors or, as it is commonly known, 'traffic'?

It is very important that your website is up to the standard of those in your industry and that your site compares well with those of your competitors and peers. This does of course still not mean that your site will get the traffic it requires. Unfortunately just having a website is no longer good enough. Now you have to market your website as well.

This means you have to take a number of steps to ensure that your website gets noticed, and that way your site can really start working for you. How do you go about doing this? Below are but a few suggestions on how to achieve this.

Online

Search engine optimisation: In order for your website to be search engine friendly, it is essential for it to be optimised for the various search engines. This will involve reviewing your keywords, search phrases, Meta tags and other design and development elements, making it easier for the 'crawlers' and 'spiders' to find your website.

167

Search engine submission: Regular, planned and structured submissions to all the major search engines. Submissions have to be done in a manner so as not to cause your site to get blacklisted for too many submissions, yet ensuring that it is listed where it matters. Consider using words familiar to overseas visitors to describe your guest house, such as 'Inn' 'boutique hotel' and so forth, as the term guest house is not recognised in all countries.

Reciprocal links: These are more important today than submissions. Links from and to your website hugely improve its chances of being indexed and 'seen' by search engine crawlers and can do a great deal to create extra awareness of your website. Links also show your potential clients what company you keep. Link to other sections and pages of your own website as well. Ask for links to your site to be placed on the websites of the local tourism organisation and link back to them and to the guest house associations. The more links from your site and to your site, the better is the chance of your site being seen and found by searchers.

Domain names: The domain name is the most visible part of the address that consumers use to find a website, e.g. www.travelinafrica.com. If you want a domain name, you will need to do the following:

* Decide on organisation branding (hotel.com) versus descriptive (safariinafrica.com). This depends on the branding strategy of the organisation as well as brand awareness.
* Consider the availability and cost of buying domain names.
* Check that new domains include .info, .biz, and .us.
* Register multiple domain names or suffixes or point to one internet address or multiple copies of the same website.

Banner advertising and sponsorships: A great deal of good and bad has been said about banner advertisements. In the heyday of the dotcom explosion, banner ads were made out to be the answer to all your problems. Banner ads do, however, still have a place today in very much the same way printed adverts have. Essential to keep in mind are the following:

❀ Place your advertisement on a website that you know is visited by your target market.
❀ In the case of a campaign, ensure that your banner has an offer.
❀ When you only want to create brand awareness, just having your company's name on a banner will be good enough.
❀ A well-designed banner with a good offer is much more likely to be 'clicked' on.
❀ Ensure that the details of the offer are clearly stated on the page to which the banner is linked.
❀ Don't attempt a campaign unless your website is up to standard.

The positive aspect of a banner advertising or pay per click campaign is that the results are easily measurable. Costs vary, but are reasonably cheap per impression on most websites. This means that for R2 000 your banner will be viewed 10 000 times (at a cost of 20 cents per impression).

Arrange to get regular feedback from your web host about the number of visits to your website, the time spent on the site and the pages visited. If some pages are not visited or are only scanned briefly, change them or cut them.

Put an email link on the site for potential guests to contact you for more information.

Add a link or a button to the reservations page on every page on the site.

Test your website on friends or guests to see how effective it is.

Remember to refresh your website regularly, as people can get bored with it. Change something on it as often as possible. To encourage return visits, add a news section with special offers or news about the area, an archive of older material, or a feedback questionnaire.

Consider incentives on your website such as online discounts, a free giveaway, competitions, and so on.

Email marketing: Use email to market your site and send special offers to your existing database, or to set up a regular email newsletter to previous guests. Great success can be achieved by having a well-planned email marketing campaign directed at your current clients or database. Your website could also contain an opt-in email facility where users can submit their details in order to receive your news. Be sure to have regular and relevant news should you choose to offer this service.

Viral marketing: Viral marketing describes any strategy that encourages individuals to pass on a marketing message to others, creating the potential for exponential growth in the message's exposure and influence. Clients know others like themselves, with similar interests, needs, and lifestyles. Moreover, loyal clients are your best advocates.

Referral marketing: Referral marketing motivates your best customers by offering them rewards in exchange for helping to recruit other customers on your behalf. The result is a new pool of qualified prospects and sales leads that were hand-picked by existing, loyal customers from among their own colleagues, friends, and family. Referral marketing can help you to reduce new customer acquisition costs, increase market share, and build stronger brand relationships with your customers.

Offline

Marketing and promotions: Whenever a marketing campaign is initiated or any promotion undertaken, your website address should be incorporated. Material for trade and consumer shows, competitions, sponsorship of events and the like should always be utilised to market your website.

Branded gifts such as T-shirts and pens should always contain your web address. Corporate clothing, corporate vehicles and banners are also great tools for promoting your internet presence.

Stationery: All letterheads, notepads, compliments slips, business cards, invoices, emails and brochures, etc. should always state the guest house's website address.

Advertising: What good is it if you have a website but don't tell anyone about it? Ensure that your web address is printed not only on your business cards and letterheads, but on every printed advert, mentioned with every radio advertisement and viewable with every television spot.

Brochures

An attractive brochure can be very useful to market your guest house and, despite the growing importance of having a website, it can still play a valuable role in conveying the image and identity of your guest house. There are times and places where it is appropriate to use a hard copy brochure, for example at a trade show. Use the brochure to promote your website as well. It should not simply be a written copy of the website but could be a much shorter statement of the features that differentiate your guest house, using the website to provide full details.

The role of the brochure in the marketing strategy of guest houses is often greatly over-rated, because it is sometimes perceived as the most important marketing tool. Many guest house owners make the mistake of thinking that they cannot start marketing if they do not have a brochure. This is not true.

Apart from the fact that a full-colour brochure can be very costly, running into thousands of rands, it is often printed at a time – right at the start of the business – when it can probably be least afforded. However, with the development of websites it is no longer necessary, if you have a website, to produce an expensive and glossy brochure.

> Remember to budget for funds for the distribution of your brochure as you don't want boxes of your brochure simply standing around. Consider innovative distribution points such as other tourism service providers, for example tour guides or adventure operators, in addition to the more usual tourism information offices.

The purpose of a brochure is simply to impart clear and concise information about the guest house to the target market in order to entice them to stay there. It should say a lot about you and your guest house, but your target market should dictate the style and content. While it is not necessary for a small bed and breakfast establishment to use the most expensive glossy paper on the market, cheap paper will not be appropriate for a luxury guest house. Preferably use stylish colours that are eye-catching but soothing, and avoid unusual shapes. The grammar and spelling of your brochure must be 100 per cent correct; steer clear of clichés and flowery language. Keep it simple, avoid jargon or slang, and use words in the second person as you would in normal conversation. Remember that the most powerful word in English is 'you'.

In addition, although your careful market research has already identified certain characteristics of your target market, your actual experience of what people enjoy and find satisfying in your guest house will lead to your having a better understanding of what you want your brochure to look like and what you want to say in it after you have been operating for a while. However, make sure that you highlight the points of difference and your own attractions clearly.

A brochure is a form of advertising and, as it will in all probability compete with the brochures of other guest houses in the area, it will have to be effective to be noticed above the rest. Do not leave essential information out, as you want to make it as easy as possible for a potential guest to realise that you offer everything he or she wants and needs.

What should you include in a brochure? These content suggestions also apply to your website:

❀ Professional photographs of your guest house, taken on a sunny summer's day. You will need photographs of at least the front view of your establishment and a bedroom interior. Consider photographs of an enticingly laid out breakfast buffet, a sparkling clean *en suite* bathroom, the patio or garden, guests relaxing at the pool and even the smiling host and hostess. Use a professional photographer, as the quality is very important, and avoid misleading pictures, as guests should not be disappointed when they see your guest house. Don't make yourself look better than you are, and don't over- or undersell. Photographs of the guest house at dusk or sunset may be very artistic but may not convince the prospective guest to make a reservation, as he or she cannot see enough of the establishment.

❀ Include information about the guest house's location that may be relevant (and as indicated in your market research), such as its position near a highway, a shopping centre, an airport or an educational institution.

❀ Give grading and assessment information with dates and categories, details of your membership of appropriate associations, and an indication of any awards you may have won.

❀ Provide information about the number of rooms available (essential for group reservations), including the allocation of beds (e.g. double beds only) and all facilities on offer (e.g. *en suite* bathrooms with a bath and/or shower). Also indicate whether you can provide for the needs of disabled individuals.

❀ Say whether bedrooms have telephones and television sets and whether the guest house has satellite TV, a swimming pool, office facilities and internet access.

❀ Provide information about all services available, such as dinner on request, laundry and airport transfers.

❀ Include a clear and easy-to-follow map, with written directions from the nearest highway or main road.

❀ Provide your postal and physical addresses; your email and website details; your telephone, fax and cellphone numbers, including after-hours emergency numbers; and a contact name for the person dealing with reservations and enquiries.

❀ Indicate any international languages, such as French and German, spoken by your staff.

❀ Indicate whether children are welcome or not.

❀ Provide details of your smoking policy, bearing legislation in mind.

❀ Provide information about your ability to cater for special requests such as *Kosher*, *Halaal* or vegetarian meals.

❀ Include a call to action – tell your readers what you want them to do next. You would like them to call and book, wouldn't you? Tell them so.

Electronic brochures

With growing international interest in South Africa as a tourist destination and an increase in the number of reservations being made via the internet, it is vital that you have instantly available information and photographs that you can forward to enquirers as email attachments if you cannot refer them to a website. People have become used to being able to see the product before committing themselves, and you will lose business if you cannot provide them with instant visual material.

An electronic brochure that can be attached in reply to an email enquiry is much cheaper, quicker and easier to design and change and, if you do not have a website, it is an essential marketing tool today. The characteristics of an e-brochure are similar to those of a traditional hard-copy brochure, apart from the obvious advantages of being able to update and change it easily and cheaply. There are many desk-top publication programs available that could be used for this. Of course, if you do have a hard-copy brochure, it is easy to simply have an electronic copy in a PDF format available to email.

A rates list

A separate rates list is less expensive to change and is handy to forward to anyone who makes an enquiry. Do not include the rates in your printed brochure, as you will not be able to change them to allow for specials or increases during the lifetime of the brochure. Do not forget to update the rates list regularly, as it could be very embarrassing if you quote a higher rate to a guest! You can of course simply have the rates listed on your website, which makes it easy to keep them up to date.

Travel agents recommend including the following additional details to ensure clarity about a booking:

- ❀ Indicate next to every rate quoted whether it is per person, per person sharing or per room, etc. If applicable, include the cost of a third adult sharing. Specify the periods (dates) during which your rates are applicable, for example high season rates from September to March, low season in June and July and so on.
- ❀ Be specific about whether you offer specials throughout the season or during certain periods only. State clearly whether a minimum period applies. Include discount rates for weekends and public holidays. Provide rates for groups and, possibly, free accommodation for the tour leader. Define your peak-season and out-of-season rates clearly, and list the periods, seasons and public holidays during which you will be closed.
- ❀ Give details of your deposit and cancellation policies, as well as of how and when payment must be made. Also indicate which methods of payment you accept, for example credit card payments (in which case, specify which credit cards are acceptable), electronic payments, etc.
- ❀ Indicate whether you will pay commission to an agent. This is usually 10 per cent, but can be as much as 20 per cent. If you wish to do business with a travel or other agent, do not add commission onto your usual rates. It must be paid out of your normal rates.
- ❀ List any inclusions and/or exclusions, such as breakfast, drinks, VAT, a tourism levy and other levies, etc.
- ❀ Indicate check-in and check-out times.

Information leaflet

An easily designed information leaflet, which can be printed on any desktop computer and copied cheaply, is sometimes all that is necessary when you start out or offer only limited accommodation, as in a one-room rural, cultural or township B&B. This should contain your contact details, a high quality photograph and your main selling points.

Advertising

Advertising is one of the most common marketing tools and is often mistakenly thought of as the only method of marketing. Most guest houses rely more on new guests than on repeat reservations, so it is necessary to advertise to attract new guests. Advertising should also be considered when you want to promote a new service or a special offer. It gets the message out that you are open for business, builds your profile and customers' awareness of you, and complements your other promotional activities. Sometimes you need to advertise to compete and keep up with competitors.

Even the best advertisement will not succeed if it does not promote something that potential buyers want. List the most appealing aspects of your guest house, such as its excellent location and value-for-money rates, a rural experience, or a view of the sea. This is an ideal opportunity to state your competitive advantages clearly.

Advertising is a very expensive form of marketing, and unwise decisions could cost you thousands. It is important to keep careful note of the effectiveness of any advertisements you place by asking every customer where they found out about you, so that you can decide whether to continue with some forms of marketing or not. Also remember that people are bombarded by literally thousands of advertising messages daily. Why should your message appeal to and reach your target market?

However, remember that advertisements on the whole are not very effective for a guest house. The simple reason for this is that people do not believe the advertisements. Unfortunately, too many people have had unpleasant service or facilities experiences in establishments run by unscrupulous and unprofessional owners. This is why quality assurance and membership of a reputable accommodation association that guarantees the standards of their members are so important. Having two or three stars will reassure potential guests about the wisdom of choosing your establishment and the quality of the service and facilities they can expect. Do not expect quality assurance on its own to bring you business, but use it as a marketing tool in your promotional activities and be sure to mention it in your advertising.

Designing your advertisement

To be effective, an advertisement must be repeated regularly, which makes it even more expensive. A print advertisement must have an eye-catching headline, an attractive photograph and your top three marketing strengths. Don't forget to include your full contact details as well as your grading level and guest house association membership.

While some media companies offer free assistance with designing and developing advertisements, it is nevertheless important that you have an idea of what will work and what appeals to you. An advertisement should contain the following:

❖ *Pictures:* Photos, diagrams, drawings, sketches, cartoons and maps help to catch attention. Research shows that readers' eyes will go to pictures first. If the advertisement is just a whole lot of writing, people may decide not to bother reading it.
❖ *Headings:* Readers' eyes will go for the heading next. The heading for the advertisement should be your main message. It should not be the name of your guest house but rather what you are offering to the customer. However, don't forget to include the name and contact details somewhere on the advertisement!
❖ *Keep it simple:* Limit the advertisement to just one message if possible, perhaps your strongest selling point or the one most applicable to the target market.

- Use *plenty of space* so the print is easy to read.
- Always offer your *unique selling* point that sets you apart from the other places readers might go to.
- Always try to include an *incentive* (such as 10 per cent discount, or a free glass of wine) so you can measure the effectiveness of the advertisement.

Where to advertise

To advertise successfully, the advertisement should be targeted to get the best value for your money. Fortunately there are many dedicated tourism media aimed at tourists.

- If you don't know where to start advertising, start closest to your guest house, for example in your local schools' circulatory letters to parents, or your suburb's local newspaper.
- Ignore the 'in-between' magazines and guides that will undoubtedly contact you on an almost daily basis to sell their product. You cannot afford to support advertising entre-preneurs who need you to get their own businesses established. If you have agreed to place an advertisement and it does not work for your business at all, you have no claim against the advertising company.
- Advertise in reputable guides such as the AA Travel Guides and Portfolio of Places which have proven themselves over the years and which can guarantee the quality of their products.
- Make use of the free advertising offered by many local and provincial tourism associa-tions' publications and websites. Ensure that they have the correct contact details of your establishment.
- Don't forget about the obvious places in which people look for information – a bold entry in your local telephone directory or in the Yellow Pages is highly likely to pay off.
- You should advertise only where your target market will see the advertisement. For example, if you have a guest house in Mpumalanga near tourist attractions, it would be inappropriate to advertise in a journal for lawyers. However, if your guest house is situ-ated near the court, this could be an ideal choice.
- Take note of the *economic preferences* of your target market. An expensive, luxury guest house will not attract business if it advertises in a magazine read by hikers.
- A useful tip that will save you lots of money is to ask current advertisers in a particular medium whether their advertisements have succeeded in gaining business for them. This way you will quickly find whether there is any truth in the claims of the advertisement recruiters.
- Don't try to evaluate the success of the advertisement after only one placement, but do not sign a contract for a full year either. If your initial advertising proves unsuccessful, think again about the ways in which your guest house meets the needs of your guests and accentuate one or more of these strengths in your next advertising message.
- Correct language and spelling are prerequisites. Critically evaluate your advertise-ment's appearance, impact and message before automatically blaming the media for the poor response you received to it.

Choosing the right media to advertise in

- *Newspaper advertisements:* Nothing is as old as yesterday's newspaper. It reaches a wide variety of readers, but it is often difficult to establish whether it is reaching your target market.

- *Magazines:* Magazines have a longer shelf life and a more specifically targeted readership. Speciality magazines, such as travel magazines and travel trade magazines, could be worth considering.
- *Radio and television:* Radio and television advertisements can often be too expensive for the small entrepreneur.
- *Books and brochures:* You will be inundated with requests for advertisements in a variety of tourism brochures and books. Be very sceptical and careful. Some deliver what they promise, but many do not live up to their promises of distribution and the large target market they claim to reach. Place yourself in your customer's shoes. For example, would an international business person realistically arrive from overseas for appointments and only decide on the aeroplane or at the airport where to stay? Would the local brochure with advertisements for the butchery and the bakery also reach a potential guest? More suitable is probably the local tourism authority's brochures, which may be free marketing for you. The most important consideration is the distribution of these publications.

Remember:

If you do not provide excellent service, good facilities, the right price and a convenient location, advertising on its own will not succeed in gaining more business for you.

Measuring the success of your advertising

When you open your guest house, you will receive many requests to advertise in a variety of media, all claiming to reach your target market. Consider these proposals very carefully as they could cost a lot of money without showing any results.

The new business generated by an advertisement should, at the very least, pay for the cost of the advertisement. For example, if you are approached to advertise in a bridal magazine at a rate of R4 000 per advertisement, and your rate is R250 for your special bridal room, you will have to sell 16 rooms (R4 000 ÷ R250 = 16) to brides to cover the cost of the advertisement. Bear in mind that most people get married on a Saturday in spring or summer. This might take care of 16 brides in 16 weeks, but will you be able to sell enough rooms during the remaining 36 Saturdays to make a profit on the advertisement? Of course, if your establishment caters especially for brides, with a small wedding chapel and reception hall and even a beauty salon, it could be well worth your while to advertise.

The success of your advertising should be seen in and be measurable by

- more reservations,
- more enquiries,
- better customer awareness,
- better brand awareness, and
- increased profit.

Publicity

Free publicity is when a newspaper or magazine publishes an article and/or photograph of your guest house if the editor of the medium concerned is convinced that it is newsworthy. Publicity has much more credibility than an advertisement, but you will need a strong news angle, such as a unique offer or a national accommodation award, in order to get the editor interested.

'Advertorials' are paid-for advertisements that look like normal editorial articles. These are very effective and are usually more credible than a normal advertisement. Should you place a paid-for advertisement, certain media might be prepared to offer you an advertorial as added value.

Advertisements will always be read with a certain degree of suspicion by readers, whereas a news story is usually taken to be the truth. Free coverage in the media is worth gold to you and gains you the attention of the general public.

Gaining free publicity involves getting the media to report on your business. This can be through any of the following:

* local newspapers,
* city newspapers,
* national newspapers,
* local television,
* national television,
* lifestyle magazines,
* national magazines,
* airline magazines,
* local radio stations, or
* national radio stations.

Many of these will reach a much wider audience than your target market, but this doesn't matter as it doesn't cost you anything, and the wider your media audience, the more credibility you will have.

People-orientated marketing: Personal marketing, networking, previous guests, referrals

Personal marketing

Personal marketing is one of the most effective marketing tools of a guest house because it combines so well with the personal nature of the product. It is time consuming and takes up a lot of energy, but it is highly cost effective and has excellent results. Personal marketing will enable you to make use of the most powerful marketing tool in the industry, word-of-mouth referrals.

It is so successful because it directly addresses the fear and hesitation of people, and they can see for themselves how well you will be able to satisfy their needs and requirements. Personal marketing starts at your own front gate, in your own neighbourhood.

Set time aside to do *direct personal marketing* in companies and organisations that have a regular inflow of possible guests to your area. The best way to make them aware of your services is to invite a few senior personnel of different companies over for a breakfast at your guest house. However, the person who is ultimately responsible for making reservations on behalf of senior personnel in an office is usually the secretary or personal assistant, who would be most likely to make reservations at an establishment that he or she has been to or heard about. Therefore it is also important to invite the secretaries or personal assistants of various companies to your guest house on a separate occasion. Your brochure can play a significant role in supporting your personal marketing activities.

Make use of quiet times over weekends to invite key personnel to stay in your guest house on a complimentary basis and treat them to a luxurious breakfast the next morning, so that they can evaluate your facilities and services on a first-hand basis. Secretaries and personal assistants also often work hard to coordinate reservations for large groups of guests, and a small token of appreciation from you after a substantial reservation would certainly be welcomed. Invite potential customers to your guest house and present the attractions to them so that they are clear about how your establishment will satisfy their needs. Get to know them on a personal level.

Make appointments to go and see or call your potential customers, as identified in your market research. Compile a list of them to establish your own database, which is a very valuable business asset. New guests could also be identified by a telephonic survey of likely sources of business. The chances are excellent that the businesses in your immediate vicinity will be a good source of business for you.

Keep in contact. Remind potential customers regularly that you still exist. Keep your database up to date. The secretary who regularly made reservations with you may have been transferred. Write personally to potential guests (this is known as a direct mail shot). Include your brochure or name card and forward a calendar or sticker with your telephone number on it at Christmas time.

Make sure that everyone in the neighbourhood, including friends and family, knows about your new guest house and think of original ways to show off your guest house. What about arranging a music evening (it may be advisable to do this on a quiet night when your guests will not be bothered by the noise), or a lunch for the local chamber of business committee members?

Famils or familiarisation visits

Famils are a promotional tool used by the tourism industry to increase awareness and promote specific countries, regions, and even individual businesses. They are designed to familiarise potential purchasers such as travel agents or travel writers (to increase public awareness) with an area or business so that over time more people will visit or encourage others to do so.

You can organise a famil for your own guest house, but unless you are a large business, it is unlikely to be successful. For individual businesses, it is probably essential that you are a member of a local tourism association as in this way you can keep in touch with planned famils to your area and try to get included on the next one.

As with any promotional activity, there is a cost. Some of this is time in helping to organise, but there is often a real cost in providing free accommodation, travel or entry to those on the famil. You need to determine what the benefit will be for you and whether it will outweigh the costs. This can be quite difficult to determine with travel writers, as it is unlikely that you will remember to ask people whether an article in a travel magazine was the reason for someone's use of your facility perhaps some time after the article appeared. With travel agents who may book directly through you, it will be easier to assess the returns.

To assist in determining whether it will be worthwhile being involved, ask some of the following questions of the organisers:

* Will they provide a profile of those on the famil, including their current business, to assess the likely benefit of your involvement?
* Are they appropriate for your market?
* What will you be expected to provide?
* When and where will any articles be published?
* What other businesses are part of the famil and how does this influence your decision?

Just as in any other promotional activity, you need to determine whether famils should be a part of your promotion. You will probably need to make individual decisions on each one, as they are bound to be different.

Networking

Be an active member of your local tourism and guest house associations, as this will keep you informed about developments that could affect your business. Should a major event such as a sporting tournament or international conference take place in the area, your guest house will automatically be considered for accommodation placements, as you will already be on the database.

Members of a guest house association often refer their guest overflow to other members. This is particularly valuable when you start your business and are not yet well known. Remember that it is usual for members to charge each other a 10 per cent commission for such referrals, as a contribution towards marketing expenses. They will provide support and invaluable information about the industry and market in the area. Membership of a respected organisation will reassure potential guests about your standards and level of service.

A group of guest houses can promote themselves together by producing a combined brochure, website or advertisement, making advertising cheaper for all. They can also arrange a guest house morning and combine their personal marketing efforts. They can exhibit together at major tourism trade fairs, sharing costs that may be too high for a single guest house.

They not only offer a wider and better choice to guests and a more comprehensive product, but more rooms than a single guest house. This can accommodate larger groups and increase your market share by competing with other accommodation providers for conference delegates or tour groups.

You will become well known in the tourism industry in your area and will get to know other tourism service providers, who may all be in a position to refer business to you, while you can add value to your services by referring your guests to them in return.

A group of guest houses has more negotiating power than a single guest house in matters relating to the industry, by negotiating discounted rates on credit card commissions with major banks, for instance. You will find out about special suppliers and services to the industry, which could save you money. For example, safety and security information about payment bilkers or fraudsters is circulated amongst members.

Referrals

The objective is to link with existing tour operators in your region in order to gain additional business, as most tourism businesses are great sources of referrals for complementary business.

There are three instances where you can link with other tourist-oriented businesses:

* Link with other accommodation providers or event providers that are less than one day's drive away; that is, hotels, motels, adventure companies, rental car companies, etc. Display their flyers, and ask them to distribute yours. Get them to stamp the back of your brochure with their company stamp, and include some incentive in the brochure (e.g. a free souvenir). Count how many brochures come back and continue to use those businesses that provide the best referrals.
* Develop a relationship with tour operators, taxi drivers and information centres. It is essential that these people have experienced your establishment so they can recommend you when the opportunity arises. This requires your giving them some vouchers or inviting them for a champagne breakfast, for example, so they can do this. As you are not likely to be referring business back to them, you need to establish an incentive scheme to reward them for the referrals. For example, for every 20 customers they refer, they get a free meal at a local restaurant or a bottle of wine. How do you know who referred the customers? When you get tourists in, you can ask them how they found out about you. The reward scheme is very important as it provides good motivation for the referrer and creates a win/win situation.
* Of course the ultimate tourist operator is the tour bus driver. If you can convince him or her (or whoever makes the decision) to regularly stop their bus at your guest house, referring overflow guests to nearby guest houses, you will have a captive market. Often you will have to provide a commission for them to do this. This might be a certain amount per passenger or a percentage of the passenger spend at your business. Whether or not it is commercially feasible for you to pay this commission depends on what other forms of promotion you would have to pay for to get other customers.

You can assess the success of each of these tactics by recording the amount of business they bring in. You then need to make sure the tactic is cost effective. For example: A tour bus company charges you a flat commission of R5.00 a head for their buses to stop at your business. Say your average cost per person to provide a service such as a snack is R25.00 and your gross profit margin is 33 per cent. You make a gross profit of R8.25; less the R5.00 commission, this equals R3.25. We suggest this represents a lot of hard work for a relatively small return. To improve your return, you could try renegotiating the commission, try to increase the average spend, or work on improving your net profit margin. If none of these is successful, you should look to see if there are other promotional tactics available to you.

Clusters

The idea of similar businesses getting together with the idea of joining forces to improve their business performance is not a new one, but it has not been tried to any great extent in the tourism industry until now.

What is a 'cluster'?

The concept can be developed in a number of different ways:

* Similar guest houses can get together to pool their product and market it with the benefit of being able to target larger markets than they could individually.

- Complementary businesses involved in different stages of a product or service process – from accommodation to tour guiding – cooperate to provide a more cost-effective and potentially higher quality end product.
- Like-minded businesses cooperate to identify new products or markets that individually they would not be able to do.

A key benefit for many small businesses is that a cluster enables them to operate like a large company, while retaining the benefits of a small one.

How does a cluster work for accommodation businesses?

There are already some examples, with visitor attractions in the same city marketing under one banner. Specific sectors such as the convention sector cooperate to market a city. At present most of the clustering, whether formal or informal, seems to revolve around marketing.

Starting a tourism cluster

Initially there has to be a recognition by businesses that there are benefits in working together.

Key questions include the following:

- What disadvantages are there for me as a small business that the development of a tourism cluster could address (e.g. small marketing budget, narrow product range, short season, limited public awareness)?
- Can I identify other businesses that could help me to overcome some of the disadvantages?
- Do they match my guest house in terms of quality, size, markets, pricing, desire to grow, etc?
- What specific advantages will there be for my business and is clustering the only way to achieve them?

Once you have dealt with these, you are on your way and now need to address the structure of the cluster and how it will operate. You will probably need at the minimum an exchange of letters between the businesses involved outlining the rules of the cluster. It may even be appropriate to set up a new legal entity (e.g. a company, or an incorporated society) which participants belong to. A business plan outlining what the expectations are for the cluster will need to be prepared and results monitored.

Previous guests

Do not forget your satisfied previous guests; you should focus on getting more business from them. They tend to spend more, and they tend to be less price sensitive once they have had a good experience with you. In addition, they can refer other business to you, and less time and effort is required on your part. Think of them as a lifelong investment worth thousands, as a happy previous customer is worth his or her weight in gold.

Keep in touch with them through direct mail and a regular newsletter. Remember their needs and let them know when a special offer may be particularly interesting to them, such as an offer of free accommodation on a Sunday night to regular business guests.

Reward loyalty with room upgrades at no extra cost or some other thoughtful gesture.

Celebrities

Do you know any celebrities (even minor ones like the local sports star)? If you don't know any, ring up an agent who coordinates speaking or appearance functions for celebrities and pay for one to visit your premises. If possible, get the celebrity for free (they also like the publicity) or provide him or her with free product and services (not cash). An example might be a regional sports captain or your local representative player of a national sports team. Arrange for the celebrity to be on your premises on a certain day for a certain time. Then do the following:

* Send out flyers to all the local sports clubs.
* Promote a free photo with the celebrity (or make a small charge to cover costs).
* Offer prizes signed by the celebrity (entry conditional on a purchase).
* Follow up every entry form with an invitation to join the Customer Club.
* Advertise in the local papers when the celebrity will be at your premises.
* Notify as many organisations as possible that may wish to send their members to your premises to visit the celebrity, such as sports clubs or local businesses.
* Announce the celebrity in your newsletter.
* Arrange a joint venture with another business that has a large database, such as a local bookseller, computer shop, or jeweller. This other business can then provide products to on-sell at your premises and assist with any costs.
* Ring people on the day to remind them to attend.
* Send a press release to the local papers about the visit, hoping the story will be printed on the day the celebrity arrives. If not, take a photo of the celebrity at your premises and send the press release again about his or her visit.

You may have noticed that this sales promotion has integrated a number of methods into one. In other words, the sales promotion that uses a celebrity 'on-site' also covers direct mail, telemarketing, joint ventures, press releases, word of mouth, window displays and advertising.

Another version could be to offer your guest house as the location for a television shoot of a popular programme.

Outside marketing sources: Marketing, reservation and travel agents, exhibitions

Agents

There are a number of central reservation organisations, many of them internet-based. This is also a well-known concept abroad. They normally advertise widely, have a solid client base, and undertake marketing actions that may not be feasible for the individual guest house owner. They may, for example, be able to market for large tour groups that cannot be accommodated in only one guest house.

Agents normally charge a *commission* of between 10 and 20 per cent on reservations made, and impose a variety of conditions on associated guest houses. These conditions range from requiring national accreditation as a minimum standard to undergoing personal inspection, and sometimes the guest house is prevented from recruiting business on its own initiative.

Make sure that you are dealing with a reputable agent. Are you comfortable with the conditions, the commission charged, and possibly an annual fee? Does the agent specialise in your type of establishment? Would the agent protect your interests?

A relationship of trust is essential. No agent can fill all your beds every month, but they can make a substantial contribution from time to time.

However, be careful of agents or agencies with no minimum requirements. They are not primarily concerned with the interests of the customer, and you may find yourself associated with an inferior type of establishment. It is also not acceptable for an agent to impose the requirement that you pay commission on all the business that you get, whether referred by the agent or recruited by yourself.

Although an agent should recommend acceptable rates – after all, how can they sell your beds if your rates are not market-related – and you should heed their advice, too severe limits on what you may ask are not acceptable.

Travel agents are a vital part of the tourism industry and will be able to channel many customers to you. Many large companies have in-house travel agents that could be a fruitful source of business for you. They require excellent and fast service, and a minimum commission of 10 per cent.

Remember that you are a very small fish compared to the hotels. Should you do business with a large travel agency, be prepared to wait for payment – three months is not unusual, because they also often receive payment only after two months. Take note that travel agents demand the same rate as your other clients. This is your so-called *rack rate*. It is unacceptable to ask agents to add their commission onto your rate (and in fact illegal in many parts of the world) and places them in an invidious position with regard to the guests they send to you. Commission is an excellent marketing expenditure, as you pay only for actual business received. Pay it promptly, and you will be rewarded with regular referrals. Commission is normally charged on bed and breakfast only, and not on other meals or services.

Exhibitions and shows

There are many and varied tourism and holiday shows annually all over South Africa as well as abroad. Exhibiting at a show that targets your specific target market may be well worth your while. An added value of taking part is the contacts that you will build up over the years. Exhibiting at a trade show can not only be time consuming but also costly. As a result, it is wise to make sure that the trade show will be worth your while, in terms of the quantity and quality of the attendees. It is expensive, and it is recommended that you join forces with other guest houses to share the costs and the long hours of stand duty.

Most local provincial tourism authorities take part in these shows. Find out whether they will market your guest house for you and, even better, if you could join them on their stand or have a table at a reduced cost. Make sure your details are included in their publicity material for the show.

Successful marketing at a show is not only about waiting for interested people to come to you but also about actively seeking out potential clients, such as travel agents also exhibiting. Remember that all trade show business would mean that you would have to pay commission on business flowing from agents. Making contacts at trade shows does little good if you don't follow up on leads properly. Consider establishing a lead-tracking system; such systems provide broadened prospects and customer bases, higher lead-to-sales ratios, and enhanced market analyses.

Designing your exhibition space

The design depends on several factors, not the least of which will be location. Location is an all-important consideration and can mean the difference between success and failure at a trade show, which explains the wide price range among booths at most large shows.

If you're unfamiliar with the exhibition hall, consult show management and choose a location according to price, paying the most you can afford. A smaller stand in a prime location will produce more results than a large stand in an obscure corner. According to industry experts, stand location is a factor responsible for at least 50 per cent of overall success.

However you design your stand, the design must catch the eye. You only have a few seconds to attract the attention of those passing.

Effective exhibition, of course, is the result of meticulous planning that begins weeks – perhaps months – before the show begins. Make sure you have enough copies of your brochures and/or leaflets and that your pull-out banners are finished. These are excellent to use as they can be easily set up anywhere and are portable and not too expensive. They also save time in setting up an attractive stand.

During the show, keep an eye on activity; notice what works and what doesn't. Be flexible and make changes as they become necessary. While your employees work, take frequent tours of the show, observing other exhibitors' displays and marketing techniques, the degree of interest they seem to be generating, their location, and the interaction between booth workers and visitors, for instance. Jot down your observations and immediately use any new ideas you get. You can also use these notes in planning your attendance at upcoming exhibitions.

After the show, compare your objectives with the results in a meeting with employees, as well as an internal company report. Did you reach your goals and stay within your budget? Was it the right show for your market? Did you target that market effectively? Were your exhibit and its location effective? Did you have too little or too much space? Only by analysing these and similar factors can you adequately judge whether to exhibit at the same show again and, if so, how to improve your results.

Start planning next year's show while this year's exhibition is fresh in your mind. For example, plan to rent a better space at a more strategic location, keeping in mind the show's traffic patterns, or change marketing collateral such as your banners, posters or brochures.

Quality assurance: Star-grading, association memberships, competitions

Star-grading

To reassure your potential guests about the quality of your guest house and the experience they will enjoy there, quality assurance is a vital tool to use. It may not get you business on its own, but you may and will lose business if you do not have it. To domestic and international visitors it is a well-known and instantly recognisable sign of your quality. A good grading gives you a competitive edge. Use it in all your other promotional material.

Membership of a local association

Belonging to a local association also gives you standing and credibility as a serious business and not a fly-by-night operator. It is another important tool to reassure guests of the wisdom of their choice in booking with you.

Competitions and awards

Your guest house would benefit from receiving an award in a local or national accommodation competition. Apart from the publicity that you would receive, you could use the accolade positively in your own marketing activities in order to convince potential guests of the excellent accommodation you are offering.

The annual AA Travel Guides and American Express Accommodation Awards programme is an example of such a competition. As a small business, you would find it difficult to afford the type of publicity that you would get from becoming a finalist. The entry form explains the benefits.

> ### Benefits of being in the awards programme
>
> Firstly, you will benefit hugely if you get your staff involved. When they have a goal to strive towards you will find everyone trying harder than usual to attain that goal. Secondly, we send you your scores and guest comments at the end of the programme, so you have priceless management information, which can assist you in running your business. Thirdly, should you become a semi-finalist or better, you will benefit a great deal from the PR we will do on your behalf. Our PR company sends press releases to regional and national newspapers, radio & TV stations and other media on a regular basis, especially after the announcement of semi-finalists, finalists and after the awards dinner. They also arrange promotions in major magazines throughout the year that benefit those who have attained semi-finalist status or better. Fourthly, you will benefit because you will be able to market your establishment as being a semi-finalist or better in a prestigious and trusted Awards Programme. Lastly, and most importantly, you have a chance to appear in the 'South Africa's Best' publication. We print 200 000 copies of this publication, distributed through various channels, including travel trade and consumer shows, via the establishments appearing in it and through the missions of the Department of Foreign Affairs.
> Source: Quoted from *AA Travel Guides*

In this competition, guests are asked their impressions of the guest house, ranging from bad to excellent, on the physical facilities and the quality of the service rendered to them. The questions in a nutshell embody your product and show what hospitality and a guest house are about. The answers would provide invaluable feedback to you about areas where you need to improve.

The following areas, among others, are addressed in the questions asked:

❀ Experience versus expectations (promising more than you deliver or delivering more than you promised in your marketing; quality and honesty of your brochures, website, and advertisements).
❀ Value for money (the most important selling point for success).

- The ambience and décor, comfort and functionality of the rooms, quality of furniture and fabrics like towels and linen (how well did you plan in the initial phases?).
- Cleanliness of interiors and exteriors, maintenance, working order of appliances and security (efficient management).
- Quality of food and beverages served, as well as the catering service itself.
- Efficiency of check-in/out, friendliness of staff and general knowledge of staff about the area.
- The importance of word-of-mouth recommendations in marketing.

It is quite clear that a high score in all these aspects indicates a well-run, well-planned and pleasant guest house, offering excellent accommodation and value for money that cannot fail to impress a potential guest as well as reassure him or her of the wisdom of making a reservation with you. Of course, it also capitalises on the word-of-mouth method of marketing, as the results are based on the experiences of guests who actually stayed at the guest house.

Promotional strategies

Sales promotions

The use of sales promotions, especially during slow business times, can be very effective. You can offer a special discount, for example for children travelling with their parents, or you can arrange for the partner of a regular client to stay over free for a weekend. Alternatively, you can offer increased value, such as free champagne at a special brunch on Sunday morning.

A sales promotion is anything that gets the customer involved in your premises, such as competitions, active displays, giveaways, special discounts, etc. The key concept is to involve customers actively by getting them to do something, like fill out an entry form for a competition, instead of having them listen passively to, or glance at, an advertisement.

There are a number of sales promotions you can run, and these should be integrated with your other promotions. Each promotion is a once-off exercise, but can be repeated as many times as you wish. This kind of promotion should have a time limit and should not run for ever.

Try to find promotional ideas that you can use with lower acquisition costs; that is, tactics that cost you less than R5.00 to attract each customer.

Signage

This needs to be big and bold with simple lettering so people have no trouble reading it. You often don't have to include the name of your premises, just a couple of words describing what you do is sufficient.

But try to build in some competitive advantage if you can. Why not prefix all your signage with some adjective such as 'great', 'awesome', 'unparalleled' etc. (for example: 'Hearty breakfast')?

The way these messages are displayed depends on the way your building is designed, its relationship to the street, whether or not you have lots of window or wall space, and any council restrictions on signage. Generally speaking, you should place the sign perpendicular to the street so passing traffic will view it head on. If you are open at night, the signage needs to be well lit, either by neon, backlighting or spot lighting. There is no point in having a great sign if people can't read it! (The legal requirements for signage are discussed in chapter 9.)

Tourist guidebooks

There will be a range of tourist guides available for potential customers to read about you and your business. The most cost-effective tourist guide exposure is where you are reviewed and recommended in the guide for free. Identify guidebooks or newspapers that do reviews and ask them to include your guest house. Offer reviewers a familiarisation visit and make absolutely sure they enjoy themselves. Sometimes the reviewer turns up unannounced, in which case you can only hope he or she has a pleasurable experience.

These reviews are more effective than advertisements, as they are a supposedly unbiased guide and recommendation. Some tourists make their decisions based solely on these recommendations in books (such as *Lonely Planet, Let's Go* etc.).

If a review is not an option, you will have to pay to advertise. The rules for tourist guide advertisments are similar to those for tourist brochures: use full colour or spot colour. It will cost you twice as much, but you more than double the probability of its being read.

Direct mail

Direct mail can be productive if you first target and segment your market. The more successful your targeting, the more cost effective and productive your direct mail campaign is likely to be.

How do you begin?

Analyse the type of people who stay with you, or who are most likely to buy from you in the future. Are they of a similar age? Do they live in a definable area, have similar jobs, hobbies, etc? Are they married or single? Answering these questions is called 'segmenting the market' – splitting the total market into small segments. The reason for this exercise is obvious: it allows you to concentrate maximum effort on the right people.

Targeting means approaching only the customers you've identified using segmentation. If you decide, for example, that your prime customers are likely to be professional women in the 30 to 45 age group, your direct mail campaign becomes much easier and more cost effective. So now you need to find out where these people live or work. Your own sales records should provide a starting point.

To get started, you should therefore

✿ build a customer profile based on existing customers, and
✿ find out where there are more people like your existing customers.

Ideas for building a list quickly

You can rent a list of people's names from various list brokers or contact the Direct Marketing Association for help. These organisations collect names and addresses from sources of all types. This option costs money, so make sure the list you rent is relevant and up to date. Ask to speak to a previous renter of the list so that you can obtain their opinion on its efficacy.

Draw up your own list through existing contacts, lawyers, accountants, family, friends etc.

Other sources include business directories. Don't neglect newspapers (for example, advertisers, classifieds, engagement notices). In all cases involving lists, however, remember that you must respect privacy requirements.

Summary

- ❀ Every business, large or small, can use direct marketing.
- ❀ Direct mail is the most common form of direct marketing.
- ❀ To get started, you need first to develop a list of names.
- ❀ It's cheaper and more efficient to collect names yourself.

Local organisations

Get involved with local organisations that have your target market as a member base, such as sports clubs and community groups. Donate your time or product and services to help these organisations. Display their posters or membership details at your premises. Sell their raffle tickets at your premises or provide prizes for them to raffle to help with their fund-raising.

Ask your staff what organisations they belong to. If one of these is appropriate, support it. Not only will the organisation be happy, so will your staff member (and you can get him or her to do all the liaising and coordinating).

Donating to charities

Give something back to the community you live in. But get some mileage out of it through some acknowledgement in their newsletter, free advertising in their in-house newsletter or a press release from them to the media praising your virtues.

Writing a tip column for the local press

Contact the local newspapers to see whether they are interested in having a regular restaurant/café/bar column (once a month would be fine). This will make you better known and will help you develop a reputation as an expert, which will have a positive effect on your guest house.

Attending seminars

By attending seminars you get to talk to all the other participants during the breaks. You may be able to introduce your business to the group. Select a seminar that your target market will be attending (like business seminars or Business after Five networks).

Sponsorships

Sponsorship of local events such as a charity golf game can be effective in making your guest house known. The same applies to sporting contests and promotional items such as T-shirts, pens, calendars or banners. You could also offer an award to the guest or the agent making the booking, such as a free upgrade for loyal or regular customers, or a gift such as a pen or keyring bearing your name and contact details.

Evaluate your progress: Troubleshooting

The criteria discussed here will help you to establish whether your guest house is successful or not and what issues to address in your marketing and promotional plans.

Imagine that in a few months from now your guest house is up and running. Guests are enjoying their stay and are returning or referring others to your establishment. You may also be starting to make an adequate profit. The danger is that you could now become complacent and over-confident about your success. Be aware that running your own business is always a risk and that nothing ever remains the same. The guest house and tourism industries are particularly lively, if not volatile, and change is inherent to these industries. The competition is tough and unforgiving.

Constantly take note of new opportunities or new threats, of what your competitors are doing, and of changes in the market. *Reassess your position at regular intervals*, even though you may currently be enjoying success. Check up on all the aspects that you examined when you did your initial market research.

If you do not keep abreast of all the factors that could influence your business, you could find that your occupation levels are decreasing and regular guests are staying away. How do you determine the problem, and where do you start to correct matters?

The following checklist points to potential problems and what you can do to rectify the situation.

- ✿ *Location:* There is not a great deal that can be done about an unsuitable location at this stage. Your best option is probably to ensure that your guest house becomes an attraction on its own, either by offering a special service or facility such as a small conference venue, or by offering unbeatable value for money, or by creating an exceptional environment so that potential clients will ignore the inconveniences of your location.
- ✿ *Service:* Bad or indifferent service chases customers away. Go through all the elements of your service and run a refresher course for the service providers in your establishment. Ensure that your service is of the highest possible standard.
- ✿ *Facilities:* Ensure that your facilities keep up with those of your competitors and with your clients' needs and expectations. Cast a critical eye over every aspect of your guest house and replace/update/refresh anything tired or worn.
- ✿ *Marketing:* Pay attention to your marketing. You may have neglected it and are now paying the price, or may have spent too much on ineffective methods or advertising. Remember that people will forget about your establishment unless you remind them, and that your competitors may be marketing very actively. Re-establish contact with your old guests and re-evaluate your marketing plan. Do your market research again to ensure that you are not missing any significant changes in the market or in your clients' needs.

How do you know that your guest house and your marketing are succeeding?

- ✿ *Word-of-mouth marketing* by satisfied guests is still the most successful marketing tool for a guest house, but it usually does not work that well within the first two years – it takes most guest houses approximately two years to get established in the market. Word of mouth is the best and cheapest form of marketing available, so make sure that you give each and every guest a wonderful experience at your guest house.
- ✿ The most certain way to establish whether you are successful or not is to see whether your *guests remain loyal* to you, and return time and time again to your guest house.
- ✿ The second proof of success is that you manage to *retain your competent, trained staff*.
- ✿ Finally, you will know that you are successful when you are making a satisfying profit from your business as planned.

Legal
and other
requirements

Introduction

There are legal and other statutory requirements for setting up your guest house and for its daily running that you will have to comply with. Please note that the contents of this chapter are indicative only of the requirements that may apply to you. We recommend that you contact your lawyer for further and more specific advice relating to your own individual situation. The legal requirements may change from time to time.

Local land-use regulations

Before converting an existing property into a guest house, it is important to establish what local requirements there are regarding application procedures to use your property as a guest house. The prescribed professional town planner fees involved in lodging a rezoning or a consent use application – whichever is applicable in your case – should be taken into account. Contact the town planning section of your local authority for full details of their requirements and to establish whether the town planning scheme permits the activity on the site you have chosen, as these may differ from town to town.

To change the land-use conditions, the following may be required:

❁ You may be required to advise your neighbours of your intentions and to take note of their complaints and objections. However, they must motivate their complaints and give reasons for their objections. It is suggested that you tactfully reassure them that your plans will not have a negative effect on their properties or lifestyles but may in fact be beneficial to the area, as you will be improving the property substantially and working from home means there is someone in the area all day.

❁ You will have to provide reasons for the change in land-use restrictions.
❁ Other parties involved can also object in writing.
❁ You may have to submit the title deeds, prints of the locality plan, the rezoning plan, and a copy of the legally required advertisement.
❁ The parking arrangements and layout and access to the guest house must be finalised with the city engineer according to the requirements of parking areas for the number of guest rooms in your guest house.
❁ Your mortgage conditions may require you to obtain the consent of the mortgage holder for the change of use of the house.
❁ Substantial structural changes will require building approval.
❁ The establishment of a new enterprise in which the present land use is substantially changed may require a scoping report to be prepared in terms of the National Environmental Management Act (107 of 1998). The Provincial Department of Agriculture and Environmental Affairs should be consulted in this regard.
❁ In the case of the establishment of a Special Consent in terms of the Planning and Development Act (5 of 1998) permission must be obtained from the local council prior to establishment.

You will also need compliance with local authority regulations regarding building regulations, a fire safety certificate, and a certificate of compliance for food preparation from the Health Department.

Signage requirements

If your guest house has been zoned, you generally do not need permission to put up a sign. However, if you wish to erect a road sign advertising your business in the road reserve area (as distinct from on your own property), you will need approval from

* the Department of Transport in the case of national roads,
* the Facility Signs Committee in the Provincial Department of Transport in the case of secondary roads, or
* the local municipal engineer in the case of local roads within a local council area.

A licence to carry on a business

In terms of Schedule 1 of the Business Act 71 of 1991, you have to apply for a licence if you sell or supply any foodstuffs in the form of meals for consumption on or off the guest house's premises. The relevant *Provincial Gazette* governs the operation of this act in each of South Africa's provinces, and therefore the requirements, charges and renewal procedures will differ from region to region.

In all areas, you must apply to the local council for a trading licence. Your application for a trading licence will be circulated by the local council to the health, fire and building inspectors, the town planning department, and in some cases the Development Services Board (DSB). These bodies will ensure that your plans comply with their regulations before the application can be approved. This can take a few weeks to complete. You are advised to contact your local municipality for information about the exact details applicable.

Approach the town planning department of the local council for permission to go ahead with your plans.

Tax considerations

As each business structure is different, we recommend that you get expert advice on your legal tax obligations and required structures. Your guest house must be registered with the Receiver of Revenue as

* a taxpayer to pay the required tax on the income,
* an employer, for the collection of employees' tax, and
* a vendor, for value-added tax (VAT) registration if the turnover justifies it.

Keep full records for tax purposes of proof of all your income as well as expenses:

* all credit notes,
* bank statements,
* deposit slips,
* paid cheques,
* payments received, including cash,
* wages paid,
* supplies and equipment bought,
* financial expenses in running the guest house, professional fees paid, etc., and
* VAT paid.

Value-added tax

Discuss the pros and cons of registering for VAT with your accountant before starting to build or convert your property and before you start buying anything for the guest house.

If you pay VAT, you will have to issue VAT invoices to your guests. Note that the rate and amount charged may be different depending on the length of stay. Your VAT invoice must contain the following:

❀ the words 'tax invoice' printed prominently on the invoice,
❀ the name, address and your VAT registration number,
❀ the date of the invoice,
❀ an individualised serial number of the invoice,
❀ the description of the services and accommodation supplied as well as the quantity,
❀ the VAT amount, or statement that VAT is included in the price and the rate at which it was charged, and
❀ the name and address of the recipient.

Below is an example of a VAT invoice:

Wind in the Willows

Address 62 Willow Lane, Willowmore 1234

PO Box 3300 Willowmore

Tel 0432 44 543   **Fax** 0432 44 542

Email windwillow@guesthouse.co.za
Website www.windwillow.co.za

TAX INVOICE

Dr H van der Merwe

Check-in date: 15 Sep 2009

Check-out date: 18 Sep 2009

Reservation 5280

Confirmation date: 4 May 2009

Guest/group ID: VM

Home phone:

Business phone: 085 111 111

Fax: 099 338 1111

Tax ID/VAT #

Vat number 4750208540

VAT TAX INVOICE 1759		Charges	Credits
16/09/09	Deposit		R100
16/09/09	One night at R250.00 per night	R250.00	
16/09/09	Value added tax (14%)	R35.00	
Statement totals		R185.00	
Balance due		R185.00	

Payment can be made into the following bank account:

Wind in the Willows Guest House cc

National Bank

Lynnwood Branch 123 456

Account No.: 456 789 000

Kindly fax through a copy of the deposit slip for our records.

Thank you for staying with us.

Kind regards,

Peter Jones

Wind in the Willows Guest House

Public liability insurance

A personal domestic insurance policy is of no use for your guest house when it is no longer purely a private residence. Your domestic policy will not cover you. Before you receive your first guest, you need to take out special insurance cover. This is not an area where you should try to make any savings, because you cannot afford not to have insurance. A disaster or a personal claim can close your business down. You are also required to have appropriate public liability insurance in place if you want to be star graded.

You can be held liable for claims against you, for example, if

- ❁ your food and beverages cause illness to your guests, such as food poisoning, as it is a condition that your food should be fit for consumption;
- ❁ your guests get hurt on the premises, for example if a guest slips on a wet floor or falls down steps due to bad lighting or a blown bulb;
- ❁ something is stolen from the guest, or
- ❁ one of your employees injures the guest or damages his or her property, for example by burning clothes when ironing them or spilling coffee on a guest's shirt.

Recommendations for public liability insurance requirements

Correct and adequate liability insurance means that it is designed specifically for a guest house. Adequate cover is dependent on the profile of the guests of your guest house. If you have mostly foreign guests, the limit of the liability insurance should be as high as is available but certainly no less than at least R25 million.

There are specialised tailor-made insurance policies available for the guest house and B&B industry, designed in cooperation with the national associations, which can be recommended. Your policy will need to cover the following:

Contents insurance

Your contents insurance must be designed to recognise that the establishment is a guest house and not a private home. A specialist policy will recognise that such requirements as 'forcible and violent entry' are almost impossible to comply with, given that guests come and go at all hours. In addition, it is imperative that the policy covers such eventualities as 'bilking' – when guests disappear without paying.

Many establishment owners also have a commercial-type policy issued when they as owners also live on the premises. This means that they lose all the cover they would require for their personal situation and also do not have all the extensions required in the specialised business of running a guest house.

Loss of revenue insurance

Your loss of revenue insurance must cater for the many risks of a guest house. There are many different ways in which a guest house can stop operating. Apart from the usual risks of fire, storm and flood a multitude of other risks are associated with a guest house. Examples are murder, rape, suicide, traumatic event, death of a spouse, failure of essential equipment, contagious diseases, staff stay-aways, or hospitalisation of a key member such as a spouse or manager.

Licences and permits

Operating licence or permit for operating a public transport service

If you want to offer a transport service to your guests for payment, you should apply for the necessary permit or operating licence in terms of the National Land Transport Transition Act 22 of 2000. Application for the transportation of guests within a specific province should be made to the Public Transport Licensing Board of the province in which the guests will be transported. Without this licence, you will not be covered against any third party claims in the event of an accident.

An operating licence is not necessary if you provide a courtesy or free service for your guests using your own vehicle. However, you must have passenger liability insurance in place if you are transporting guests. The driver will be required to hold a special driver's licence and the vehicle must have a special permit.

193

Liquor licence

The Liquor Act of 1989 prescribes that an establishment that provides accommodation for payment and keeps or displays liquor with the intent to sell or offer to guests must hold a liquor licence, irrespective of whether the liquor is sold or offered free of charge or is otherwise included in the price of accommodation or meals. Such a licence must also be issued in the name of the current owner. The Act makes provision for heavy penalties of a fine up to R100 000 in the event of non-compliance.

You must therefore have a liquor licence to sell liquor, and this applies even if you only intend serving complimentary drinks. The application process is fairly complicated and lengthy. It is recommended that you use a lawyer specialising in this field to assist you. Bear in mind that it is expensive for a small establishment, and it may not be worth your while financially to offer the service and to pay for the licence.

Television and satellite licences

As a business, you need a licence for every television set in every guest room and elsewhere on the property, as well as a special agreement for satellite coverage in the rooms. Contact your service providers for the details, depending on the service you want to provide.

Smoking laws

You must abide by the non-smoking laws. Smoking may be allowed only in specifically designated areas and not in public areas such as the guest dining room. Signs must be displayed.

SAMRO licence to play music

If you play music in your guest house by means of a radio, television or CD/DVD player, you will have to apply for a licence from the South African Music Rights Organisation (SAMRO) in Pretoria, as it is regarded as a public performance.

Quality assurance requirements

Star grading by the Tourism Grading Council of South Africa is obligatory if you want to be involved in providing accommodation for major international events, such as a world cup sports tournament. In addition, all government departments are required to procure accommodation from graded establishments only. It is therefore clear that you will lose business if you are not graded.

You are strongly advised to get a grading, as it provides clear guidelines to you as owner of what you are expected to provide. With growing international tourism, it is important to confirm your level of standards by means of the star grading system. It assures potential guests of what they can expect, and it is a useful marketing tool.

The facilities and services requirements for star grading provide a useful checklist for what you offer in your own guest house. However, if you follow the guidelines for setting up your guest house and the required services in chapters 3 and 5, you will meet, if not exceed, the grading standards.

The Basic Conditions of Employment Act

When you employ staff, you need to take note of the conditions of employment and, as the hours of work in a guest house – late evenings, weekends and so forth – differ considerably from a domestic house, it is most important that you are aware of your legal obligations. Employers are saddled with the responsibility of complying with the provisions of the legislation applicable to the labour market and, more often than not, carry the responsibility in disputes to show and prove that they have done so. Ignorance of the law will not be an excuse, and the sooner employers comply with this legislation, the sooner they will be able to protect themselves as well.

The Basic Conditions of Employment Act (BCEA) determines and prescribes minimum standards with regard to the employee's conditions of employment. Employers cannot contract themselves out of these provisions, even with the consent of the employee. The following guidelines for some of the important standards should be considered:

Definition of an employee: The Act's broad definition of an employee includes any person who assists in carrying out or conducting the business of an employer or who works for another person and who receives or is entitled to receive any remuneration. An employee who works more than 24 hours per month enjoys all the protection and minimum standards set by the Act, and employers should be careful of words like 'casual' and 'temporary' when categorising an employee, as the Act does not use these descriptions.

Hours of work: An employee can be requested to work no more than 45 hours of normal time and 10 hours of overtime during a week (Monday to Saturday). Saturday is a normal working day, but Sundays are regarded as different. Work on Sundays is remunerated at double the normal rate of pay, unless the business is normally operating on a Sunday, in which case the rate of pay is one-and-a-half times the normal rate of pay. Employees are not allowed to work seven days a week and must enjoy at least one break of 36 hours per week or 72 hours every fortnight. Public holidays are remunerated at double the rate of normal time.

Overtime: Overtime is worked voluntarily and unless an employer contractually binds (as a general rule) an employee to work overtime on request, the employee has the option to refuse.

Annual leave: 21 calendar days or the number of working days normally worked in a three-week period, or one day for every 17 days worked (normally used for fixed-term employees).

Sick leave: In the first six months it is one day per month and thereafter it is 30 or 36 days (number of working days in a normal six-week period $30 = 6 \times 5$, $36 = 6 \times 6$) in a three-year cycle starting from the first day of employment.

Family responsibility leave (for compassionate reasons): three days per year in total for any of the following reasons: death in the direct family, paternity leave, child being sick.

Maternity leave: four months' unpaid leave. Employee may not work four weeks prior to and six weeks after the birth.

Notice periods: one week for employment of less than six months, two weeks for employment of less than one year and four weeks for employment of longer than one year.

Payslip/deductions: Employees must be issued with payslips indicating the various monies earned as well as any deductions made. Please note that you may not deduct any money from an employee's salary without written permission, unless permitted by law (e.g. UIF) to do so.

Contract of employment: You must provide your employees with contracts that reflect the agreement between you in terms of these conditions of employment. Remember that you carry the onus of proof in any dispute about conditions of employment.

Registers: Employers must have a time register, indicating days and hours worked (with signatures), lunch and any leave taken.

The new employee form below captures essential employee information:

New employee personal information			
General information		**Family information**	
Surname		**Father**	
		Name	
Initials		Surname	
		Cell number	
First names		Address	
Address			
		Mother	
		Name	
		Surname	
Tel. number		Cell number	
		Address	
Cell number			
I.D. number			
		Other	
Date of birth		Name	
		Cell number	
Licence code		Relation	
Bank account details		Name	
Name		Cell number	
Bank		Relation	
Branch code			
Account no.		Name	
Type of acc.		Cell number	
		Relation	

The summary attempts only to provide you, as an employer, with a bird's-eye view of these topics covered by the Act. Employers must obtain copies of the Act, and it is recommended that you consult a labour law specialist before making any decisions, for example when terminating the appointment of a staff member, as mistakes could be costly.

The Labour Relations Act

The Labour Relations Act (LRA) regulates the relationship in the workplace and the processes involved in dealing with disputes.

Employee rights: Employees have the right to join trade unions, to strike and to be represented in most matters dealt with under this Act. Employees have the right not to be unfairly dismissed and not to be discriminated against.

Dismissals: Three forms of dismissal are recognised by the LRA. These are for misconduct, incapacity due to ill-health/injury or poor performance and operational requirements (e.g. retrenchment).

Determining the fairness of a dismissal: All dismissals are judged on two aspects, namely substance and process. The LRA clearly prescribes certain procedures that need to be complied with should an employer wish to terminate any contract of employment. In cases of misconduct, the employer has to conduct a disciplinary hearing in accordance with the rules determined in the Act before the contract may be terminated. Dismissal for first-time offences is allowed only in serious cases, for example theft, assault and serious insubordination. In cases of incapacity and operational requirements, the procedures are based on consultation, again in accordance with very specific rules laid down by the Act. In every instance, the employer needs to show that he or she has complied with the procedural requirements and has a fair, substantive reason to dismiss the employee.

Onus of proof: Once cause for dismissal has been proved by the employee, the onus is on the employer to show that the dismissal was fair in procedure and substance. The CCMA (Commission for Conciliation, Mediation and Arbitration) or Labour Court may award up to 12 months of salary as compensation for an employee, should they rule that the employer has not proven the fairness of the dismissal, whether substantially or procedurally.

Disciplinary hearing: The employee needs to be notified of his rights and the charges against him. The employee has the right to be represented, but this may be limited to 'inside' representation (i.e., a fellow-worker). The employer cannot be prosecutor and judge. In a small business, an outside person is normally appointed as chairperson of the hearing. During the hearing, each side states its case and has the right to cross-examine the other side's witnesses.

Below is an example of a written letter of warning to an employee:

Wind in the Willows

Address 62 Willow Lane, Willowmore 1234
PO Box 3300 Willowmore
Tel 0432 44 543   Fax 0432 44 542
Email windwillow@guesthouse.co.za
Website www.windwillow.co.za

Written warning

Name of employee: _____

Date: _____

1st/2nd/3rd written warning for the following:
[Description of incident]

☐	Insubordination:	
☐	Dereliction of duties:	
☐	Theft (instant dismissal):	
☐	Breaking of employment contract:	
☐	Repeatedly late for work:	
☐	Other:	

Signed by

Employer: _____
Date: _____

Employee: _____
Date: _____

Witness 1: _____
Date: _____

Witness 2: _____
Date: _____

CCMA/Labour Court: Employees have the right to refer unfair dismissal and unfair labour practice disputes to the CCMA for conciliation. The referral needs to comply with certain prescriptions of the CCMA, which are found in the 'CCMA Rules'. At conciliation, the CCMA attempts, through an appointed commissioner, to mediate and settle the dispute. Should this be unsuccessful, the employee may refer the matter to the CCMA for arbitration. The CCMA now adjudicates the dispute and makes a ruling as to the fairness and compensation payable. In the case of retrenchment, the matter proceeds to the Labour Court after conciliation. The employee has 30 days after dismissal to lodge a dispute with the CCMA and 90 days after conciliation to lodge a dispute for arbitration.

Apart from these two Acts, the employer needs to take cognisance of the following legislation that impacts on the labour market:

❀ the Employment Equity Act,
❀ the Skills Development Act,
❀ the Unemployment Insurance Fund Act (UIF),
❀ the Occupational Health and Safety Act, and
❀ the Compensation for Occupational Injuries and Diseases Act.

Recommended policy for HIV/Aids

Please adapt the following HIV/Aids workplace policy to suit your guest house's particular needs. (Note that policy documents typically contain legal jargon. However, you can use more user-friendly language if you wish, and also replace the corporate terms with terms that reflect your own management structure. Use the example below as a guide to set your own policy.)

HIV/Aids Workplace Policy for _____

[Insert your company's name]

1. **Policy purpose**

    (a) To ensure that the company uses a consistent approach when dealing with employees who are living with HIV/Aids.

    (b) To ensure that this approach is legally compliant and does not infringe on the constitutional rights of employees.

2. **Responsibility**

    _____

    _____

    [Insert the department/the job title of the person/people responsible for this policy]

3. **Effective date**

    _____

    [Insert the date on which this policy becomes effective. As and when you make any changes to your policy, so you will change this effective date.]

4. **Background**

    [This section provides a background on HIV/Aids. Adapt this according to your needs.]

    HIV/Aids is widespread throughout southern Africa. With the dramatic rise in Aids deaths, the socio-economic impact on employers, families and communities will become an increasing burden. This will impose a threat to the ability of our company to deliver services to our clients. We recognise this burden and are committed to dealing with this socio-economic problem.

---

5. Principles

The company affirms the principles of equality and equity and further states that:

- This policy has been developed and implemented in consultation with employees and their representatives.

- Employees living with HIV/Aids have the same rights and responsibilities as all other employees. Therefore the company will do everything in its power to protect employees living with HIV/Aids against discrimination and ensure confidentiality regarding their HIV status.

- Testing for HIV infection will not be imposed on employees (HIV is not classified as a notifiable disease, and transmission through the handling of food is impossible). Where HIV testing is done at the request of the employee, this will be with his/her informed consent, accompanied by counselling, and the results will be available only to the employee.

6. Coordination and management strategies

A dedicated HIV/Aids person will be nominated and situated at _____ (e.g. head office) and supported by an HIV/Aids task team with representation from

_____

[List applicable department and divisions]

_____.

Regular _____ (monthly, biannual, etc.) progress reports on the strategy will be made to _____.

[Specify owner/supervisor/management, etc.]

The leadership of the company will utilise all appropriate opportunities to demonstrate support for the HIV/Aids workplace policy and strategy.

7. Human resources issues

The company will regularly review employee benefits in the context of the impact of the epidemic. In addition, a skills succession plan will be developed.

Recruitment

In accordance with Employment Equity legislation, an employee will not be denied employment if he/she is HIV positive, provided that he/she is deemed fit to perform the job for which he/she has applied. Furthermore, prospective employees will not be required to undergo HIV testing.

Medical benefits

[Provide details of your company's medical aid and medical aid benefits offered to employees, i.e. who has access to these benefits, what do these benefits offer in terms of HIV/Aids, etc.]

Details of the company's medical aid and the particular scheme are as follows:

Name of medical aid	Medical aid benefits including HIV/Aids treatment	Beneficiaries of medical aid benefits

Public health care

[*If your company does not offer all employees medical aid benefits, we recommend that you include information on the nearest public health service(s) available to your employees.*]

The nearest hospital and/or clinic to the workplace that offers HIV/Aids medical assistance is:

Name of hospital or clinic	Address	Contact telephone number	Hours of operation

Pension/provident fund

[*Provide details of pension/provident fund benefits offered to employees, i.e. who has access to these benefits, what these benefits offer in terms of HIV/Aids, etc.*]

Details of the company's pension/provident fund are as follows:

Name of pension/provident fund	Fund benefits including grants for employees living with HIV/Aids	Beneficiaries of fund benefits

Unemployment Insurance Fund (UIF)

[*If your company does not offer all employees pension/provident fund benefits, we recommend that you provide information on the nearest UIF office.*]

The nearest UIF office to the workplace is:

Name of UIF office	Address	Contact telephone number	Hours of operation

Sick leave

Employees who require sick leave as a result of illness related to chronic/life-threatening diseases, including HIV/Aids, will be entitled to the same sick leave allocation as all other employees. Information on sick leave is available at/on/in _____.

[*Specify where employees can access this information, e.g. HR, the intranet, each employee's employment contract.*]

According to the Basic Conditions of Employment Act, employees are entitled to paid sick leave equivalent to the number of days worked in a six-week working period, during a three-year cycle.

Family responsibility leave

Employees who require time off work to attend to the needs of immediate family members who are seriously ill or have died, will be entitled to _____ days' family responsibility leave per calendar year. Information of this leave is available at/on/in _____.

[*Specify where employees can access this information, e.g. HR, the intranet, each employee's employment contract.*]

According to the Basic Conditions of Employment Act, employees are entitled to a minimum of three days per year for family responsibility leave.

Loans

[*If applicable, provide information on your company's loan policy for employees with chronic/life-threatening diseases.*]

8. Legal compliance

The company undertakes to consider employees living with HIV/Aids in terms of their contract of employment and fair and reasonable labour practices. The company commits to compliance with the following laws:

- the Employment Equity Act
- the Labour Relations Act
- the Occupational Health and Safety Act
- the Basic Conditions of Employment Act (or employment law applicable to your business)
- the Compensation for Occupational Injuries and Diseases Act.

Unfair discrimination is against company policy and procedures and therefore discrimination against an employee on the grounds of his/her HIV status should be reported to _____ [*Managing Director, CEO, Human Resources Manager, HIV/Aids task team, etc.*], or go through the company's grievance procedure.

9. Existing employees

HIV/Aids is not a notifiable disease and therefore employees who contract the disease are not obliged to inform the company. However, there is a duty to notify the company of incapacity or disability once an employee's health deteriorates to such an extent that the employee is unable to perform his/her duty in an adequate manner, or

- the disease manifests itself in excessive absenteeism, or
- the employee takes more than the standard amount of sick leave, or
- the employee displays irregular behaviour (e.g. Aids dementia).

In the event that an employee eventually develops symptoms to the extent that he/she is unable to perform as required, the company's incapacity policy would then be implemented. Information on the company's incapacity policy is available at/on/in _____.

[*Specify where employees can access this information, e.g. HR, the intranet, each employee's employment contract.*]

The company is obliged to provide a safe working environment for all employees in line with the requirements laid down by prevailing legislation.

10. Confidentiality

Persons living with HIV/Aids have the right to confidentiality and privacy concerning their health and HIV status. There should be no indicator on an employee's records if their HIV status is known.

- All personal details of all employees, including the actual or suspected HIV status of any employee, shall remain strictly confidential.

- Any information about an employee's HIV status shall be revealed only with his/her written consent.

- An employee who contracts HIV will not be obligated to inform management. If an employee with HIV/Aids decides to disclose his/her diagnosis to a colleague, superior or manager, the person will take all reasonable measures to ensure that this information remains private and confidential.

- The company will not tolerate any breaches in confidentiality. Any employee who breaches such confidentiality shall be subjected to appropriate disciplinary procedure. Speculation regarding another person's medical status will also not be tolerated.

11. Reasonable accommodation

Employees who become unfit for work as a result of Aids will be dealt with compassionately and in a just, humane and life-affirming way. The company will attempt to reasonably accommodate such individuals in less strenuous and stressful tasks, if possible. Failing this, the employee will be offered early retirement in accordance with standard company procedures and be entitled to appropriate benefits. Should early retirement not be applicable (i.e. the employee is not within 10 years of normal retirement age of 65), then the pension/provident fund benefit rules, as they pertain to permanent or temporary disability due to illness, will apply.

12. Colleagues of employees who are HIV positive

The company will ensure that effective educational programmes informing employees of the facts of HIV infection and Aids are implemented. Should an employee, after reassurance and with all appropriate safety and health precautions being taken and supplied by the company, remain unwilling to work with an HIV-positive employee, he/she will be warned that his/her reaction is unreasonable and scientifically unjust. He/she will be informed that his/her own employment situation is in jeopardy and that disciplinary action may be instituted.

13. Employees at risk

The company will ensure that correct protective equipment is provided in all first-aid boxes and that employees are trained in the correct use of this equipment.

The company will ensure that all first-aid and healthcare workers are educated regarding HIV and Aids infections as well as other potentially infectious diseases; and that they understand and adhere to these standard operating procedures.

In addition to training on the facts of HIV/Aids, the company will ensure that all employees will receive the following training to help them deal with HIV/Aids in the workplace:

- how to deal with body fluids,
- how to deal with stained linen,
- how to deal with sanitary bins,
- how to deal with used hypodermic needles,
- how to deal with guest queries regarding HIV/Aids and food,
- how to deal with guest queries regarding HIV/Aids in general,
- knowledge about HIV/Aids and cutlery, crockery, food preparation, etc.,
- knowledge about HIV/Aids and sharing toilets, and
- how to deal with a colleague or guest who may be wounded, etc.

Where necessary, the company will provide all relevant employees with appropriate protective clothing.

Safety in the guest house

Your property and wellbeing, and those of your guests and staff, are at risk from the dishonest, the opportunist, and the deliberate troublemaker. Remember to verify all personal details of guests and staff.

General duties of employers to their employees

The law requires that every employer shall provide and maintain, as far as is reasonably practicable, a working environment that is safe and without risk to the health of his or her employees. The Occupational Health and Safety (OHS) Act outlines the duties of both employers and employees in terms of safety at the workplace, and these are listed below:

✿ Provide and maintain 'systems of work, plant and machinery' that are 'safe and without risks to health'.
✿ Take all reasonable steps to 'eliminate' or reduce any hazard or potential hazard 'before resorting to personal protective equipment'.
✿ Make arrangements for ensuring 'the safety and absence of risk to health in connection with the production, processing, use, handling, storage of articles or substances'.
✿ Reasonably establish the existence of hazards to health or safety and the precautionary measures required, and then provide the necessary means to apply such precautionary measures.
✿ Provide the required health and safety information, training and supervision.
✿ Do not permit any employee to carry out any action or activity unless it complies fully with the prescribed precautionary measures.
✿ Make sure that the requirements of the OHS Act are complied with by everyone on the premises, and enforce all prescribed measures.
✿ Ensure that all activities are carried out 'under the general supervision of a person trained to understand the hazards' and who has 'the authority to ensure that precautionary measures taken by the employer are implemented'.
✿ Inform all employees of the scope of their authority.
✿ Every employer and every user of machinery shall make an evaluation of the risk attached to any condition or situation which may arise from the activities of such employer or user, as the case may be, and to which persons at a workplace or in the course of their employment or in connection with the use of the machinery are exposed, and he or she shall take such steps as may under the circumstances be necessary to make such condition or situation safe.
✿ The employer must provide and maintain all the equipment that is necessary to do work and all the systems according to which work must be done.
✿ The employer must provide the necessary information, instructions, training and supervision, keeping the extent of the employees' competence in mind, in what the employees do.
✿ Personal protective equipment must be issued where necessary, dependent on the work environment:
 − adequate and protective clothing, and
 − appropriate footwear for working on slippery surfaces.

General duties of employees at work

Every employee shall

* take reasonable care for the health and safety of himself and of other persons who may be affected by his acts or omissions,
* carry out any lawful order given to him and obey any health and safety rules and procedures laid down by his employer or by anyone authorised thereto by his employer in the interests of health and safety, and
* if any situation which is unsafe or unhealthy comes to his attention, as soon as practicable, report such situation to his employer.

Basic security measures

The building

* Entrances – reduce the number of public entrances to the minimum.
* Public areas and car parks should be well lit.
* Key control – sign in and out any keys issued to staff, limiting access to master keys.
* Mark fire exits clearly.

Fire risk

Fire-fighting equipment: Consult your fire department for advice on the positioning and number of extinguishers and fire hoses required. Your staff must be familiar with the operation of fire extinguishers.

Hoses: Fire hose reels must be installed in any building of two or more storeys in height or in any single-storey building of more than 250 m^2 at a rate of one hose reel for every 500 m^2 or part thereof of floor area of any storey. Any hose reel installed must comply with the SABS requirements.

 205

Fire extinguishers: Any building must contain one 4 kg fire extinguisher per 200 m^2 of floor area. Many fire authorities will recommend dry powder extinguishers, as they are effective for all types of fire. Fire extinguishers must be kept in approved, accessible positions, and must be routinely inspected, at least monthly, and maintained by an approved service engineer to be kept in good working order.

Fire blankets: Fire blankets are not stipulated in the regulations, but they are highly recommended by the fire authorities. They are much easier to use for small fires, and the establishment can keep on trading, as opposed to having to clean up the mess made by a fire extinguisher.

Grease filters: Are filters clean and free from greasy deposits? The fire departments are very cautious about extraction canopies. Filters have to be cleaned at least twice a week. If this does not happen, they will not extract grease, and it will accumulate in the entire ventilation system. Should a fire occur, this is a highly flammable hazard, and could cause untold damage to a building. The entire extraction system has to be cleaned out annually.

Gas installation

This may be installed only by a registered gas installer. Your insurance will not pay out if this has not been done.

Lighting

Emergency routes must have artificial lighting with a minimum illuminance of 50 lux at any time when the building is occupied.

Electricity

✿ Are electrical cords in good condition?
✿ Are there enough plugs in the wall to eliminate the use of double adapters?
✿ Are all workers' hands dry when working with electrical equipment?
✿ Are all electrical switches switched off before plugs are pulled out of wall sockets?
✿ Do all appliances comply with safety measures?
✿ Is equipment in good working order?

Disaster management

By law, all local authorities (e.g. municipalities) have to have a division that regulates disaster management. This may be the local fire department, the town clerk or the traffic police. Investigate who the authority is, and consult with them when determining escape routes, evacuation procedures, or any such matters. Ensure that emergency numbers are posted at telephones wherever possible.

Your emergency measures must be displayed prominently in your reception area and behind the doors of every bedroom. Make sure that you point them out to guests on arrival.

General safety requirements

First-aid requirements

Taking into account the types of injury that are likely to occur at a workplace, the nature of the activities performed and the number of employees employed at the workplace, you must make sure that the first-aid box contains suitable first-aid equipment. This includes at least the equipment listed below. You must also make sure that only articles and equipment or medicines are kept in the first-aid box or boxes. It is recommended that you also take a basic first-aid course, if possible.

Contents of a first-aid kit

- Wound cleaner or antiseptic (100 ml)
- Swabs for cleaning wounds
- Cotton wool for padding (100 g)
- Sterile gauze
- One pair forceps (for splinters)
- One pair of scissors (minimum size 100 mm)
- One set of safety pins
- Four triangular bandages
- Four roller bandages (75 mm × 5 m)
- Four roller bandages (100 mm × 5 m)
- One roll of elastic adhesive (25 mm × 3 m)
- One non-allergic adhesive strip (25 mm × 3 m)
- One packet of adhesive dressing strips (minimum quantity: 10 assorted)
- Four first-aid dressings (75 mm × 100 mm)

- Four first-aid dressings (150 mm × 200 mm)
- Four straight splints
- Two pairs large and two pairs medium disposable latex gloves
- Two CPR mouthpieces or similar devices

Equipment and procedures

Security equipment and procedures can do much to reduce the risks, but all too often the problem occurs because of inadequate training, poor supervision, or unwillingness to take action. You must provide and maintain, as far as is reasonably practicable, a working environment that is safe and without risk to the health of your employees.

Human factors

Human factors are often the cause of accidents. They include

- tiredness,
- recklessness,
- hastiness,
- poor vision,
- carelessness,
- insufficient knowledge or training,
- poor concentration,
- working under the influence of alcohol, anaesthetics, or drugs,
- faulty handling of equipment, such as electrical stoves, hot water urns, ovens, steam pots and steam ovens and deep fat fryers,
- unsafe use of electrical appliances and equipment,
- unsafe handling of sharp utensils, such as knives and tin openers,
- hastiness and unsafe movements with glassware, and
- faulty handling of chemicals.

Safety equipment

- You must instruct your employees in the proper use, maintenance and limitations of the safety equipment provided and not require or permit any employee to work unless he or she uses the required safety equipment or facility provided in terms of this regulation.
- Suitable goggles, caps, gloves, aprons, jackets, sleeves, leggings, protective footwear, protective overalls or any similar safety equipment of a type that will effectively prevent bodily injury must be provided.
- Mats, barriers and safety signs are required, or any similar facility that will effectively prevent slipping, unsafe entry or unsafe conditions.

General safety rules

- Remove all obstructions to passageways, paths and working areas, such as equipment boxes and cartons of rubbish.
- Clean up spillages immediately after they occur, especially chemicals, fat, grease and water.
- Faults in the equipment used must immediately be reported to you and attended to, and the equipment must not be used until it has been repaired.

- ❀ Keep machinery guarded, especially where there are sharp edges and bits of debris flying off.
- ❀ Work in good lighting and attend to any broken light bulbs. Bad lighting increases the likelihood of accidents.
- ❀ Store all items, especially chemicals, according to the manufacturer's instructions and away from heat and sunlight, and keep food and chemicals separate.
- ❀ Make sure the shelves you use can hold what you put on them. Some shelves can support only lightweight items. Make sure the shelves cannot tip towards you and never climb up or on shelves.
- ❀ Wear protective clothing suitable for the job you are doing. Remember to wear hard, closed footwear, so that if something drops, your feet won't get crushed.
- ❀ Use the correct lifting technique – bend the knees, not the waist, and keep your back straight. Use a trolley or forklift for heavy items.
- ❀ Compile a safety checklist, in order to promote and manage safety in your guest house and to minimise hazards.

Useful contacts

Guest house catering: Foodlink

Demonstrations, recipe development, staff training

Carolie de Koster

Telephone: 011 468 2973

Email: carolie@mweb.co.za

Quality assurance: Hospitality consultation services

Tourism Grading Council assessor

André Burger

Telephone: 012 331 0706

Cell: 082 639 8077

Email: burgan@mweb.co.za

Online reservation and management system: GuestWise

Enterprise Management Systems

Adri de Koster

Telephone: 011 468 2973

Cell: 083 629 7519

Email: imsystem@mweb.co.za

Public liability and insurance for guest houses: BnB SURE

Dave Jack

Telephone: 011 886 6066

Cell: 082 444 0442

Email dave@bnbsure.co.za

Labour law consultant: Employment-informed

Jan Rhoodie

Telephone: 012 362 2556

Cell: 082 577 7512

Email: jan@employmentinfo.co.za

E-marketing

Tourism e-marketing strategist

Japie Swanepoel

Telephone: 011 361 6020

Cell: 082 443 3033

Email: japie@longtail.co.za

Website: www.longtail.co.za

National Accommodation Association

Email: info@naa.co.za

Website: www.naa.co.za

AA Travel Guides

Telephone: 011 713 2000

Email: info@aatravel.co.za

Website: www.aatravel.co.za

Tourism Grading Council of South Africa

Telephone: 011 895 3108

Email: enquiries@tourismgrading.co.za

Website: www.tourismgrading.co.za

Guest House Accommodation of South Africa

Telephone: 021 762 0880

Email: lyndsay@ghasa.co.za

Website: www.ghasa.co.za

Guest houses featured

Aan de Oever Guest House

21 Faure Street

Swellendam, Western Cape

TGCSA 4 Stars, AA Accommodation Awards Winner 2004

Telephone: 028 514 1066

Email: info@aandeoever.com

Website: www.aandeoever.com

Foodlink at Beauvilla Guest House

508 Krause Street

Beaulieu, Midrand, Gauteng

Telephone: 011 468 2973

Email: carolie@mweb.co.za

Website: www.beauvilla.co.za

Oystercatcher Lodge

1st Avenue, Shelley Point

St Helena Bay, Western Cape

TGCSA 4 Stars, finalist. AA Awards, 2005, 2006, 2007

Telephone: 022 742 1202

Email: info@oystercatcherlodge.co.za

Website: www.oystercatcherlodge.co.za

Plumbago Guest House

Off R40, Nelspruit to Hazyview,

Mpumalanga

TGCSA 5 Stars AA Superior

Telephone: 013 737 8806

Email: plumbagoguesthouse@mweb.co.za

Website: www.plumbagoguesthouse.co.za

Sandals Guest House

39 Chartwell Drive

Umhlanga, KwaZulu-Natal

TGCSA 5 Stars, Finalist AA Travel Guides and American Express Accommodation Awards 2007 – Runners Up – Highly Commended

Telephone: 031 561 3973

Email: iain@sandalsumhlanga.co.za

Website: www.sandalsumhlanga.co.za

Index

Entries pertaining to diagrams, tables, checklists or contact details appear in italics.

Effective Guest House Management

Index

Index

Effective Guest House Management